UNIVERSITY OF HAWAII-WEST OAHU
LIBRARY

B1649
P633
A9413
1992

Popper, Karl Raimund, Sir

In search of a better world

DUE DATE

UNIVERSITY OF HAWAII-WEST OAHU
LIBRARY

8/27/93

B1649
P633
A9413
1992

Popper, Karl Raimund, Sir 1902-
[Auf der Suche nach einer besseren Welt. English]
In search of a better world : lectures and essays from thirty years / Karl Popper ; translated by Laura J. Bennett, with additional material by Melitta Mew. -- London ; New York : Routledge, 1992.
x, 245 p. ; 22 cm.

Includes bibliographical references and indexes.
ISBN 0-415-08774-0
1.Philosophy. I.Title.

B1649.P633A9413 1992 192
92-5394

©1993 BRODART
000 365 LC-MARC

IN SEARCH OF
A BETTER WORLD

IN SEARCH OF A BETTER WORLD

Lectures and essays from thirty years

Karl Popper

Translated by Laura J. Bennett,
with additional material by Melitta Mew.
Translation revised by Sir Karl Popper and Melitta Mew.

London and New York

First published in English in 1992
by Routledge
11 New Fetter Lane, London EC4P 4EE

Simultaneously published in the USA and Canada
by Routledge
a division of Routledge, Chapman and Hall, Inc.
29 West 35th Street, New York, NY 10001

© 1984, 1992 Karl R. Popper

Typeset in 10 on 12 point Bembo by
Computerset, Harmondsworth, Middlesex
Printed in Great Britain by
TJ Press (Padstow) Ltd, Padstow, Cornwall

All rights reserved. No part of this book may be reprinted or reproduced or utilized in any form or by any electronic, mechanical, or other means, now known or hereafter invented, including photocopying and recording, or in any information storage or retrieval system, without permission in writing from the publishers.

British Library Cataloguing in Publication Data
A catalogue record for this book is available from
the British Library

Library of Congress Cataloging in Publication Data
Popper, Karl Raimund, Sir
[Auf der Suche nach einer besseren Welt. English]
In search of a better world: lectures and essays of thirty years/
Karl Popper.
p. cm.
Translation of: Auf der Suche nach einer besseren Welt.
Includes indexes.
1. Philosophy. I. Title.
B1649.P633A9413 1992
192–dc20 92-5394

ISBN 0-415-08774-0

CONTENTS

* For a translation of this title, please see the footnote on page 171.

A SUMMARY BY WAY OF A PREFACE

All things living are in search of a better world.

Men, animals, plants, even unicellular organisms are constantly active. They are trying to improve their situation, or at least to avoid its deterioration. Even when asleep, the organism is actively maintaining the state of sleep: the depth (or else the shallowness) of sleep is a condition actively created by the organism, which sustains sleep (or else keeps the organism on the alert). Every organism is constantly preoccupied with the task of solving problems. These problems arise from its own assessments of its condition and of its environment; conditions which the organism seeks to improve.

An attempted solution often proves to be misguided, in that it makes things worse. Then follow further attempts at solutions – further trial and error movements.

We can see that life – even at the level of the unicellular organism – brings something completely new into the world, something that did not previously exist: problems and active attempts to solve them; assessments, values; trial and error.

It may be supposed that, under the influence of Darwin's natural selection, it is the most active problem solvers, the seekers and the finders, the discoverers of new worlds and new forms of life, that undergo the greatest development.

Each organism also strives to stabilize its internal conditions of life and to maintain its individuality – an activity whose results biologists call 'homoeostasis'. Yet this too is an internal agitation, an internal activity: an activity that attempts to restrict the internal agitation, a feedback mechanism, a correction of errors. The homoeostasis must be incomplete. It must restrict itself. Were it completely successful, it would mean the death of the organism, or, at the very least, the temporary cessation of all its vital functions. Activity, agitation, search are essential for life, for perpetual restlessness, perpetual imperfection; for perpetual seeking, hoping, evaluating, finding, discovering, improving, for learning and for the creation of values; but also for perpetual error, the creation of negative values.

Darwinism teaches that organisms become adapted to the environment through natural selection. And it teaches that they are passive throughout this process. But it seems to me far more important to stress that the organisms find, invent and reorganize new environments in the course of their search for a better world. They build nests, dams, little hills and mountains. But their most momentous creation has probably been the transformation of the atmosphere surrounding the earth by enriching it with oxygen; this transformation was, in turn, a consequence of the discovery that sunlight can be eaten. The discovery of this inexhaustible food supply and of the countless ways of trapping the light created the kingdom of plants; and the discovery that plants can be eaten created the animal kingdom.

We ourselves have been created by the invention of a specifically human language. As Darwin says (*The Descent of Man*, part 1, chapter III), the use and development of the human language 'reacted on the mind itself'. The statements of our language can describe a state of affairs, they can be objectively true or false. So the search for objective truth can begin – the acquisition of human knowledge. The search for truth, particularly in the natural sciences, no doubt counts among the best and greatest things that life has created in the course of its long search for a better world.

But have we not destroyed the environment with our natural science? No! We have made great mistakes – all living creatures make mistakes. It is indeed impossible to foresee all the unintended consequences of our actions. Here science is our greatest hope: its method is the correction of error.

I do not want to end this preface without saying something about the success of the search for a better world during the eighty-seven years of my life, a time of two senseless world wars and of criminal dictatorships. In spite of everything, and although we have had so many failures, we, the citizens of the western democracies, live in a social order which is better (because more favourably disposed to reform) and more just than any other in recorded history. Further improvements are of the greatest urgency. (Yet improvements that increase the power of the state often bring about the opposite of what we are seeking.)

I would like to mention briefly two things that we have improved.

The most important one is that the terrible mass poverty which still existed in my childhood and in my youth has now disappeared. (Unfortunately, this is not the case in places like Calcutta.) Some may object that there are people in our society who are too rich. But why should that bother us, if there are sufficient resources – and the good will – to struggle against poverty and other avoidable suffering?

The second is our reform of the criminal law. At first we may have hoped that if punishments were lessened, then crime would also lessen. When things did not work out like this, we nonetheless decided that we ourselves, individually and collectively, would rather suffer the effects of crime, corruption, murder, espionage and terrorism, than take the very questionable step of trying to eradicate these things by means of violence, and so run the risk of turning innocent people into victims. (Unfortunately, it is difficult to avoid this completely.)

Critics accuse our society of corruption, although they may admit that corruption is sometimes punished (Watergate). Perhaps they are not aware of the alternative. We prefer an order that guarantees full legal protection even to evil criminals so that they are not punished in cases where there is doubt. And we prefer this order to another order in which even those who are innocent of any crime cannot find legal protection and are punished even when their innocence is undisputed (Sakharov).

Yet perhaps in making this decision we may have chosen still other values. Perhaps we have, quite unconsciously, applied Socrates' wonderful teaching that 'It is better to suffer injustice than to commit an injustice.'

K. R. P.
Kenley
Spring 1989

TRANSLATOR'S ACKNOWLEDGEMENTS

I am greatly indebted to Sir Karl Popper for his detailed responses to all my queries, and for his translations of the verse passages throughout the text. My thanks are also due to Mrs Melitta Mew for her patient assistance with many aspects of the translation and for allowing me to include her translation of chapters 7 and 14.

Mr David Miller has very kindly discussed earlier versions of the translation with me and has made many invaluable suggestions. Mr Greg Hunt has been most helpful with the technical niceties of producing the translation.

Whilst I have been working on the translation, I have been sustained by encouragement, support and advice from both family and friends. I should like to take this opportunity to thank them all. I am especially grateful to my parents, my husband Steve, Joanne and Gary Pellow, and Jan Tapdrup.

Laura J. Bennett

Part I
ON KNOWLEDGE

1

KNOWLEDGE AND THE SHAPING OF REALITY

The search for a better world

The first half of the title of my lecture was not chosen by me, but by the organizers of the Alpbach Forum. Their title was: 'Knowledge and the Shaping of Reality'.

My lecture consists of three parts: *knowledge*; *reality*; and *the shaping of reality* through knowledge. The second part, which deals with reality, is by far the longest, since it contains a great deal by way of preparation for the third part.

1. KNOWLEDGE

I shall start with knowledge. We live in a time in which irrationalism has once more become fashionable. Consequently, I want to begin by declaring that I regard *scientific knowledge* as the best and most important kind of knowledge we have – though I am far from regarding it as the only one. The central features of scientific knowledge are as follows:

1. It begins with problems, practical as well as theoretical.

One example of a major practical problem is the struggle of medical science against avoidable suffering. This struggle has been extremely successful; yet it has led to a most serious unintended consequence: the population explosion. This means that another old problem has acquired a new urgency: the problem of birth control. One of the most important tasks of medical science is to find a genuinely satisfactory solution to this problem.

It is in this way that our greatest successes lead to new problems.

An example of a major theoretical problem in cosmology is how the theory of gravitation may be further tested and how

A lecture given in Alpbach in August 1982. The sub-title – 'The search for a better world' – was added by the author.

unified field theories may be further investigated. A very great problem of both theoretical and practical importance is the continued study of the immune system. Generally speaking, a theoretical problem consists in the task of providing an intelligible explanation of an unexplained natural event and the testing of the explanatory theory by way of its predictions.

2. Knowledge consists in the search for truth – the search for objectively true, explanatory theories.

3. It is not the search for certainty. To err is human. All human knowledge is fallible and therefore uncertain. It follows that we must distinguish sharply between truth and certainty. That to err is human means not only that we must constantly struggle against error, but also that, even when we have taken the greatest care, we cannot be completely certain that we have not made a mistake.

In science, a mistake we make – an error – consists essentially in our regarding as true a theory that is not true. (Much more rarely, it consists in our taking a theory to be false, although it is true.) To combat the mistake, the error, means therefore to search for objective truth and to do everything possible to discover and eliminate falsehoods. This is the task of scientific activity. Hence we can say: our aim as scientists is objective truth; more truth, more interesting truth, more intelligible truth. We cannot reasonably aim at certainty. Once we realize that human knowledge is fallible, we realize also that we can *never* be *completely certain* that we have not made a mistake. This might also be put as follows:

There are uncertain truths – even true statements that we take to be false – but there are no uncertain certainties.

Since we can never know anything for sure, it is simply not worth searching for certainty; but it is well worth searching for truth; and we do this chiefly by searching for mistakes, so that we can correct them.

Science, scientific knowledge, is therefore always hypothetical: it is *conjectural knowledge*. And the method of science is the *critical method*: the method of the search for and the elimination of errors in the service of truth.

Of course someone will ask me 'the old and famous question', as Kant calls it: 'What is truth?' In his major work (884 pages), Kant refuses to give any further answer to this question other than that truth is 'the correspondence of knowledge with its object' (*Critique of Pure Reason,* 2nd edition, pp. 82 f.[1]). I would say something very similar: *A theory or a statement is true, if what it says corresponds to reality*. And I would like to add to this three further remarks.

1. Every unambiguously formulated statement is either true or false; and if it is false, then its negation is true.

2. There are therefore just as many true statements as there are false ones.

3. Every such unambiguous statement (even if we do not know for certain if it is true) either is true or has a true negation. It also follows from this that it is wrong to equate the truth with definite or certain truth. Truth and certainty must be sharply distinguished.

If you are called as a witness in court, you are required to tell the truth. And it is, justifiably, assumed that you understand this requirement: your statement should correspond with the facts; it should *not* be influenced by your subjective convictions (or by those of other people). If your statement does not agree with the facts, you have either lied or made a mistake. But only a philosopher – a so-called relativist – will agree with you if you say: 'No, my statement is true, for I just mean by truth something other than correspondence with the facts. I mean, following the suggestion of the great American philosopher William James, utility; or, following the suggestion of many German and American social philosophers, what I mean by truth is what is accepted; or what is put forward by society; or by the majority; or by my interest group; or perhaps by television.'

The philosophical relativism that hides behind the 'old and famous question' 'What is truth?' may open the way to evil things, such as a propaganda of lies inciting men to hatred. This is probably not seen by the majority of those who represent the relativist position. But they should have and could have seen it. Bertrand Russell saw it, and so did Julien Benda, author of *La Trahison des Clercs* ('The Treason of the Intellectuals').

Relativism is one of the many crimes committed by intellectuals. It is a betrayal of reason and of humanity. I suppose that the alleged relativity of truth defended by some philosophers results from mixing-up the notions of truth and certainty; for in the case of certainty we may indeed speak of degrees of certainty; that is, of more or less reliability. Certainty is relative also in the sense that it always depends upon what is at stake. So I think that what happens here is a confusion of truth and certainty, and in some cases can be shown quite clearly.

All this is of great importance for jurisprudence and legal practice. The phrase 'when in doubt, find in favour of the accused' and the idea of trial by jury show this. The task of the jurors is to judge whether or not the case with which they are faced is still doubtful. Anyone who has ever been a juror will understand that truth is something objective, whilst certainty is a matter of subjective judgement. This is the difficult situation that faces the juror.

When the jurors reach an agreement – a 'convention' – this is called the 'verdict'.[2] The verdict is far from arbitrary. It is the duty of every juror to try to discover the objective truth to the best of his knowledge, and according to his conscience. But at the same time, he should be aware of his fallibility, of his uncertainty. And where there is reasonable doubt as to the truth, he should find in favour of the accused.

The task is arduous and responsible; and it demonstrates clearly that the transition from the search for truth to the linguistically formulated verdict is a matter of a *decision*, of a *judgement*. This is also the case in science.

Everything I have said up to now will doubtless lead to my being associated with 'positivism' or with 'scientism' once again. This does not matter to me, even if these expressions are being used as terms of abuse. But it does matter to me that those who use them either do not know what they are talking about or twist the facts.

Despite my admiration for scientific knowledge, I am not an adherent of scientism. For scientism dogmatically asserts the authority of scientific knowledge; whereas I do not believe in any authority and have always resisted dogmatism; and I continue to resist it, especially in science. I am opposed to the thesis that the scientist must believe in his theory. As far as I am concerned 'I do not believe in belief', as E. M. Forster says; and I especially do not believe in belief in science. I believe at most that belief has a place in ethics, and even here only in a few instances. I believe, for example, that objective truth is a value – that is, an ethical value, perhaps the greatest value there is – and that cruelty is the greatest evil.

Nor am I a positivist just because I hold it to be morally wrong not to believe in reality and in the infinite importance of human and animal suffering and in the reality and importance of human hope and human goodness.

Another accusation that is frequently levelled against me must be answered in a different way. This is the accusation that I am a sceptic and that I am therefore either contradicting myself or talking nonsense (according to Wittgenstein's *Tractatus* 6.51).

It is indeed correct to describe me as a sceptic (in the classical sense) in so far as I deny the possibility of a general criterion of (non-tautological) truth. But this holds of every rational thinker, say, Kant or Wittgenstein or Tarski. And, like them, I accept classical logic (which I interpret as the organon of criticism; that is, not as the organon of proof, but as the organon of refutation, of *elenchos*). But my position differs fundamentally from what is usually termed sceptical these days. As a philosopher I am not interested in doubt and uncertainty, because these are subjective states and because long ago I gave up as superfluous the search for subjective certainty. The problem that interests me is that of *the objectively critical rational grounds* for preferring one theory to another, *in the search for truth*. I am fairly sure that no modern sceptic has said anything like this before me.

This concludes for the moment my remarks on the subject of '*knowledge*'; I now turn to the subject of '*reality*', so that I may conclude with a discussion of '*the shaping of reality through knowledge*'.

2. REALITY

I

Parts of the reality in which we live are material. We live upon the surface of the earth which mankind has conquered only recently – during the eighty years of my life. We know a little about its interior, with the emphasis upon 'little'. Apart from the earth, there are the sun, the moon and the stars. The sun, the moon and the stars are material bodies. The earth, together with the sun, the moon and the stars, furnishes us with our first idea of a universe, of a cosmos. The investigation of this universe is the task of cosmology. All sciences serve cosmology.

We have discovered two kinds of bodies on earth: animate and inanimate. Both belong to the material world, to the world of physical things. I will call this world 'world 1'.

I shall use the term 'world 2' to refer to the world of our experiences, especially the experiences of human beings. Even this terminological and provisional distinction between worlds 1 and 2, that is, between the physical world and the world of experiences, has aroused much opposition. All I mean by this distinction, however, is that world 1 and world 2 are at least *prima facie* different. The connections between them, including their possible identity, are among the things that we need to investigate using hypotheses, of course. Nothing is prejudged by making a verbal distinction between them. The main point of the suggested terminology is to facilitate a clear formulation of the problems.

Presumably animals also have experiences. This is sometimes doubted; but I do not have the time to discuss such doubts. It is perfectly possible that all living creatures, even amoebae, have experiences. For as we know from our dreams or from patients with a high fever or similar conditions, there are subjective experiences of very different degrees of consciousness. In states of deep unconsciousness or even of dreamless sleep we lose consciousness altogether, and with it our experiences. But we may suppose that there exist also unconscious states, and these too can be included in world 2. There may perhaps also be transitions between world 2 and world 1: we should not rule out such possibilities dogmatically.

So we have world 1, the physical world, which we divide into animate and inanimate bodies, and which also contains in particular states and events such as stresses, movements, forces and fields of force. And we have world 2, the world of all conscious experiences, and, we may suppose, also of unconscious experiences.

By 'world 3' I mean the world of the objective products of the human mind; that is, the world of the products of the human part of world 2. World 3, the world of the products of the human mind, contains such things as books, symphonies, works of sculpture, shoes, aeroplanes, computers; and also quite simple physical objects, which quite obviously also belong to world 1, such as saucepans and truncheons. It is important for the understanding of this terminology that all planned or deliberate *products* of man's mental activity are classified within world 3, even though most of them may also be world 1 objects.

In this terminology, therefore, our reality consists of three worlds, which are interconnected and act upon each other in some way, and also partially overlap each other. (The word 'world' is obviously not being used here to mean the universe or cosmos, but rather parts of it.) These three worlds are: the physical world 1 of bodies and physical states, events and forces; the psychological world 2 of experiences and of unconscious mental events; and the world 3 of mental products.

There were and there are some philosophers who regard *only* world 1 as real, the so-called materialists or physicalists; and others who regard *only* world 2 as real, the so-called immaterialists. Even some physicists were or are among these opponents of materialism. The most famous was Ernst Mach, who (like Bishop Berkeley before him) regarded only our sensory impressions as real – although perhaps not always. He was an important physicist, but his way of resolving difficulties in the theory of matter was to assume that matter does not exist: in particular, he insisted that there are neither atoms nor molecules, and that these mental constructions are unnecessary and highly misleading.

Then there were the so-called dualists. They supposed that both the physical world 1 and the psychological world 2 are real. I am going still further: I assume not only that the physical world 1 and the psychological world 2 are real, and therefore, of course, all the *physical* products of the human mind, such as, for example, cars or toothbrushes and statues; but also that mental products which belong neither to world 1 nor to world 2, are equally real. In other words, I assume that there exist immaterial inhabitants of world 3, which are real and very important; for example, *problems*.

The order of worlds 1, 2 and 3 (as indicated by these numbers) corresponds to their age. According to the current state of our conjectural knowledge, the inanimate part of world 1 is by far the oldest; then comes the animate part of world 1, and at the same time or somewhat later comes world 2, the world of experiences; and then with the advent of mankind comes world 3, the world of mental products; that is, the world that anthropologists call 'culture'.

II

I now want to discuss each of these three worlds in greater detail, starting with the physical world 1.

Since my present theme is *reality*, I would like to begin by saying that the physical world 1 is entitled to be regarded as the most obviously 'real' of my three worlds. By this I mean in fact only that the word 'reality' obtains its meaning first by being applied to the physical world. I mean no more than that.

When Mach's predecessor Bishop Berkeley denied the reality of physical bodies, Samuel Johnson said 'I refute him thus', kicking at a stone with all his might. It was the *resistance* of the stone that was intended to demonstrate the reality of matter: the stone pushed back! By this I mean that Johnson felt the resistance, the reality as a repercussion, a kind of repulsion. Although Johnson could not of course prove or refute anything in this way, he was nevertheless able to show how we comprehend reality.

A child learns what is real through effect, through resistance. The wall, the railing is real. Anything that can be picked up or put in the mouth is real. Above all, solid objects that get in our way or act in opposition to us are real. Solid material things give us our central and most basic conception of reality, and the conception broadens out from this centre. So we include everything that can change solid material things or can act upon them. This makes first water and air real; also attractive magnetic and electric forces, and gravity; heat and cold; motion and rest.

Hence everything is real that can kick, such as radar, either us or other real things, and can be kicked back; or anything that can have an effect upon us or upon other real things. I hope that this is sufficiently clear. It includes the earth and the sun, the moon and the stars. The cosmos is real.

III

I am not a materialist, but I admire the materialist philosophers, especially the great atomists, Democritus, Epicurus and Lucretius. They were the philosophers of the great enlightenment of antiquity, the opponents of superstition, the liberators of mankind. But materialism has transcended itself.

We human beings are familiar with *one kind* of effect: we reach for an object, such as a switch, and press it. Or we push or shove an armchair. Materialism was the theory that reality consists *solely* of material things, which act upon each other through pressure, push or action by contact. There were two versions of materialism: first, atomism, which taught that tiny particles, too small to be visible, interlink with each other and bump into each other. Between the particles there is a void. The other version taught that there is no void. Things move in a 'full' world – perhaps full of 'ether' – rather like tea leaves in a cup full of tea that has been stirred.

It was fundamental to both theories that there are no incomprehensible or unfamiliar modes of operation – just pressure, shove and push; and that even pull and attraction are explicable in terms of pressure and push: when we pull a dog on a leash, then in reality the effect is that his collar exerts pressure upon or pushes him. The leash acts like a chain, of which the links are pressing against or pushing each other. Pull, attraction, must somehow be explained by pressure.

This materialist philosophy of pressure and push, also put forward by others, notably René Descartes, was shaken by the introduction of the notion of force. First came Newton's theory of gravity as an attractive force operating at a distance. Then came Leibniz, who showed that atoms must be centres of repulsive force if they are to be impenetrable and capable of pushing. Then came Maxwell's theory of electromagnetism. And finally even push, pressure and action by contact were explained by the electrical repulsion of the electron shell of the atoms. That was the end of materialism.

In place of materialism came physicalism. But this was something completely different. In place of a conception of the world that held that our *everyday experiences of pressure and push* explain all other effects and thereby the whole of reality, there came a philosophy in which effects were described by differential equations, and ultimately by formulae that the greatest physicists, such as Niels Bohr, declared to be inexplicable and, as Bohr repeatedly insisted, incomprehensible.

The history of modern physics can be described in the following, oversimplified, manner: materialism expired, unnoticed, with Newton, Faraday and Maxwell. It transcended itself when Einstein, de Broglie and Schrödinger directed their research programme towards the explanation of the nature of matter itself; in terms of oscillations, vibrations and waves; not oscillations of matter, but rather vibrations of an immaterial ether consisting of fields of forces. But this programme became obsolete too and was replaced by still more abstract programmes: for example by a programme that explains matter as vibrations of fields of probability. At every stage the various theories were extremely successful. Yet they were overtaken by still more successful theories.

That is, roughly speaking, what I call the self-transcendence of materialism. It is also precisely the reason why physicalism is something completely different from materialism.

IV

It would take far too long to describe the rapidly changing relationship that has developed between physics and biology. But I would like to point out that, from the point of view of the modern Darwinian theory of natural selection, the same situation can be represented in two fundamentally different ways. One mode of representation is traditional; the other, however, seems to me to be by far the better of the two.

Darwinism is usually regarded as a cruel philosophy: it depicts 'Nature, red in tooth and claw'; that is, a picture in which nature poses a hostile threat to us and to life in general. My claim is that this is a prejudiced view of Darwinism, which has been influenced by an ideology that existed before Darwin (Malthus, Tennyson, Spencer) and has almost nothing to do with the actual theoretical content of Darwinism. It is true that Darwinism places great emphasis upon what we call 'natural selection'; but this too can be interpreted in a quite different manner.

As we know, Darwin was influenced by Malthus, who tried to demonstrate that the increase in population, combined with a shortage of food, would lead to cruel competition, to selection of the strongest and to the cruel annihilation of those who are not as strong. But according to Malthus, even the strongest are put under pressure by the competition: they are *forced* into exerting all their energies. Hence, on this interpretation, the competition results in the *limitation of freedom*.

But this can be seen in another way. *Men seek to extend their freedom*: they are in search of new possibilities. Thus competition can clearly be regarded as a process that favours the discovery of new ways of making a living and with them new possibilities of life, together with the discovery and the construction of new ecological niches, including niches for such individual human beings as physically handicapped people.

These possibilities entail choice between alternative decisions, increased freedom of choice and more freedom.

The two interpretations are therefore fundamentally different. The first is pessimistic: *limitation of freedom*. The second is optimistic: *extension of freedom*. Both are, of course, oversimplifications, but both can be regarded as good approximations to the truth. Can we claim that one of them is *the better interpretation*?

I think that we can. The great success of the competitive society and the great extension of freedom to which it has led can be explained *only* by the optimistic interpretation. It is the better interpretation. It is closer to the truth, it explains more.

If this is the case, then individual initiative, pressure from within, the search for new possibilities, for new liberties, and the activity that seeks to realize these possibilities, is more effective than the selection pressure from without, which results in the elimination of the weaker individuals and in the curtailment of freedom, even of the strongest.

Throughout these remarks I am taking for granted the pressure that is caused by the increase in population.

Now, the problem of interpreting Darwin's theory of evolution through natural selection seems to me to be quite like the problem of interpreting Malthus's theory.

The old, pessimistic and still accepted view is this: the role played by the organisms in adaptation is purely passive. They constitute a very heterogeneous population, from which the struggle for existence, the competition, selects those (on the whole) best-adapted individuals, by elimination of the others. The selection pressure comes from without.

Great emphasis is usually put on the fact that all evolutionary phenomena, especially the phenomena of adaptation, can be explained only by reference to this selection pressure from without. Nothing is thought to come from within except the mutations, the variability (of the gene-pool).

My new optimistic interpretation stresses (as does Bergson) the activity of all living creatures. All organisms are fully occupied with problem-solving. Their first problem is survival. But there are countless concrete problems that arise in the most diverse situations. And one of the most important problems is the search for better living conditions: for greater freedom; for a better world.

According to this optimistic interpretation, it is through natural selection and (we may suppose) through an external selection pressure that a strong internal selection pressure comes into being at a very early stage; a selection pressure exerted by the organisms upon their environment. This selection pressure manifests itself as a kind of behaviour that we may interpret as *searching for a new ecological niche*. Sometimes it is even the *construction* of a new ecological niche.

This pressure from within results in a *choice* of niches; that is, in forms of behaviour that may be regarded as a *choice of lifestyles* and of surroundings. This must be taken to include choice of friends, symbiosis, and above all, perhaps most importantly from a biological point of view, the choice of a mate; and the preference for certain kinds of food, especially sunlight.

So we have an internal selection pressure; and the optimistic interpretation regards this selection pressure from within as *at least* as important as the selection pressure from without: the organisms seek new niches, even without having undergone any organic change themselves; and they mutate later as a result of the external selection pressure, the selection pressure of *the niche that was actively chosen by them*.

We might say that there is a circle, or rather a spiral of interactions between the selection pressure from without and that from within. The question that is answered differently by the two interpretations is: which loop in this circle or spiral is active and which is passive? The old theory locates the activity in the selection pressure from without; the new in the selection pressure from within: it is the organism that chooses, that is active. It may be said that both interpretations are ideologies, ideological interpretations of the same objective content. But we can ask: is there anything that can be better explained by one of the two interpretations than by the other?[3]

I think that there is. I would describe it briefly as the victory of life over its inanimate surroundings. The essential fact is as follows: there was, so most of us suppose – hypothetically, of course – a primordial cell from which all life gradually developed. According to Darwinian evolutionary biology this is best explained by the hypothesis that nature worked on life with a desperately cruel chisel, which then chiselled out every living adaptation at which we marvel.

However, we may point to one fact that contradicts this view: *the primordial cell is still alive*. We are all the primordial cell. That is not an image, nor a metaphor, but rather the literal truth.

I want to give only a very brief explanation of this. There are three possibilities for a cell; the first is death, the second is cell division; the third is fusion: a union, a merging with another cell, which almost always causes a division. Neither division nor union means death: it is a reproductive process, the changing of one living cell into two living cells that are virtually the same. They are both the living continuations of the original cell. The primordial cell came into being billions of years ago, and the primordial cell has survived in the form of trillions of cells. And it lives on still in every single one of all the cells alive now. And all life, everything that has ever lived and everything that is alive today, is the result of divisions of the primordial cell. It is therefore composed of the primordial cell, which is still alive. These are matters that no biologist can dispute and that no biologist will dispute. We are all the primordial cell, in a very similar sense (genidentity) to that in which I am the same person now as I was thirty years ago, even though perhaps not one atom of my present body existed in my body in those days.

In place of a picture of the environment that attacks us with 'tooth and claw', I see an environment in which a tiny little living creature has succeeded in surviving for billions of years and in conquering and improving its world. If, therefore, there is a struggle between life and the environment, then life has triumphed. I believe that this somewhat revised conception of Darwinism leads to a completely different view from that of the old ideology, namely to the view that we inhabit a world that has become more and more agreeable and more and more favourable to life, thanks to the activity of life and its search for a better world.

But who wants to admit this? Today everyone believes in the persuasive myth of the total maliciousness of the world and of 'society'; just as formerly everyone in Germany and Austria believed in Heidegger and in Hitler, and in war. But the mistaken belief in maliciousness is itself malicious: it disheartens young people and leads them astray into doubts and into despair, and even into violence. Although this mistaken belief is essentially political, the old interpretation of Darwinism has nevertheless contributed to it.

A very important thesis forms part of the pessimistic ideology, namely, that the adaptation of life to the environment and all these (to my mind wonderful) inventions of life over billions of years, which we are not yet able to recreate in the laboratory today, are not inventions at all, but the product of sheer chance. It is claimed that life has invented nothing at all, it is all the mechanism of purely chance mutations and of natural selection; the internal pressure of life is nothing more than self-reproduction. Everything else comes about through our struggle, indeed *blind* struggle, against each other and against nature. And things (in my view, wonderful things) like the use of sunlight as food are the result of chance.

I maintain that this is once again just an ideology, and indeed a part of the old ideology. To this ideology, by the way, belong the myth of the selfish gene (for genes can only function and survive by co-operating), and the revived social Darwinism that is currently being presented as a brand-new and naively deterministic 'sociobiology'.

I should now like to put together the main points of the two ideologies.

1. Old: Selection pressure from without functions by killing: it eliminates. The environment is therefore hostile to life.

   New: The active selection pressure from within constitutes the search for a better environment, for better ecological niches, for a better world. It is favourable to life in the highest degree. Life improves the environment for life, it makes the environment more favourable to life (and friendlier for man).

2. Old: Organisms are completely passive, but they are actively selected.

   New: Organisms are active: they are constantly preoccupied with problem-solving. Life consists in problem-solving. The solution is often the choice or the construction of a new ecological niche. Not only are the organisms active, their activity is constantly on the increase. (The attempt to deny activity in humans – as the determinists do – is paradoxical, especially with regard to our critical mental activity.)

   If animal life began in the sea – as we may suppose – then its environment was in many respects fairly uniform. Nevertheless the animals (with the exception of the insects) developed into vertebrates before they went on to land. The environment was equally favourable to life and relatively undifferentiated, but life itself diversified into an unforeseeably large number of different forms.

3. Old: Mutations are a matter of pure chance.

New: Yes; but the organisms are constantly inventing wonderful things that improve life. Nature, evolution and organisms are all inventive. They work, as inventors, in the same way that we do: using the method of trial and the elimination of errors.

4. Old: We live in a hostile environment that is changed by evolution through cruel eliminations.

New: The first cell is still living after billions of years, and now even in many trillions of copies. Wherever we look, it is there. It has made a garden of our earth and transformed our atmosphere with green plants. And it created our eyes and opened them to the blue sky and the stars. It is doing well.

V

I now turn to world 2.

Improvements in the organism and in its environment are associated with an extension and improvement of animal consciousness. Problem-solving, invention, is never a *completely* conscious act. It is always achieved by means of trial and error: by means of tests and the elimination of error; that means, through interaction between the organism and its world, its surroundings. And in the course of this interaction consciousness sometimes intervenes. Consciousness, world 2, was presumably an *evaluating and discerning consciousness*, a problem-solving consciousness, right from the start. I have said of the animate part of the physical world 1 that all organisms are problem solvers. My basic assumption regarding world 2 is that this problem-solving activity of the animate part of world 1 resulted in the emergence of world 2, of the world of consciousness. But I do not mean by this that consciousness solves problems all the time, as I asserted of the organisms. On the contrary. The organisms are preoccupied with problem-solving day in, day out, but consciousness is *not only* concerned with the solving of problems, although that is its most important biological function. My hypothesis is that the original task of consciousness was to anticipate success and failure in problem-solving and to signal to the organism in the form of pleasure and pain whether it was on the right or wrong path to the solution of the problem. ('Path' is initially – as in the case of the amoeba – to be understood quite literally as the physical direction of the *path* of the organism.) Through the experience of pleasure and pain consciousness assists the organism in its *voyages of discovery*, and in its *learning processes*. It thus intervenes in many of the mechanisms of memory, which – again for biological reasons – cannot all be conscious. It is, I believe, very important to realize that it is not possible for the majority of the mechanisms of memory to be conscious. They would interfere with each other. It is for precisely this reason – this can be shown almost *a priori* – that there are conscious and unconscious events that are quite closely related to one another.

Hence, almost inevitably, a domain of the unconscious comes into being, fundamentally linked to our memory apparatus. It contains above all a kind of unconscious map of our surroundings, of our local biological niche. The organization of this map and of the *expectations* that it contains, and the subsequent linguistic formulations of expectations, that is, of *theories*, constitute the task of the cognitive apparatus, which has therefore conscious and unconscious aspects interacting with the physical world, world 1, the cells; in man, with the brain.

So I do not regard world 2 as what Mach described as the sensations, visual sensations, aural sensations, etc.: I regard all of these as thoroughly unsuccessful attempts to describe or classify our varied experiences systematically and, in this way, to arrive at a theory of world 2.

Our fundamental starting point should be the question of what the biological functions of consciousness are, and which of these functions are the most basic. We must also ask how we, in the course of the active search for information about the world, invent our senses: how we learn the art of touching, develop phototropy, vision and hearing. Thus we are confronted with new problems and respond with new expectations and with new theories about the environment. Hence world 2 comes into being through interaction with world 1.

(Naturally, there is then the further problem of discovering signals for rapid actions; and our senses play an important role in this.)

VI

I will soon return to world 1 and world 2; but first I want to say a few words about the beginning of the physical world, world 1, and about the idea of emergence, which I would like to introduce with the help of the idea of phase.

We do not know *how* world 1 came into being and *if* it came into being. Should the big bang theory be true, then the first thing to come into existence was probably light. 'Let there be light!' would have been the first stage in the creation of the world. But this first light would have had a short wavelength, well beyond the ultra-violet region, and would have therefore been invisible to man. Then, so the physicists tell us, came electrons and neutrinos, and then came the first atomic nuclei – only the nuclei of hydrogen and of helium: the world was still far too hot for atoms.

Thus we may suppose that there is a non-material or pre-material world 1. If we accept the (in my opinion, very dubious) theory of the expansion of the world from the big bang, we can say that the world, thanks to its expansion, is slowly cooling down, and is therefore becoming more and more 'material' in the sense of the old materialist philosophy.

We could perhaps distinguish a number of phases in this process of cooling down:

Phase 0: Here there is only light, as yet no electrons, nor atomic nuclei.

Phase 1: In this phase there are electrons and other elementary particles as well as light (photons).

Phase 2: By now there are also hydrogen nuclei and helium nuclei.

Phase 3: In this phase there are atoms as well: hydrogen atoms (but no molecules) and helium atoms.

Phase 4: In addition to atoms, diatomic molecules can now also exist, thus including, among others, diatomic hydrogen gas molecules.

Phase 5: In this phase there is, among other things, water in a liquid state.

Phase 6: At this stage there are, among other things, and initially very rarely, water crystals, that is, ice in the diverse and wonderful forms of snow flakes, and later also solid crystalline bodies, such as blocks of ice, and still later, other crystals.

We live in this sixth phase, that is to say, in our world there are local areas, in which there are solid bodies and, of course, also liquids and gas. Further away there are, of course, also large areas that are too hot for molecular gases.

VII

What we know as life could only come into being in a sufficiently cooled down, but not too cold, area of the world in phase 6. Life can be thought of as a very special phase within phase 6: the simultaneous presence of matter in gaseous, liquid and solid states is essential for what we know as life, as is a further state, the colloid state, which lies somewhere between the liquid and the solid states. Living matter differs from (superficially) very similar but inanimate material structures in the same way as two phases of water differ from one another, such as the liquid and gaseous forms of water.

The characteristic feature of these temperature-dependent phases is that the most thorough examination of one temperature-dependent phase could not enable the greatest natural scientist to foresee the properties of the next and later phase: the examination of atoms in isolation by the greatest thinker with nothing more at his disposal for his examination but phase 3, in which there are only atoms but still no molecules, would hardly permit him, we may assume, even from the closest examination of the atoms, to infer the coming world of molecules. And the most careful examination of steam in phase 4 would indeed scarcely have allowed him to foresee the completely new properties of a fluid, like those of water or the wealth of forms of snow crystals, let alone the highly complex organisms.

Properties such as that of being gaseous, liquid or solid we call (with reference to their unforeseeable nature) 'emergent' properties. Clearly, 'living' or 'being alive' is such a property. This does not say very much, but it does suggest an analogy with the phases of water.

VIII

Thus, life is, we may assume, emergent, like consciousness; and so is what I call world 3.

The greatest emergent step that life and consciousness have taken up to now is, I suspect, the invention of *human* language. This no doubt led to the creation of mankind.

Human language does not consist in mere *self-expression* (1), nor merely in *signalling* (2): animals have these abilities too. Nor is it mere symbolism. That too, and even rituals, can be found in animals. The great step that resulted in an unforeseeable development of consciousness is the invention of *descriptive statements* (3), Karl Bühler's *representative function*: of statements which describe an objective state of affairs, which may or may not correspond to the facts; that is, of statements that may be true or false. This function is the unprecedented feature within human language.

Herein lies the difference from animal languages. *Perhaps* we could say of the language of the bees that their communications are true – except, perhaps, when a scientist misleads a bee. Misleading signs can also be found among the animals: for example, butterflies' wings may give the appearance of eyes. But only we human beings have taken the step of *checking* our own theories for their objective truth by means of critical arguments. This is the fourth function of language, the *argumentative function* (4).

IX

The invention of descriptive (or, as Bühler calls it, representative) human language makes a further step possible, a further invention: the invention of criticism. It is the invention of a *conscious choice*, a *conscious selection* of theories in place of their *natural* selection. Thus, just as materialism transcends itself, so, one might say, natural selection transcends itself. It leads to the development of a language containing true and false statements. And this language then leads to the invention of criticism, to the emergence of criticism, and thereby to a new phase of selection: natural selection is amplified and partially overtaken by critical, cultural selection. The latter permits us a conscious and critical pursuit of our errors: we can consciously find and eradicate our errors, and we can consciously judge one theory as inferior to another. This is, in my opinion, the decisive point. Here begins what is called 'knowledge' in the title I was given: human knowledge. There is no knowledge without rational criticism, criticism in the service of the search for truth. Animals have no knowledge *in this sense*. Of course they know all kinds of things – the dog knows his master. But what we call knowledge, and the most important type of knowledge, scientific knowledge, is dependent on rational criticism. This is therefore the decisive step, the step that depends upon the invention of true or false statements. And this is the step that, I suggest, lays the foundations for world 3, for human culture.

X

World 3 and world 1 overlap: world 3 encompasses, for instance, books, it contains statements; it contains above all human language. These are all *also* physical objects, objects, events, that take place in world 1. Language consists, we may say, of dispositions anchored in nervous structures and therefore in something material; of elements of memory, engrams, expectations, learnt and discovered behaviour; and of books. You can hear my lecture today because of acoustics: I am making a noise; and this noise is part of world 1.

I would now like to show that this noise is perhaps more than pure acoustics. That part of it that goes beyond world 1, of which I am making use, constitutes precisely what I have termed world 3 and has until now been only rarely noticed. (Unfortunately, I do not have the time to talk about the history of world 3; see, however, my book *Objective Knowledge*, chapter 3, section 5.) I want to try to explain the main point, that is, the immaterial part, the immaterial aspect of world 3; or, as we might also say, the autonomous aspect of world 3: what goes beyond worlds 1 and 2. At the same time I would like to show that the immaterial aspect of world 3 not only plays a role in our consciousness – in which it plays a major role – but that it is *real*, even apart from worlds 1 and 2. The immaterial (and non-conscious) aspect of world 3 can, as I hope to show, have an *effect* upon our consciousness and, through our consciousness, upon the physical world, world 1.

I would therefore like to discuss the interaction, or what we might call the spiral, of the feedback mechanisms between the three worlds and their subsequent mutual reinforcement. And I would like to show that there is something immaterial here, namely the *content* of our statements, of our arguments, in contrast to the acoustic or the written, and hence physical, formulations of these statements or arguments. And it is always the *subject matter or content* with which we are concerned whenever we use language in its truly human sense. *It is above all the content* of a book, not its physical form, that belongs to world 3.

Here is a very simple case that illustrates clearly the importance of the idea of content: with the development of human language came *numerals*, counting with the words 'one', 'two', 'three', etc. There are some languages that have only the words 'one', 'two' and 'many'; some that have 'one', 'two' . . . up to 'twenty' and then 'many'; and still other languages like ours, that have invented a method allowing us to count onwards from every number; that is, a method that is essentially not finite, but rather unbounded in the sense that every number can in principle still be exceeded by adding another number. This is one of the great inventions that was made possible only *by the invention of language*: the method of constructing an endless sequence of more and more numerals. The instructions for the construction of such a sequence can be formulated linguistically or in a computer program, and they could therefore be described as something *concrete*. But our discovery that the series of natural numbers is now (potentially) infinite is totally *abstract*. For this infinite series cannot be instantiated in concrete terms in either world 1 or world 2. The infinite series of natural numbers is 'something purely ideational', as they say: it is a pure product of world 3, since it belongs *solely* to that abstract part of world 3 that consists of elements or 'inmates' that are indeed thought of, but instantiated in concrete terms neither in thinking nor in physically concrete numerals nor in computer programs. The (potential) *infinity* of the series of natural numbers is, one might say, not an invention, but rather a discovery. We discover it as a possibility; as an unintended property of a series that was invented by us.

In the same way we discover the numerical properties 'even' and 'odd', 'divisible' and 'prime number'. And we discover problems, such as Euclid's problem: is the series of prime numbers infinite or (as the ever increasing rarity of larger prime numbers suggests) finite? This problem was, so to speak, completely hidden; it was not even unconscious, rather it was simply not there, when we invented the number system. Or was it there? If it was, then it was there in an ideational and purely abstract sense, that is, in the following sense: that it lay hidden in the number system that we constructed, but was nonetheless there, without anyone's being aware of it and without its being somehow hidden in the unconscious of some person or other, and leaving no physical trace behind. No book existed in which it could be read about. It was therefore physically not there. It was also not there as far as world 2 was concerned. But it was there as a *not yet discovered, but discoverable problem*: a typical instance of a problem that belongs *only* to the purely abstract part of world 3. Incidentally, Euclid not only discovered the problem, he also solved it. Euclid found a proof for the proposition that after every prime number there must always be another prime number; from which we can conclude that the sequence of prime numbers is infinite. This proposition describes a state of affairs that is obviously, for its part, purely abstract: it is likewise an inmate of the purely abstract part of world 3.

XI

There are also many unsolved problems connected with the prime numbers, such as, for example, Goldbach's problem: is *every* even number greater than 2 the sum of two prime numbers? Such a problem may have either a positive solution or a negative solution; or it may be insoluble; and its insolubility may or may not itself admit of proof. Thus new problems arise.

These are all problems that are *real* in the sense that they have *effects*. They can above all have an effect upon the human mind. A man can see or discover the problem and then try to solve it. The grasping of the problem and the attempt to solve a problem constitutes an activity of consciousness, of the human mind; and this activity is clearly also created by the problem, by the existence of the problem. A solution of the problem may result in a publication; and hence the abstract world 3 problem can cause (via world 2) the heaviest printing presses to be set in motion. Euclid wrote down his solution to the problem about prime numbers. This was a physical act with many consequences. Euclid's proof was reproduced in many textbooks, that is, in physical objects. These are events in world 1.

Of course consciousness, world 2, plays the main role in the causal chains that lead from the abstract problem to world 1. As far as I can see, the abstract part of world 3, the world of abstract, non-physical contents, that is the actual, specific world 3, has so far never exerted a *direct* influence upon world 1; not even with the aid of computers. The link is always forged by consciousness, by world 2. (Perhaps this will be different one day.) I suggest that we speak of 'mind' when we are referring to consciousness – in its role of interacting with world 3.

I believe that the mind's mediation with the inmates of world 3 influences and shapes our conscious and unconscious life in a decisive fashion. Here, in the interaction between world 2 and world 3, lies the key to understanding the difference between human and animal consciousness.

XII

To sum up, we can say that world 3, above all that part of world 3 that is created by human language, is a product of our consciousness, of our mind. Like human language, it is our invention.

But this invention is something external to us, outside our skin ('exosomatic'). It is something objective, as are all our inventions. Like all inventions, it creates its own problems, which, although autonomous, depend upon us. (Think of the control of fire, or the invention of the motor vehicle.) These problems are unintentional and unexpected. They are typical, unintended consequences of our actions, which then in their turn react upon us.

This is how the objective, abstract, autonomous, yet real and effective world 3 comes into being.

One example, which is perhaps not altogether typical, but is nonetheless striking, is mathematics. It is, clearly, our work, our invention. Yet almost all mathematics is surely objective and at the same time abstract: it is a whole world of problems and solutions, which we do not invent, but rather discover.

Accordingly, those who have reflected upon the status of mathematics have in the main reached two opinions. And we have in effect two philosophies of mathematics.

1. *Mathematics is the work of mankind.* For it is based upon our intuition; or it is our construction; or it is our invention. (Intuitionism; constructivism; conventionalism.)
2. *Mathematics is a field that exists objectively in its own right.* It is an infinitely rich field of objective truths, which we do not create, but confront objectively. And we can discover more than a few of these truths. (This conception of mathematics is usually described as 'Platonism'.)

These two philosophies of mathematics have until now stood in direct opposition to each other. But the theory of world 3 shows that they are both right: the infinite series of natural numbers (for example) is our linguistic invention; our convention; our construction. But the prime numbers and their problems are not: these we *discover* in an objective world, which we have indeed invented or created, but which (like all inventions) becomes objectified, detached from its creators and independent of their will: it becomes 'autonomous', 'purely ideational': it becomes 'Platonic'.

From the point of view of world 3 there can be no quarrel between the two philosophies of mathematics. There remains at most the disagreement about whether a particular mathematical object – such as the infinite sequence of numbers or the universe of sets of axiomatic set theory – is the work of man, or whether we confront this field as a part of the objective world, as if given by God. But at least since 1963 (Paul Cohen) we have known that axiomatic set theory is also the work of man. We have known for a long time that even mathematicians are fallible and that we can refute our theories, but cannot always prove them.

I have tried to explain world 3. And I come now to the third and final section of my lecture: On the shaping of reality.

3. ON THE SHAPING OF REALITY

I

It is the interaction between world 1, world 2, and world 3 that may be regarded as the *shaping of reality*; the interaction that consists of multiple feedback mechanisms, and within which we operate using the method of trial and error. That is, we intervene consciously in this spiral of feedback mechanisms. We – the human mind, our dreams, our objectives – are the creator of the work, of the product, and at the same time we are shaped by our work. This is in fact the creative element in mankind: that we, in the act of creating, at the same time transform ourselves through our work. The shaping of reality is therefore our doing; a process that cannot be understood without trying to understand all three of its aspects, these three worlds; and without seeking to understand the way in which the three worlds interact with each another.

This spiral of interactions or feedback mechanisms is influenced by our developing theories and by our dreams. An example is the shaping, the creation, the invention of Leonardo's bird: of what we all know today as the aeroplane. It is important to notice that it is the dream of flying that leads to flying, and not, as the materialistic conception of history of Marx and Engels would doubtless suggest, the dream of thereby making money. Otto Lilienthal (whose brother I knew personally) and the Wright brothers and many others dreamed of flying and consciously risked their lives in pursuing their dream. It was not the hope of gain that inspired them, but the dream of a new freedom – of the expansion of our ecological niche: it was in the course of the search for a better world that Otto Lilienthal lost his life.

World 3 plays a decisive role in the shaping of reality, in the attempt to realize the world 2 dream of flying. The decisive factor is the plans and descriptions, the hypotheses, the trials, the accidents and the corrections; in a phrase, the method of trial and the elimination of errors through criticism.

This is the spiral of the feedback mechanism; and within it the world 2 of the researchers and the inventors also plays a great role. But even more important are the emergent problems and above all world 3, which has a constant feedback effect upon world 2. Our dreams are constantly corrected by means of world 3, until they can one day be finally realized.

Pessimists have pointed out to me that Otto Lilienthal, the German glider pilot, like Leonardo, dreamed of a mode of flying like a bird. They would probably have been horrified if they could have seen our Airbus.

This remark is correct in so far as our ideas are no doubt never realized in *quite* the way we imagine them. But nevertheless the remark is false. Anyone who wants to fly today in exactly the way that Leonardo and Lilienthal wanted to fly need only join a gliding club. Provided that he has the courage, it is not too difficult. Those others who fly in the Airbus or in a Boeing 747 will no doubt have their reasons for preferring this way of flying, despite its great dissimilarity to the glider; preferring it to the latter or to the railway or to the boat or to the motor vehicle. Even flying in the cramped conditions of a giant aeroplane has created many new possibilities and many new and valuable liberties for many people.

II

Giant aeroplanes are without a doubt consequences of Leonardo's and Lilienthal's dreams, but probably unforeseeable consequences. Using our language, our scientific knowledge and our technology, we are able to predict the future consequences of our dreams, our wishes and our inventions, better than do plants and animals, but certainly *not a great deal better*. It is important that we realize just how little we know about these unforeseeable consequences of our actions. The best means available to us is still *trial and error*: trials that are often dangerous, and even more dangerous errors – which are sometimes dangerous to humanity.

The belief in a political Utopia is especially dangerous. This is possibly connected with the fact that the search for a better world, like the investigation of our environment, is (if I am correct) one of the oldest and most important of all the instincts of life. We are right to believe that we can and should contribute to the improvement of our world. But we must not imagine that we can foresee the consequences of our plans and actions. Above all we must not sacrifice any human life (except perhaps our own if the worst comes to the worst). Nor do we have the right to persuade or even to encourage others to sacrifice themselves – not even for an idea, for a theory that has completely convinced us (probably unreasonably, because of our ignorance).

In any case, one part of our search for a better world must consist in the search for a world in which others are not forced to sacrifice their lives for the sake of an idea.

III

I have come to the end of my lecture. I would like to add just one final optimistic reflection, with which I also ended my contribution to *The Self and Its Brain*, a book that my friend Sir John Eccles and I wrote together.

As I have tried to show above, Darwinian selection, the ideas of natural selection and selection pressure, are generally associated with a bloody struggle for existence. This is an ideology that should be taken seriously only in part.

But with the emergence of human consciousness and of the mind and of linguistically formulated theories this all changes completely. We can leave it to the competition between theories to eliminate the unusable ones. In previous times the upholder of the theory was eliminated. Now we can let our theories die in our place. From a biological point of view – the point of view of natural selection – the main function of the mind and of world 3 is that they make possible the use of conscious criticism; and consequently, the selection of theories without the killing of their proponents. This non-violent use of the method of rational criticism is made possible through biological development; through our invention of language and the subsequent creation of world 3. In this way natural selection overcomes or transcends its original no doubt rather violent character: with the emergence of world 3 it becomes possible to select the best theories, the best adaptations, even without violence. We can now eliminate false theories using non-violent criticism. Doubtless, non-violent criticism is still seldom employed: criticism is usually still a semi-violent activity, even when it is fought out on paper. But there are no longer any biological reasons for violent criticism, only reasons against it.

Hence the currently predominant, semi-violent criticism could be a temporary stage in the development of reason. The emergence of world 3 means that non-violent cultural evolution is not a utopian dream. It is a biological and entirely feasible consequence of the emergence of world 3 through natural selection.

A shaping of our social environment with the aim of peace and non-violence is not just a dream. It is a possible, and from the biological point of view obviously necessary, objective for mankind.

NOTES

1 Translator's note: The page numbers refer to Kant's *Critique of Pure Reason*, trans. Norman Kemp Smith, Macmillan, London, 2nd edn 1933 (reprinted 1990).

2 Translator's note: The English term 'verdict' does not express the element of truth contained in the jury's judgement as explicitly as does the German *Wahrspruch* (literally 'true saying'). However, the English word is derived from the Latin *veredictum* (literal meaning 'spoken truly').

3 There are of course also facts that support the old interpretation; such as *catastrophic changes of the niches*, say, through the introduction of a poison like DDT or penicillin. In these cases, which have nothing to do with the preferences of the organisms, it is in fact the chance existence of a mutant that may determine the survival of the species. The situation is similar in the famous case in England of 'industrial melanism'; that is, the development of dark varieties (of moths) by way of adaptation to industrial pollution. These striking and experimentally repeatable, but very specific, cases may perhaps explain why the interpretation of Darwinism that I describe as 'pessimistic' is so popular among biologists.

2

ON KNOWLEDGE AND IGNORANCE

Mr President, Mr Dean, ladies and gentlemen, let me first thank the Faculty of Economic Sciences of the Johann Wolfgang Goethe University for the great honour they have bestowed on me in making me a *doctor rerum politicarum honoris causa*. With Johann Wolfgang Goethe's great first monologue of Doctor Faust, I can now say:

> They call me a master, and a doctor to boot . . .
> But in teaching my students I can do no good.

But I really must ask you for your permission to recite a dozen lines from the beginning of the monologue in full; you will find that they are highly relevant.[1]

> I have studied philosophy
> Many a night,
> Eager and earnest
> And hopeful of light;
> Also medicine and law
> Which were mainly a grind,
> And it all conspired to close up my mind.
> Thereafter I turned to theology.
> But this subject, by God! was sheer blasphemy.
> And now I stand here,
> A poor foolish bore,
> Knowing no more
> Than ever before.
> They call me a master,

A lecture given on 8 June 1979 in the Great Hall of the University of Frankfurt am Main on being awarded an honorary doctorate.

And a doctor to boot,
But in teaching my students
I can do no good.
I have longed to find
The great powers that bind
Together the world.
Now I see we are blind.
For I see that true knowledge
Cannot be achieved.
And my heart almost breaks:
I am deeply aggrieved.

As you see, what Doctor Faust says is highly relevant: he leads us towards the very topic announced by the title of my talk, the topic of Knowledge and Ignorance.[2] I intend to deal with this subject historically, though only very briefly, and to make its focal point the teachings of Socrates; and so I shall begin with the finest philosophical work I know, Plato's *Apology of Socrates Before His Judges*.

I

Plato's *Apology* contains Socrates' defence speech and a short report on his condemnation. I regard the speech as authentic.[3] In it, Socrates describes how astonished and alarmed he was when he heard that the Oracle of Delphi upon being asked the bold question 'Is there anyone who is wiser than Socrates?', replied: 'No one is wiser.'[4] 'When I heard this,' said Socrates, 'I asked myself: What can Apollo possibly mean? For I know that I am not wise; neither very wise, nor even only a little.' Since Socrates found that he could not work out what the god meant by the judgement of the oracle, he decided to try to refute it. So he went to someone who was regarded as wise – to one of the politicians of Athens – to learn from him. Socrates describes the result as follows (*Apology* 21 D): 'I am certainly wiser than this man: it is true that neither of us knows anything that is good. But *he* supposes that he knows something, and yet knows nothing. It is true that *I* too know nothing; but I do not pretend to know anything.' After speaking to the politicians, Socrates went to the poets. The result was the same. And then he went to the craftsmen. Now these indeed did know things of which he had no understanding. But they were under the impression that they also knew many other things, even the greatest things. And their arrogance more than offset their genuine knowledge.

Hence Socrates finally reached the following interpretation of the intention of the Delphic Oracle: clearly, the god did not want to say anything at all about Socrates; he had made use of this name only for the purpose of claiming that 'The wisest of men is the one who, like Socrates, recognizes that in reality he is not wise.'

II

Socrates' insight into our ignorance – 'I know that I know almost nothing, and hardly that' – is, in my opinion, of the utmost importance. This insight was never expressed more clearly than in Plato's *Apology of Socrates*. This Socratic insight has often not been taken seriously. Under Aristotle's influence, it was regarded as ironical. Plato himself ultimately (in the *Gorgias*) rejected the Socratic teaching of our ignorance, and with it the characteristic Socratic stance: the call for intellectual modesty.

This becomes clear if we compare the Socratic theory of the statesman with the Platonic theory. This particular point should be especially significant to a *doctor rerum politicarum*.

Both Socrates and Plato require the statesman to be wise. But this has a fundamentally different meaning for each of them. For Socrates, it means that the statesman should be fully aware of his indisputable ignorance. Hence Socrates advocates intellectual modesty. 'Know thyself!' means for him: 'Be aware of how little you know!'

By contrast, Plato interprets the demand that the statesman be wise as a demand for the rule of the wise, for the rule of the sophists. Only the well-educated dialectician, the learned philosopher, is competent to rule. This is the meaning of the famous Platonic insistence that philosophers must become kings and kings become fully trained philosophers. Philosophers have been deeply impressed by this Platonic stipulation; the kings, one may suppose, rather less so.

One can scarcely imagine a greater contrast between two interpretations of the requirement that the statesman be wise. It is the contrast between intellectual modesty and intellectual arrogance. And it is also the contrast between fallibilism – the recognition of the fallibility of all human knowledge – and scientism – the theory that authority should be conferred upon knowledge and the knower, upon science and the scientists, upon wisdom and the wise man, and upon learning and the learned.

It is clear from this that a contrast in the assessment of human knowledge – that is, an epistemological contrast – can result in contrasting ethico-political objectives and requirements.

III

At this stage I should like to discuss an objection to fallibilism; an objection that, in my opinion, could almost be used as an argument *in favour of* fallibilism.

This is the objection that knowledge, unlike opinion or supposition, is intrinsically a matter of authority; and further, that general linguistic usage supports the theory of the authoritative nature of knowledge. Thus it is only grammatically correct to use the expression 'I know' in the presence of the following three things: first, the truth of what I am claiming to know; second, its certainty; and third, the availability of sufficient reasons for it.

Such analyses can often be heard in philosophical discussions and read in philosophy books.[5] And these analyses really do show what we mean by our everyday use of the word 'knowledge'. They analyse a concept that I should like to call the classical concept of knowledge: this classical concept of knowledge implies the truth and the certainty of what is known; and also that we have sufficient reasons for holding it to be true.

It is precisely this classical concept of knowledge that Socrates is using when he says 'I know that I know almost nothing – and hardly that!' And Goethe is using the same classical concept of knowledge when he has Faust say:

> And now to feel that nothing can be known!
> This is a thought that burns into my heart.

Hence it is precisely this classical concept of knowledge, the concept of knowledge of everyday language, which is also used by fallibilism, the doctrine of fallibility, to emphasize that we are always or almost always capable of error and that we therefore know nothing or only very little in the classical sense of 'knowledge'; or, as Socrates says, that we know 'nothing that is good'.

Of what was Socrates likely to have been thinking when he said that we know 'nothing that is good' or, more literally translated, 'nothing that is beautiful and good' (*Apology* 21 D)? Here Socrates was thinking particularly of ethics. He was far from declaring ethical knowledge to be impossible; on the contrary, he tried to find a basis for it. His method of doing so was a critical one: he criticized anything that seemed to himself and to others to be certain. It was this critical method that led him to fallibilism and to the insight that he and others were far from having knowledge in ethical matters. Nevertheless Socrates is a innovative moral philosopher. It is from him and from his contemporary Democritus that we have the valid and important rule of life: 'It is better to suffer injustice than to inflict it.'

IV

But to return to the *Apology*; when Socrates says there that nothing good is known by him or by others, he is perhaps thinking also of the philosophers of nature, of those great Greek thinkers whom we now call the Presocratics, the forefathers of the natural sciences as we know them today. Socrates may have been thinking in particular of Anaxagoras, the philosopher of nature mentioned in his *Apology* a little later, as it happens in a not very respectful manner: for he says that the work of Anaxagoras, which he describes as 'unsuccessful' (*atopos*), will fetch a drachma at most at the Athenian booksellers (*Apology* 26 D). Furthermore, another of Plato's works, the *Phaedo*, intimates that Socrates was greatly disappointed by Anaxagoras' philosophy of nature – and by philosophy of nature in general. Hence we have reason to suppose that when Socrates said 'I know that I know almost nothing – and hardly that', he was thinking of the many grave and unsolved problems that he had encountered; from ethical and political problems to those of the philosophy of nature.

Socrates, to be sure, does not have all that much in common with Goethe's Faust. Nevertheless, we may suppose that the insight that we can know nothing burned into Socrates' heart too: that he, like Faust, suffered intensely from the unfulfilled desire of all true scientists:

> To know what forces there might be
> That hold this word in unity.

But modern natural science has nevertheless brought us somewhat closer to this unrealizable goal. Hence we must ask whether the stance of Socratic ignorance has not been shown by modern natural science to have been transcended.

V

In fact, Newton's theory of gravitation created a completely new situation. This theory can be regarded as the realization, after more than two thousand years, of the original research programme of the Presocratic natural philosophers. And Newton himself may have been thinking of his theory in this light when he chose the title of his book: *Mathematical Principles of Natural Philosophy*. It was a realization that left the boldest dreams of the ancient world far behind.

It was an unprecedented step forward. Descartes' theory, which Newtonian theory gradually displaced, does not stand comparison. It provided only a very vague qualitative explanation of planetary movement, but nevertheless, it contradicted facts that were well established even in those days. Among other things, Descartes' theory had the disastrous consequence that the planets furthest away from the sun move the fastest, thus contradicting not only observations but also, and most importantly, Kepler's third law.

By contrast, Newton's theory not only could explain Kepler's laws, but also corrected them, since it yielded correct quantitative predictions of minor deviations from these laws.

VI

Thus Newton's theory created a new intellectual situation; it was an unparalleled intellectual triumph. The predictions of Newtonian theory were corroborated with unbelievable accuracy. And when minor deviations from the orbit predicted by Newton for the planet Uranus were discovered, it was from precisely these deviations that Adams and Leverrier, with the help of Newton's theory (and a great deal of luck), calculated the position of a new and unknown planet, which was then promptly discovered by Galle. Furthermore, Newton's theory explained not only the movement of the heavenly bodies, but also terrestrial mechanics, the movements of bodies at the surface of the earth.

It seemed that here indeed was knowledge; true, certain and sufficiently justified knowledge. There could surely be no further doubt about it.

It took a remarkably long time before the novelty of the intellectual situation was grasped. Few realized what had happened. David Hume, one of the greatest philosophers, saw that a great step forward had been taken, but he did not understand just how great and how radical this advance in human knowledge really was. I am afraid that even today many people still do not fully understand this.

VII

Immanuel Kant was the first thinker to understand it fully. Converted to scepticism by Hume, he saw the paradoxical, almost illogical nature of this new knowledge. He asked himself how something like Newtonian science could ever be possible at all.

This question, and Kant's answer, became the central issue of his *Critique of Pure Reason*. In this book Kant raised the questions:

How is pure mathematics possible?

and

How is pure science of nature possible?

And he wrote: 'Since these sciences actually exist, it is quite proper to ask *how* they are possible; for that they must be possible is proved by the fact that they exist.'[6]

Kant's astonishment – his legitimate astonishment at the existence of Newton's theory, which he characterized as 'pure natural science' – is unmistakable.

Unlike everyone else who had an opinion on the matter, Kant saw that Newton's theory was not the result of an experimental or inductive method, but a creation of human thought, of the human intellect.

Kant's answer to the question 'How is pure natural science possible?' was as follows:

> Our intellect does not draw its laws [the laws of nature] from nature, but imposes its laws upon nature.

In other words, Newton's laws are not read off from nature, but are rather Newton's work, they are the product of his intellect, his invention: the human intellect invents the laws of nature.

This extremely novel epistemological position held by Kant was described by Kant himself as the Copernican Revolution in the theory of knowledge. Newton's science is, in Kant's view, knowledge in the classical sense: true, certain and sufficiently justified knowledge. Moreover, knowledge such as this is possible because human experience itself is the product of active processing and interpretation of sense data by our cognitive apparatus, especially by our intellect.

This Kantian theory of knowledge is important and for the most part correct. But Kant was mistaken in his belief that his theory answered the question of how knowledge, that is, knowledge in the classical sense, is possible.

The classical notion of science as true, secure and sufficiently justified knowledge still flourishes even today. But it was overtaken sixty years ago by the Einsteinian Revolution; by Einstein's gravitational theory.

The outcome of this revolution is that Einstein's theory, whether true or false, demonstrates that knowledge in the classical sense, secure knowledge, certainty is impossible. Kant was right: our theories are free creations of our intellect, which we try to impose upon nature. But we are only rarely successful in guessing the truth; and we can never be certain whether we have succeeded. *We must make do with conjectural knowledge.*

VIII

I must make some brief comments here upon the logical connections between Newton's gravitational theory and Einstein's.

Newton's theory and Einstein's logically contradict each other: there are specific consequences of the two theories that are incompatible given particular background knowledge. Hence it is impossible for both theories to be true.

Nevertheless the two theories are related to each other through *approximation*. The discrepancies between their empirically verifiable consequences are so small that all the countless observed instances that corroborate and support Newton's theory simultaneously corroborate and support Einstein's theory.

Newton's theory was, as I have already mentioned, backed by splendid empirical corroboration; it might indeed be said, optimal corroboration. But the discovery, or invention, of Einstein's theory makes it impossible for us to regard these splendid corroborations as reasons for regarding even just one of these two theories as true and certain. For the very same reasons we would then also support acceptance of the other theory as true and certain. Yet it is logically impossible for two incompatible theories both to be true.

Hence we learn from this that it is impossible to interpret even the best-corroborated scientific theories as knowledge in the classical sense. Even our best-tested and best-corroborated scientific theories are mere conjectures, successful hypotheses, and they are for ever condemned to remain conjectures or hypotheses.

IX

Knowledge is the search for truth; and it is perfectly possible that many of our theories are in fact true. But even if they are true, we can never know this for certain.

This had already been realized by the poet and bard Xenophanes, who wrote approximately a hundred years before Socrates and five hundred years before the birth of Christ (the translations are mine):

> But as for certain truth, no man has known it,
> Nor will he know it; neither of the gods,
> Nor yet of all the things of which I speak.
> And even if by chance he were to utter
> The perfect truth, he would himself not know it:
> For all is but a woven web of guesses.

Yet even in those days Xenophanes taught that there can be progress in our search for truth; for he writes:

> The gods did not reveal, from the beginning,
> All things to us; but in the course of time,
> Through seeking we may learn, and know things better.

These fragments of Xenophanes that I have quoted might perhaps be encapsulated in the following two theses:

1. There is no criterion for truth; even when we have reached the truth, we can never be certain of it.

2. There is a rational criterion for progress in the search for truth, and hence a criterion for scientific progress.

I believe that both theses are correct.

But what is the rational criterion for scientific progress in the search for truth, for progress in our hypotheses, in our conjectures? When is one scientific hypothesis better than another hypothesis?

The answer is: science is a critical activity. We examine our hypotheses critically. We criticize them so that we can find errors, in the hope of eliminating the errors and thus getting closer to the truth.

We regard one hypothesis, a new hypothesis for example, as better than another if it fulfils the following three requirements. First, the new hypothesis must explain all the things that the old hypothesis successfully explained. That is the first and most important point. Second, it must avoid at least some of the errors of the old hypothesis: that is, it should, where possible, withstand some of the critical tests that the old hypothesis could not withstand. Third, it should, where possible, explain things that could not be explained or predicted by the old hypothesis.

This is therefore the criterion of scientific progress. It is employed very widely and usually unconsciously, particularly in the natural sciences. A new hypothesis is only taken seriously if it explains at least everything that was successfully explained by its predecessor, and if, in addition, it either promises to avoid particular errors of the old hypothesis or makes new predictions – where possible, testable predictions.

X

This criterion for progress can also be regarded as a criterion for approximation to the truth. For if a hypothesis satisfies the criterion for progress and therefore withstands our critical tests at least as well as its predecessor did, then we do not regard this as a coincidence; and if it withstands the critical tests even better, then we assume that it comes closer to the truth than its predecessor did.

Truth is therefore the aim of science: science is the search for truth. And even if, as Xenophanes saw, we cannot know if we have achieved this aim, we nevertheless have very good reasons for supposing that we have come closer to the truth; or, as Einstein says, that we are on the right track.

XI

I would like to end by drawing some conclusions from what I have said.

The Socratic doctrine of ignorance is, in my view, extremely important. We have seen that Newtonian natural science was interpreted by Kant in terms of the classical concept of knowledge. This interpretation has been unacceptable since Einstein. We now know that even the best knowledge acquired in the natural sciences does not constitute knowledge in the classical sense, that is, it is not the 'knowledge' of ordinary language. This leads to a genuine revolution of the concept of knowledge: the knowledge of the natural sciences is *conjectural knowledge*; it is bold guesswork. So Socrates is right, despite Kant's sympathetic evaluation of Newton's monumental achievement. But knowledge is guesswork disciplined by rational criticism.

This turns the struggle against dogmatic thinking into a duty. It also makes the utmost intellectual modesty a duty. And above all, it makes a duty of the cultivation of a simple and unpretentious language: the duty of every intellectual.

All the great natural scientists were intellectually modest; and Newton speaks for them all when he says: 'I do not know what I may appear to the world, but to myself I seem to have been only a boy playing on the seashore, and diverting myself in now and then finding a smoother pebble or a prettier shell than ordinary, whilst the great ocean of truth lay all undiscovered before me.'[7] Einstein called his general theory of relativity a nine-day wonder.

Moreover, all the great scientists realized that every solution to a scientific problem raises many new and unsolved problems. Our knowledge of the problems that are as yet unsolved, our Socratic knowledge of our ignorance, becomes increasingly conscious, detailed and precise, the more we learn about the world. Scientific research is the best method we have for obtaining information about ourselves and about our ignorance. It leads us to the important insight that there may be great differences between us with regard to the minor details of what we may perhaps know, yet we are all equal in our infinite ignorance.

XII

The charge of scientism – that is, of having a dogmatic belief in the authority of the method of the natural sciences and in its results – is therefore completely inappropriate if it is levelled at the critical method of the natural sciences or against the great natural scientists; especially since the reform of the concept of knowledge, which we owe to such men as Socrates, Nicolas da Cusa, Erasmus, Voltaire, Lessing, Goethe and Einstein. Goethe was, as all great scientists are too, an opponent of scientism, of the belief in authority; and he fought against it in the context of his criticism of Newton's *Optics*. His arguments against Newton were probably invalid, but all great natural scientists have sometimes made mistakes; and Goethe's polemic against Newton's dogmatic belief in authority was certainly appropriate. I would even go so far here as to conjecture that the charge of scientism – that is, the charge of dogmatism, of belief in authority and of the arrogant presumption of knowledge – is far more frequently applicable to the adherents of the sociologies of knowledge and of science than to their victims, the great natural scientists. In fact, many people who regard themselves as critics of scientism are in reality dogmatic, ideological and authoritarian opponents of the natural sciences, of which they sadly understand all too little.

First and foremost, they do not know that the natural sciences have an objective and non-ideological criterion of progress: of progress towards the truth. It is that simple and rational criterion that has dominated the development of the natural sciences since Copernicus, Galileo, Kepler and Newton, since Pasteur and Claude Bernard. The criterion is not always applicable. But natural scientists (except when they have fallen victim to fashions, as has happened even to some good physicists) generally use it confidently and with accuracy, even though they are rarely wholly conscious of doing so. In the social sciences, the power of this rational criterion is much less assured. Thus fashionable ideologies and the power of great words developed, together with opposition to reason and to natural science.

Goethe was also acquainted with this anti-scientific ideology, and he condemned it. The Devil himself is waiting for us to embrace it. The words that Goethe makes the Devil say are unambiguous:

Reason and science you despise,
The highest powers of the mind?
Hell's willing slave with others of your kind,
You are the profits of my enterprise.

Ladies and gentlemen, I hope that you will not condemn me if this time I let the Devil himself have the last word.

NOTES

1 Note that my English version of Faust's speech is in some places extremely free; see the Endnote below.

2 Translator's note: Up to this point, the English text of this address is due to the author, and so are all the later verse translations.

3 Of course there is no proof of the authenticity of Plato's *Apology*: even prominent scholars have spoken out against it. But there are important grounds for accepting it. I am sure that Plato intended it to be regarded as genuine, and that it numbers amongst his early works, so that many witnesses were still alive when Plato wrote the *Apology*. As in all the early dialogues (at least before the *Gorgias*), Socrates employs in the *Apology* the method of *refutation by practical examples* (*elenchos*: 21 B–C); and he stresses his *ignorance*.

4 This judgement of the oracle is obviously historical too. Chaerephon, who put the question to the oracle, and was a friend and admirer of Socrates in his youth, is a historical figure, a militant opponent of the Thirty Tyrants, falling in the battle of Piraeus. His brother was cited by Socrates as a witness and was present throughout his trial. Since Plato was an opponent of democracy, the crucial role played in the *Apology* by Chaerephon, a follower of democracy, supports the authenticity of Plato's report.

5 Cf. W. T. Krug, *Fundamentalphilosophie*, 1818, p. 237; J. F. Fries, *System der Logik*, 1837, pp. 412 f. A possible English replacement for these inaccessible German references: Bertrand Russell, *The Problems of Philosophy*, Williams & Norgate, 1912, OUP paperback 1967, ch. XIII.

6 Kant, *Critique of Pure Reason*, trans. Norman Kemp Smith, 2nd edn, Macmillan, London, 1933 (reprinted 1990), p. 56.

7 Translator's note: The English version of this quotation is taken from *Brewster's Memoirs of Newton*, vol. II, ch. 27.

Endnote In my very free translation of Faust's monologue (lines 354–65, with an adaptation of lines 382–3 inserted in place of 362–3), I have tried to make the translation close whenever I could, but I have in general made two (but in one or two places more lines) out of one German line, in order to catch the mood and something of the rhythm of Faust's speech. In one place – the two lines on theology and blasphemy – I have gone beyond Goethe's one short line (356), because I felt it impossible otherwise to translate the utter condemnation and contempt compressed and hidden in the two harmless sounding German words '*leider auch*'. I must thus stress my responsibility for sharpening Goethe's attack, but I wish also to refer the reader to Faust's lines 3428 and 3429 in his comments on Margarete's question 'Do you believe in God?'

3

ON THE SO-CALLED SOURCES OF KNOWLEDGE

Thank you for the great honour that you have bestowed on me by making me a Doctor of Philosophy in the Faculty of Arts of your University. I am deeply grateful for this honour and I accept it with real pleasure.

I have also taken on a difficult task, at very short notice, namely the task of giving a short lecture. Before I begin this lecture, however, I should like to tell you a true story from my days in New Zealand.

In Christchurch, New Zealand, I was friendly with the physicist Professor Coleridge Farr, who was roughly the same age when I arrived there as I am now. He was a very witty and amusing man and a Fellow of the Royal Society of London. Professor Farr was a public-spirited man, and used to give lectures on popular science in the most varied circles, including, among others, prisons. Once he began his lecture in a prison with the words: 'Today I am giving exactly the same lecture as I gave here six years ago. So if anyone has already heard it, then it jolly well serves him right!' Scarcely had he uttered these rather provocative words, when the light in the lecture hall went out. He said afterwards that he had felt rather ill at ease until the light came back on.

I was reminded of this situation when Professor Weingartner told me last Saturday – that is, right at the last minute – that I was expected to give a lecture here today. You see, he added that I could, of course, repeat one of my old lectures. Naturally, I thought of Professor Farr, and also that I could obviously *not* say here 'If anyone has already heard my lecture, then it serves him

Lecture given on 27 July 1979 at the University of Salzburg when the author was awarded an honorary doctorate.

right.' So I am in an even worse position than Professor Farr; for, since I had very little time, I had no option, after several unsuccessful attempts, but to revamp a larger old work of mine,[1] give it a new introduction and, above all, shorten it by about seven-eighths. I do apologize therefore, particularly because my lecture is still far too long. But I hope that, with the exception of one or two members of my honourable audience, no one will recognize my lecture. The subject of my lecture is: 'On the So-called Sources of Human Knowledge'.

There has been something like a theory of knowledge for almost 2,500 years. And the fundamental question of this theory of knowledge which concerned philosophers from the Greeks to the members of the Vienna Circle was *the question of the sources of our knowledge*.

Even in one of the later works of Rudolf Carnap, one of the leaders of the Vienna Circle, we can read something on the following lines: If you make an assertion, then you must also justify it. And this means that you must be able to answer the following questions:

How do you know that? What is the *source* of your assertion? What *observations* underlie your assertion?

I find this string of questions quite unsatisfactory, and, in the course of this lecture, I want to try to indicate some of the reasons *why* I find these questions so unsatisfactory.

My main reason is that these questions presuppose an authoritarian attitude to the problem of human knowledge. They presuppose that our assertions are reliable if, and only if, we can appeal to the authority of *sources of knowledge* and in particular to *observations*.

By contrast, I claim that there are no such authorities and that a *moment of uncertainty* clings to *all* assertions; even to all assertions based upon *observation*, indeed even to all *true* assertions.

That is why I shall suggest here that the old question about the sources of our knowledge should be replaced by a completely different question. The traditional question of the theory of knowledge has a certain similarity with the traditional question of political theory, and this similarity can help us to find a new and more appropriate question for the theory of knowledge.

That is to say, the traditional fundamental question about the authoritarian sources of knowledge corresponds to the traditional fundamental question of political theory according to Plato. I am referring to the question 'Who should rule?'

This question demands an authoritarian answer. The traditional answers were: 'the best' or 'the wisest'. But different and apparently liberal answers to the question, such as 'the people' or 'the majority', also lurk within the authoritarian formulation of the question.

It also leads us, incidentally, into such silly alternatives as: 'Who should be our rulers: the capitalists or the workers?' (This question is analogous to the epistemological question: 'What is the ultimate source of knowledge: the intellect or the senses?')

The question 'Who should rule?' is obviously wrongly put, and the answers which it elicits are authoritarian. (They are also paradoxical.)

I propose that this question should be replaced by an entirely different and much more modest question such as: 'How can we organize our political institutions so that bad or incompetent rulers (whom we should try to avoid, of course, but whom we might get all the same) can do the minimum amount of damage?'

I believe that unless we change our question in this way we can never hope to proceed towards a reasonable theory of the state and its institutions.

In my opinion, the only theoretical foundation for democracy lies in the answer to this much more modest question. The answer is: The democratic institutions are designed to enable us to get rid of bad or incompetent or tyrannical rulers without bloodshed. (Incidentally, the survival of the term 'democracy' – which is Greek for 'rule of the people' – shows that Platonism and the question 'Who should rule?' are unfortunately still influential, although, fortunately, in practice democracy has always attempted to tackle the most important question of politics: the avoidance of despotism.)

In a similar way, the question about the sources of our knowledge can be replaced by another question. The traditional question was and still is: 'What are the best sources of our knowledge – the most reliable ones, those which will not lead us into error, and to which we can turn, in case of doubt, as a last court of appeal?'

I propose to assume that no such ideal and infallible sources of knowledge exist – no more than ideal and infallible rulers – and that all 'sources' of our knowledge may lead us into error at times.

And I propose to replace the question of the sources of our knowledge by an entirely different question, by the question: 'Is there a way of detecting and eliminating error?'

The question of the sources of our knowledge, like so many authoritarian questions, is a question about origin. It asks for the origin of our knowledge, in the belief that knowledge may legitimate itself by its pedigree. The (often unconscious) metaphysical idea behind the question is one of a racially pure knowledge, an untainted knowledge, a knowledge which derives from the highest authority, if possible from God Himself, and which therefore incorporates the authority of an independent nobility. My modified question 'How can we hope to detect error?' derives from the conviction that such pure, untainted and certain sources do not exist, and questions of origin and of purity should not be confounded with questions of validity and of truth. This view is an old one which goes back to Xenophanes. Xenophanes was aware in about 500 BC that what we call knowledge is nothing but guesswork and opinion – *doxa* rather than *episteme* –as we can see from his verses:[2]

> The gods did not reveal, from the beginning,
> All things to us; but in the course of time,
> Through seeking we may learn, and know things better.
> But as for certain truth, no man has known it,
> Nor will he know it; neither of the gods,
> Nor yet of all the things of which I speak.
> And even if by chance he were to utter
> The perfect truth, he would himself not know it:
> For all is but a woven web of guesses.

Yet the traditional question of the authoritative sources of our knowledge is still asked today – and very often even by positivists and other philosophers who are convinced that they are in revolt against all authority.

The proper answer to my question 'How can we hope to detect and eliminate error?' seems to me to be 'By criticizing the theories and conjectures of others and – if we can train ourselves to do so – by criticizing our own theories and speculative attempts to solve problems.' (Incidentally, such criticism of our own theories is highly desirable, but not indispensable; for if we don't criticize them ourselves, there will be others who will do it for us.)

This answer sums up a position which we might describe as 'critical rationalism'. It is a view, attitude and tradition that we owe to the Greeks. It is fundamentally different from the 'rationalism' or 'intellectualism' of Descartes and his school, and even from Kant's epistemology. Yet in the field of ethics and moral knowledge, Kant's *principle of autonomy* comes very close to this position. This principle expresses his realization that we must never accept the command of an authority, however exalted, as the basis of ethics. For whenever we are faced with the command of an authority, it is always up to us to judge, critically, whether it is morally permissible to obey. The authority may have the power to enforce its commands, and we may be powerless to resist. But if it is physically possible for us to choose our conduct, then we cannot escape the ultimate responsibility. For the critical decision rests with us: we can obey or disobey the command; we can accept the authority or reject it.

Kant boldly applied this idea also to the field of religion: in his opinion, the responsibility for deciding whether the teachings of a religion should be accepted as good or rejected as evil rests with us.

In view of this bold statement, it seems strange that in his *philosophy of science* Kant did not adopt the same attitude of critical rationalism, of the critical search for error. I feel certain that only *one thing* prevented Kant from taking this step: his acceptance of Newton's authority in the field of cosmology. This acceptance was based upon the fact that Newton's theory had passed the most severe tests with almost unbelievable success.

If my interpretation of Kant is correct, then critical rationalism – and critical empiricism which I also advocate – can be regarded as an attempt to carry further Kant's critical philosophy. This was only made possible by Albert Einstein, who taught us that Newton's theory may perhaps still be mistaken in spite of its overwhelming success.

So my answer to the traditional question of epistemology, 'How do you know that? What is the source or the basis of your assertion? Upon what observations is it founded?' is: 'Of course I am not saying that I *know* anything: my assertion was only meant as a conjecture, a hypothesis. Nor should we worry about the source, or the sources, from which my conjecture may have sprung: there are many possible sources, and I am by no means aware of them all. In any case, origin and pedigree have very little to do with truth. But if you are interested in the problem that I tried to solve by my tentative conjecture, then you can help me. Try to criticize it as severely and as objectively as you can! And if you can devise an experiment which you think might refute my assertion, then I am prepared to do everything in my power to help you to refute it.'

This answer applies, strictly speaking, only if the question is asked about some scientific assertion as distinct from a historical one. For if the tentative assertion has a historical reference, then any critical discussion of its validity must of course also deal with *sources* – although not with 'ultimate' and 'authoritative' sources. But my answer would remain fundamentally the same.

I am now going to summarize the results of this discussion. I will put them in the form of eight theses:

1. There are no ultimate sources of knowledge. Every source, every suggestion, is welcome; but every source, every suggestion, is also open to critical examination. As long as we are not dealing with historical matters, we usually examine the asserted facts themselves, rather than investigate the sources of our information.

2. The proper questions of epistemology are not actually concerned with sources at all; rather, we ask whether an assertion is true – that is to say, whether it agrees with the facts.

In connection with this critical examination of the truth, all kinds of arguments may be brought to bear. One of the most important procedures is to take a critical attitude towards our own theories and, in particular, to look for contradictions between our theories and observations.

3. Tradition is – apart from inborn knowledge – by far the most important source of our knowledge.

4. The fact that most of the sources of our knowledge are traditional demonstrates that opposition to tradition, that is to say, antitraditionalism, is of no importance. But this fact must not be held to support traditionalism; for every bit, however small, of our traditional knowledge (and even of our inborn knowledge) is open to critical examination and may be overthrown if need be. Nevertheless, without tradition, knowledge would be impossible.

5. Knowledge cannot start from nothing – from the *tabula rasa* – nor yet from observation. The advance of our knowledge consists in the modification and the correction of earlier knowledge. Of course it is sometimes possible to take a step forward through an observation or through a chance discovery; but the significance of

an observation or of a discovery generally depends upon whether it enables us to modify *existing* theories.

6. Neither observation nor reason is an authority. Other sources, such as intellectual intuition and intellectual imagination, are most important, but they are also unreliable: they may show us things with the utmost clarity and yet mislead us. They are the main sources of our theories and are therefore indispensable; but the vast majority of our theories are false. The most important function of observation and logical thought, but also of intellectual intuition and imagination, is to help us in the critical examination of those bold theories which we need in order to delve into the unknown.

7. Clarity is an intellectual value in itself; exactness and precision, however, are not. Absolute precision is unattainable; and there is no point in trying to be more precise than our problem demands. The idea that we must define our concepts to make them 'precise' or even to give them a 'meaning' is misleading. Every definition must make use of defining concepts; and so we can never ultimately avoid working with undefined concepts. Problems connected with the meaning or the definition of words are unimportant. Indeed, these purely verbal problems are tiresome: they should be avoided at all costs.

8. Every solution of a problem creates new unsolved problems. The harder the original problem and the bolder the attempt to solve it, the more interesting these new problems are. The more we learn about the world, and the deeper our learning, the more conscious, clear and well-defined will be our knowledge of *what we do not know*, our knowledge of our ignorance. The main source of our ignorance lies in the fact that our knowledge can only be finite, while our ignorance must necessarily be infinite.

We get an idea of the vastness of our ignorance when we contemplate the vastness of the heavens. It is true that the size of the universe is not the deepest cause of our ignorance; but it is nevertheless one of its causes.

I believe that it is worthwhile trying to discover more about the world, even if this only teaches us how little we know. It might do us good to remember from time to time that, while differing widely in the various little bits we know, in our infinite ignorance we are all equal.

If we thus admit that there is no authority beyond the reach of criticism to be found within the whole province of our knowledge, however far we may have penetrated into the unknown, then we can retain, without risk of dogmatism, the idea that truth itself is beyond all human authority. Indeed, we are not only able to retain this idea, we must retain it. For without it there can be no objective standards of scientific inquiry, no criticism of our conjectured solutions, no groping for the unknown, and no quest for knowledge.

NOTES

1 This is the 'Introduction' to my book *Conjectures and Refutations*, 1963; 5th edn, Routledge, London and New York, 1989.
2 Translated by the author.

4

SCIENCE AND CRITICISM

As an old member of the Alpbach Forum I was very pleased to be invited to its thirtieth birthday celebrations; but I only accepted this invitation after some hesitation. I thought it scarcely possible to say something sensible and comprehensible on our extremely wide-ranging basic theme of 'Intellectual and scientific development over the past thirty years' in just thirty minutes. In fact, if my mathematics are correct, this leaves me with exactly one minute for each year of intellectual and scientific development! And so I must not fritter away the time available to me with apologies, but must begin without further ado.

I

As you can see from the title I have chosen, 'Science and Criticism', I intend to let the question of intellectual development go more or less by the board and to deal mainly with the development of science. The reason for this is, quite simply, that I do not think much of the intellectual or cultural development of the past thirty years.

I am, of course, a layman in this field, since I am not a philosopher of culture. Yet it seems to me that, in spite of all the attempts to produce something new, the intellectual development of the last thirty years can be subsumed under Remarque's title 'All Quiet on the Western Front'. Moreover, I am afraid that it is also 'All Quiet on the Eastern Front' – unless you call India's transition from Mahatma Gandhi to the atom bomb an intellectual development.

Lecture given to commemorate the 30th anniversary of the so-called 'Alpbach European Forum', August 1974. Alpbach is a little village, high in the Tyrolese mountains, where since 1946 a Summer School has been held.

This development, which came to India from the West, replaced the idea of non-violence with the idea of violence. Sadly, this is nothing new to us. Some of our western philosophers of culture, the prophets of doom and of violence, have preached about this for a long time and, sure enough, their theory is now being translated into acts of violence.

But can we not report something better, something more encouraging from the realm of the spirit? I think that we can. I often reflect with pleasure that the music of the great masters of the past can be heard by far more people today and that it fills far more people with gratitude, hope and enthusiasm than one could ever dream of thirty years ago. It can truly be said of these works that:

> The incomprehensible noble works
> Are as magnificent as they were at the Creation.

In fact, it seems to me that they grow still more magnificent by the day.

One of the best things of our time is that so many people have a keen appreciation of the great works of art from the past, and this is, admittedly, partly thanks to technology – to the gramophone, to radio and to television. But in this case, such technology is serving genuine intellectual needs. Were there not such a great interest in the works of the past, they would not be played and shown so frequently. The development in this field is the most important, most revolutionary and most promising spiritual development of the past thirty years that I know of.

I would now like to turn to my two central subjects: scientific development over the past thirty years and my main subject, science and criticism.

II

If I am to talk about scientific development here today, then I must obviously adopt a very selective approach. My criterion is simple: I will discuss a few scientific developments that have interested me the most and that have had the most influence upon my conception of the world.

Of course, my selection is closely connected with my views on science and especially with my views on the criterion of scientific status which I have proposed for theories. This criterion is criticizability, rational criticism. In the natural sciences this boils down to criticizability by means of empirical tests or empirical refutation.

Clearly, I do not have time for more than a very brief discussion of criticizability.

I think that what is common to art, myth, science and even pseudo-science is that they all belong to something like a creative phase which allows us to see things in a new light, and seeks to explain the everyday world by reference to hidden worlds. These worlds of the imagination were anathema to the positivists. This explains why even Ernst Mach, the great Viennese positivist, was an opponent of atomic theory. But atomic theory survived, and the whole of our physics, not only the physics of material and atomic structure, but also the physics of electrical and magnetic fields and of gravitational fields, is a description of hypothetical worlds, which we suppose to lie hidden beyond the world of our experience.

These hypothetical worlds are, as in art, products of our imagination, of our intuition. But in science they are controlled *by criticism*: scientific criticism, rational criticism, is guided by the regulative idea of truth. We can never justify our scientific theories, for we can never know whether they will not turn out to be false. But we can subject them to critical examination: rational criticism replaces justification. Criticism curbs the imagination, but does not put it in chains.

So *science* is characterized by rational criticism which is guided by the idea of truth, whereas the imagination is common to all creative activity, be it art, myth or science. I will therefore confine myself in what follows to developments in which both these elements, imagination and rational criticism, are particularly apparent.

III

I will begin with a remark about mathematics.

As a student, I was strongly influenced by the eminent Viennese mathematician Hans Hahn, who was for his part influenced by Whitehead and Russell's great work, *Principia Mathematica*. The exciting ideological message of this work was that mathematics can be reduced to logic, or more precisely, that mathematics can be logically deduced from logic. We begin with something that is undoubtedly logic; we then proceed by strictly logical deduction, and in doing so we obtain something that is undoubtedly mathematics.

It seemed that this was not just a bold project. In *Principia Mathematica*, this research programme appeared to be realized. *Principia* began with the logic of deduction, the propositional calculus and the restricted functional calculus. From this the calculus of classes was deduced, without asserting that classes exist. Then abstract set theory was deduced, which had been established by Georg Cantor in the nineteenth century. In addition, *Principia* did much towards proving the thesis, which is rarely disputed even now, that differential and integral calculus can be constructed as part of set theory.

But it was not long before Whitehead and Russell's *Principia* came in for severe criticism, and about forty years ago the situation was still as follows. Three schools of thought could be distinguished. First, there was the school called logicism that maintained that mathematics could be reduced to logic, led by Bertrand Russell and, in Vienna, by Hans Hahn and Rudolf Carnap. Second, there was the school of axiomatics, later known also as formalism, that did not deduce set theory from logic, but wanted to introduce it as a formal system of axioms, similar to Euclidean geometry; holders of this view included Hilbert, Zermelo, Fraenkel, Bernays, Ackermann, Gentzen and von Neumann. The third school was that of the so-called intuitionists, to which Poincaré, Brouwer and later Hermann Weyl and Heyting belonged.

It was an extremely interesting situation, but at first it seemed hopeless. An enmity with strongly personal overtones developed between the two greatest and most productive mathematicians involved in the debate, Hilbert and Brouwer. Many mathematicians not only regarded the dispute over the foundations of mathematics as fruitless, but also rejected the basic project in its entirety.

Then, forty-four years ago, the Austrian mathematician Kurt Gödel entered the debate. Gödel had studied in Vienna, where logicism was strongly supported, but where the other two movements were also taken very seriously. Gödel's first major result, a proof of completeness for the restricted functional calculus, was based upon problems formulated by Hilbert and could probably be credited to formalism. His second result was his brilliant proof that established the incompleteness of *Principia Mathematica* and of the theory of numbers. All three competing schools of thought tried to take some credit for this result.

But this was in fact the beginning of the end – the end, that is, of these three schools of thought. In my opinion, it also heralded the beginning of a new philosophy of mathematics. Things are in a state of flux at the moment, but they may perhaps be summarized like this:

Russell's theory of reduction, that is, the theory that mathematics can be reduced to logic, is to be rejected. Mathematics cannot be completely reduced to logic; in fact, it has even led to a considerable refinement of logic and, it may be said, to a critical correction of logic: to a critical correction of our logical intuition and to the critical insight that our logical intuition is not all that reliable. On the other hand, it has also shown that intuition is very important and capable of development. The majority of creative ideas come about through intuition; and those that do not are the result of the critical refutation of intuitive ideas.

There does not seem to be *one* system of fundamental principles of mathematics, but different methods of constructing mathematics or the different branches of mathematics. I say 'constructing' and not 'establishing', since there seems to be no ultimate establishment or safeguard for its fundamental principles. Moreover, we can prove the consistency of our construction only in the case of weak systems. And we know from Tarski that important branches of mathematics are *fundamentally* incomplete, that is to say, these systems may be strengthened, but never to the extent that we can prove within them all true and relevant statements. Most mathematical theories are, like those of physics or biology, hypothetico-deductive: pure mathematics therefore turns out to be much closer to the natural sciences whose hypotheses are conjectures, than it seemed even recently.

Gödel and Cohen also succeeded in furnishing proofs that the so-called *continuum hypothesis* can neither be refuted nor proved with the methods of set theory employed so far. This famous hypothesis, which Cantor and Hilbert hoped to prove one day, was shown to be independent of the current theory. Of course it is possible so to strengthen the theory (by using additional assumptions) that the hypothesis becomes demonstrable; but it is equally possible so to strengthen it that the hypothesis can be refuted.

We come now to an interesting example that illustrates how mathematics can correct our uncorrected or naive or 'natural' logical intuitions.[1] German, English, Greek and many other European languages bear witness that, according to our natural logical intuition, the word 'undeniable' and perhaps even more obviously the word 'irrefutable' have the same force of meaning as 'irrefutably true' or 'quite definitely true'. If in addition the irrefutability of a statement is actually *proved* (as in Gödel's proof of the irrefutability of the continuum hypothesis), then according to our natural logical intuition, the statement itself was proved to be true, having been proved to be not refutable.

This argument is corrected and shown to be naive by the fact that Gödel, who proved the irrefutability of the continuum hypothesis, also suspected at the same time that this irrefutable proposition was also unprovable: that it could therefore be neither refuted nor proved within this system and that it was independent.[2] His suspicion was soon confirmed by Paul Cohen.[3]

The pioneering studies of Gödel, Tarski, and Cohen which I have briefly mentioned here all refer to set theory, to Cantor's magnificent theory of the *actual infinite*. This theory was, in its turn, chiefly inspired by the problem of creating a foundation for analysis, that is, for differential and integral calculus, which, particularly in their original form, employed the concept of the infinitesimal. This concept of the infinitesimal was already regarded by Leibniz and by other theoreticians of the potentially infinite merely as a helpful yet problematic concept; and it was expressly rejected as incorrect by the great Cantor, by his disciples and even by his critics: actual infinity was restricted to the infinitely large. It is therefore extremely interesting that in 1961 a 'second Cantor' (this term was used by A. Fraenkel[4]) came on the scene, who outlined a rigorous theory of the actual infinitesimal, which in 1966 he expanded in great detail.[5] Sadly, the creator of this theory, Abraham Robinson, died recently in America.

Of course, my remarks about recent achievements in mathematical logic and mathematics are very sketchy. But I have tried to point out some of the most interesting developments in this infinitely broad field of the infinite; they are developments that are based entirely upon the critical treatment of the problem. Gödel, Tarski and Robinson, in particular, are critics. Gödel's work amounts to a criticism of all the leading schools of thought forty years ago; of logicism, formalism and intuitionism. And his work also constitutes a criticism of positivism, which was strongly represented in the Vienna Circle of which Gödel was a member. And Gödel's criticism was based upon his mathematical intuition, upon the mathematical imagination which did indeed guide him, but which he never used as an authority: it always had to stand up to examination using the rational, critical-discursive method.

IV

I am now going to talk for a few minutes about cosmology, which is arguably the most philosophically important of all the sciences.

Cosmology has undergone an incredible development over the past thirty years. Even before that, the solar system, which Newton still called the System of the World, had become a local phenomenon. The first modern cosmology, the theory of stellar systems and systems of Milky Ways greatly formulated by Kant,[6] had been developed between the two world wars under the influence of Einstein's theories and Hubble's new methods of estimating stellar distances; and Hubble's theory of the expanding universe seemed to be established. The results of radio astronomy, which was first developed in England and Australia after the Second World War, seemed to fit well into this framework at first. One theory (in my view, a very fine and promising theory) of the expanding universe, which was put forward by Bondi, Gold and Hoyle, even turned out to be testable using the methods of radio astronomy; and it seems to have been refuted in favour of the (older) big bang theory of expansion. But Hubble's Constant was reduced to a tenth, and the expansion of the largest Milky Ways was multiplied by 150. Many other results were also called into question by radio astronomy; we seem to be almost as helpless in the field of cosmology in the face of some of these completely revolutionary results as we are in politics when faced with the task of making peace. Star-like objects of hitherto unprecedented mass and density appear to exist and our previous ideas of Milky Ways scattering peacefully in all directions might perhaps soon be superseded by a theory of rare yet constantly recurring catastrophes.

In any case, radio astronomy represents, contrary to all expectations, a most exciting and revolutionary episode in the history of cosmology. The revolution is comparable to the revolution started by Galileo's telescope.

A general comment may be appropriate here. It is often claimed that the history of scientific *discoveries* depends only (or mainly) upon the purely technical *inventions* of new instruments. By contrast, I believe that the history of science is essentially a history of ideas. Magnifying lenses had been around for a long time before Galileo had the idea of using them in an astronomical telescope.

Radio astronomy was similarly delayed. Radio waves were discovered by Heinrich Hertz in 1888. But in spite of the discovery of so-called cosmic rays by Victor Hess in 1912, which might have been an incentive to look out for new radiation emanating from stellar objects, it took another twenty years before radio astronomy got under way, and the invention of the instruments needed for it began. The likely explanation for the delay is that no astronomer thought of using radio waves. Of course, once the idea did occur, it led (after some fight for its survival) to a new and revolutionary development. And it was the new idea which suggested the construction of new instruments; something like huge artificial sense organs.

V

Cosmology has been, since the time of Newton at any rate, a branch of physics, and Kant, Mach, Einstein, Eddington and others continued to treat it as such. Einstein, Eddington, Erwin Schrödinger and Wolfgang Pauli (who, like Schrödinger, was born in Vienna), in particular, have made interesting remarks about the connections between material and atomic structure on the one hand and cosmology on the other.[7] That was forty years ago, and since then these ideas have been more or less abandoned, although some great physicists, notably Einstein, Dirac, Heisenberg and Cornelius Lanczos, continued to work upon a unification of physical theory.

However, Pauli's hypotheses about the link between neutrino fields and gravitation have been taken up again very recently, because of unexpected experimental results about the apparent lack of a solar neutrino flux. Hans-Jürgen Treder, the cosmologist and physicist from Potsdam, tried to derive this negative experimental result from his version of Einstein's theory of General Relativity, using a hypothesis suggested by Pauli in 1934. It is to be hoped that this may have sparked off a new phase of attempts to forge a closer link between the theory of matter and cosmology. In any case, it is worth noting that this new attempt can be traced back to an expectation that was refuted experimentally.

VI

I now turn to what is perhaps the most important example of scientific development over the last thirty years, the development of biology. I am not only thinking of the unique breakthrough in genetics due to the theory of James Watson and Francis Crick which led to a flood of new results of the most important and informative character. I also have in mind the growth of ethology, of animal psychology; the start of a biologically orientated developmental psychology and the new interpretation of Darwinism.

What was Watson and Crick's great breakthrough? The idea of the gene is relatively old: it was implicit in the work of Gregor Mendel. Yet it was questioned for longer than Lavoisier's combustion theory. Watson and Crick put forward not only a theory of the chemical structure of genes, but also a theory of chemical gene replication, and even a theory of the effect on the organism of the pattern encoded in the genes. But as if this was not enough, or more than enough, they also discovered the alphabet of the language in which the pattern is written: the alphabet of the genetic code.

The hypothesis that something like a genetic code exists was, as far as I know, first propagated by Erwin Schrödinger, whose memory is so closely associated with our Alpbach. Schrödinger wrote that 'It is these chromosomes, or probably only an axial skeleton fibre of what we actually see under the microscope as the chromosome, that contain in some kind of code-script the entire pattern of the individual's future development and of its functioning in the mature state.'[8]

This hypothesis of Schrödinger's was developed and proved in unprecedented ways over the next thirty years, and the molecular genetic code was deciphered.

As a result of Watson and Crick's theory, this scientific miracle became reality in the last year of Schrödinger's life, and shortly after his death the code was completely deciphered. We now know the alphabet, the vocabulary, the syntax and the semantics (that is, the science of meaning) of the language hypothesized by

Schrödinger. We know that every gene is an instruction to construct a particular enzyme, and we can work out the precise (linear) chemical structural formula of the enzyme in question from the instruction that is written in the genetic code. We also know about the functions of many enzymes. However, although we can work out from the coded formula of a gene the chemical formula for the corresponding enzyme, we cannot as yet determine the biological function of the enzyme from its formula: here lies the boundary of our knowledge of the meaning of the genetic code.

Finally I want to mention yet another important and welcome biological concept, which is also connected with Schrödinger's work, although Schrödinger was neither the first nor the last person to work upon this concept.[9] This is an aspect of Darwinian theory that Lloyd Morgan, Baldwin and others have described as 'organic selection'. Schrödinger spoke of a Darwinian selection, which simulates Lamarckism.

At first sight, Darwin's ideas (by contrast with Lamarck's) seem to attach little significance for evolution to the behaviour of individual plants and animals – for example, to the preference an individual animal may show for a new kind of food or for a new method of hunting. The new idea of the theory of organic selection is that these forms of individual behaviour can influence the evolution of the phylum by means of natural selection. The idea is simple: every new mode of behaviour can be regarded as the selection of a new ecological niche. For example, the preference for a new food or for nesting in a particular kind of tree signifies, even when the animal does not migrate, that it has moved into a new environment. But in adopting this new environment, this new ecological niche, the animal exposes itself and its descendants to a new environmental influence and therefore to a new selection pressure. And it is then that this new selection pressure guides genetic development and brings about adaptation to the new environment. This simple and convincing theory is in fact an old one – as Alister Hardy shows, it predates Darwin and even Lamarck[10] – but during the past thirty years it has been rediscovered, developed further and tested experimentally, by Waddington, for example. The theory demonstrates, much more clearly than Lamarck, that behaviour, such as the desire of an animal to explore, curiosity, and the likes and dislikes of an animal, can have a decisive influence upon phylogenetic gene development.

So every behavioural novelty of an individual organism has creative and often revolutionary phylogenetic consequences. This shows that individual initiative plays an active role in Darwinian development. This observation overcomes the hopeless and depressing impression that has surrounded Darwinism for so long, when it seemed that the activity of the individual organism could play no part in the selection mechanism.

Ladies and gentlemen, it only remains for me to add that we may not draw any conclusions about the future of science from the astonishing results of the most recent past. I think that the enormous new organizations for scientific research represent a serious danger to science. The great men of science were critical individuals. This was of course true of Schrödinger and Gödel and even of Watson and Crick.

The spirit of science has changed as a result of organized research. We must hope that, in spite of this, there will always be great individuals.

NOTES

1 This was first emphasized by Brouwer. See L. E. J. Brouwer, *Tijdschrift v. Wijsbegeerte*, 2, 1908, pp. 152–8.

2 See Kurt Gödel, *Am. Math. Monthly*, 54, 1947, pp. 515–25.

3 Paul J. Cohen, *Proc. Nat. Acad. Sci. USA*, 50, 1963, pp. 1143–8 and 51, 1964, pp. 105–10.

4 A. A. Fraenkel, *Einleitung in die Mengenlehre*, 3rd edn, Springer, Berlin, 1928.

5 A. Robinson, *Proc. Royal Dutch Academy*, ser. A. 64, 1961, pp. 432–40; *Non-Standard Analysis*, Amsterdam, 1966.

6 I. Kant, *Universal Natural History and Theory of the Heavens,* trans. W. Hastie, Ann Arbor Paperbacks, The University of Michigan Press, 1969 (reprinted from *Kant's Cosmogony*, Glasgow, 1900); cf. also H. J. Treder, in *Die Sterne*, 50, vol. 2, p. 67, note 4: 'Kant is the sole founder of "the theory of stellar systems".'

7 Cf. Wolfgang Pauli, *Physik und Erkenntnistheorie* ('Physics and Epistemology'), 1961, and also W. Pauli and M. Fierz, *Helv. Phys. Acta*, 15, 1939, p. 297.

8 E. Schrödinger, *What is Life?*, 1st edn, Cambridge, 1944, p. 20.

9 Schrödinger (*Mind and Matter*, 1958, p.20) attributes the idea of organic evolution to Julian Huxley; however, the idea is much older, as Sir Alister Hardy in particular has shown; cf. his book *The Living Stream*, 1965, e.g. pp. 178 ff. See also my book *Objective Knowledge*, Oxford University Press, Oxford, 1972, 7th edn 1992, chapter 7.

10 Sir Alister Hardy mentions (op. cit.) an unpublished manuscript of James Hutton, the great Scottish geologist, which contains this version of Darwinism: 'it was written eleven years before Charles Darwin was born and twelve years before Lamarck first published his evolutionary views.'

5

THE LOGIC OF THE SOCIAL SCIENCES

I propose to begin my paper on the logic of the social sciences with two theses which express the contrast between our knowledge and our ignorance.

First thesis: We have a fair amount of knowledge. Moreover, we know not only details of doubtful intellectual interest, but also, and more especially, things that are not only of considerable practical importance, but may, in addition, provide us with deep theoretical insight, and with a surprising understanding of the world.

Second thesis: Our ignorance is boundless and sobering. Indeed, it is precisely this overwhelming progress of the natural sciences (to which my first thesis alludes) that continually reminds us of our ignorance, even in the field of the natural sciences themselves.

Opening lecture at the conference of the German Sociology Society in Tübingen, 1961. My lecture was first published in the *Kölner Zeitschrift für Soziologie und Sozialpsychologie*, 2, 14, 1962, pp. 233–48. My lecture was supposed to start a debate. Professor Adorno had been invited to continue this debate in his supplementary paper, in which he essentially agreed with me. However, when the book *The Positivist Dispute in German Sociology* was published, Adorno began with two polemical pieces, which together took up approximately one hundred pages; then came my lecture, followed by Adorno's supplementary paper and by others that were not given at the conference. It is most unlikely that anyone reading the book *The Positivist Dispute* would suspect that my lecture had opened the debate and that Adorno's aggressive opening hundred pages had been written much later (specifically for the book).

Translator's note: The main body of this translation makes some use of the version printed in *The Positivist Dispute in German Sociology*, the English translation by Glyn Adey and David Frisby (Heinemann, London, 1976) of *Der Positivismusstreit in der deutschen Soziologie*. However, it has been revised and amended for this edition, particularly in those places where the German deviates noticeably from the English.

This gives a new twist to the Socratic idea of ignorance. With each step forward, with every problem we solve, we not only discover new and unsolved problems, but we also discover that just when we believed that we were standing on firm and safe ground, all things are, in reality, insecure and unstable.

Of course, my two theses about knowledge and ignorance only appear to contradict one another. The chief cause of this apparent contradiction lies in the fact that the word 'knowledge' is used in a rather different sense in each of the two theses. Yet both senses are important, and so are both theses: so much so that I propose to make this explicit in the following third thesis.

Third thesis: Every theory of knowledge has a fundamentally important task, which may even be regarded as its crucial test: it must do justice to our first two theses by clarifying the relations between our remarkable and constantly increasing knowledge and our constantly increasing insight that in reality we know nothing.

If we give it a little thought, it goes almost without saying that the logic of knowledge must address this tension between knowledge and ignorance. An important consequence of this insight is formulated in my fourth thesis. But before I present this fourth thesis, I should like to apologize for the many theses that are still to come. My excuse is that it was suggested to me that I assemble this paper in the form of numbered theses. I found this suggestion very useful despite the fact that this style may create the impression of dogmatism. Here, then, is my fourth thesis.

Fourth thesis: So far as one can say at all that science or knowledge starts from something, one might say the following: Knowledge does not start from perceptions or observations or the collection of data or facts; it starts, rather, from *problems*. One might say: No knowledge without problems; but also, no problems without knowledge. But this means that knowledge starts from the tension between knowledge and ignorance: No problems without knowledge – no problems without ignorance. For every problem arises from the discovery that there is something amiss within our supposed knowledge; or, viewed logically, from the discovery of an inner contradiction in our supposed knowledge, or of a contradiction between our supposed knowledge and the facts; or, to be more accurate, from the discovery of an apparent contradiction between our supposed knowledge and the supposed facts.

While my first three theses may perhaps, because of their abstract character, create the impression that they are somewhat removed from our topic – that is, the logic of the social sciences – I should like to say that my fourth thesis brings us right to the heart of our topic. This can be formulated in my fifth thesis as follows.

Fifth thesis: As in all other sciences, we are in the social sciences either successful or unsuccessful, interesting or dull, fruitful or unfruitful, in exact proportion to the significance or interest of the problems we are concerned with; and also, of course, in exact proportion to the honesty, directness and simplicity with which we tackle these problems. None of this restricts us to theoretical problems. Serious practical problems, such as the problems of poverty, of illiteracy, of political suppression or of uncertainty concerning legal rights, were important starting points for research in the social sciences. Yet these practical problems led to speculation, to theorizing and thus to theoretical problems. In all cases, without exception, it is the character and the quality of the problem – and also of course the boldness and originality of the suggested solution – which determine the value, or lack of value, of the scientific achievement.

The starting point, then, is always a problem; and observation becomes something like a starting point only if it reveals a problem; or in other words, if it surprises us, if it shows us that there is something not quite right about our knowledge, about our expectations, about our theories. Thus an observation only creates a problem when it contradicts certain of our conscious or unconscious expectations. But then what constitutes the starting point of our scientific work is not so much an observation pure and simple, but rather an observation that plays a particular role; that is, an observation which creates a problem.

I have now reached the point where I can formulate my *main thesis*, as thesis number six. It consists of the following.

Sixth thesis (main thesis):

(a) The method of the social sciences, like that of the natural sciences, consists in trying out tentative solutions to those problems from which our investigations start.

Solutions are proposed and criticized. If a proposed solution is not open to objective criticism, then it is excluded as unscientific, although perhaps only temporarily.

(b) If the proposed solution is open to objective criticism, then we attempt to refute it; for all criticism consists in attempts at refutation.

(c) If a proposed solution is refuted through our criticism we propose another solution.

(d) If it withstands criticism, we accept it temporarily; and we accept it, above all, as worthy of further discussion and criticism.

(e) Thus the method of science is one of tentative attempts (or brain-waves) to solve our problems which are controlled by the most severe criticism. It is a critical development of the method of 'trial and error'.

(f) The so-called objectivity of science lies in the objectivity of the critical method; that is, above all, in the fact that no theory is exempt from criticism, and further, in the fact that the logical instrument of criticism – the logical contradiction – is objective.

The basic idea which lies behind my central thesis might also be put in the following way.

Seventh thesis: The tension between knowledge and ignorance leads to problems and to tentative solutions. Yet the tension is never overcome. For it turns out that our knowledge only ever consists in suggestions for provisional and tentative solutions. Thus the very idea of knowledge involves, in principle, the possibility that it will turn out to have been a mistake, and therefore a case of ignorance. And the only way of justifying our knowledge is itself merely provisional, for it consists in criticism or, more precisely, in an appeal to the fact that *so far* our attempted solutions appear to withstand even our most penetrating criticism.

There is no positive justification: no justification which goes beyond this. In particular, our tentative solutions cannot be shown to be probable (in any sense that satisfies the laws of the calculus of probability).

Perhaps one could describe this position as *criticist*.

In order to give a better idea of my main thesis and its significance for sociology it may be useful to contrast it with certain other theses which belong to a widely accepted methodology which has often been quite unconsciously absorbed.

There is, for instance, the misguided and erroneous methodological approach of naturalism or scientism, which urges that it is high time that the social sciences learn from the natural sciences what scientific method is. This misguided naturalism establishes such demands as: begin with observations and measurements; this means, for instance, begin by collecting statistical data; proceed, next, by induction to generalizations and to the formation of theories. It is suggested that in this way you will approach the ideal of objectivity, so far as this is at all possible in the social sciences. In so doing, however, you ought to be conscious of the fact that objectivity in the social sciences is much more difficult to achieve (if it can be achieved at all) than in the natural sciences. For being objective demands that one is not biassed by one's value judgements – that is (as Max Weber called it), to be 'value-free'. But only in the rarest cases can the social scientist free himself from the value system of his own social class and so achieve even a limited degree of 'value freedom' and 'objectivity'.

Every single one of the theses which I have here attributed to this misguided naturalism is in my opinion totally mistaken: all these theses are based on a misunderstanding of the methods of the natural sciences, and actually on a myth – a myth, unfortunately all too widely accepted and all too influential. It is the myth of the inductive character of the methods of the natural sciences, and of the character of the objectivity of the natural sciences. I propose in what follows to devote a small part of the precious time at my disposal to a critique of this misguided naturalism.

Admittedly, many social scientists will reject one or other of the theses which I have attributed to this misguided naturalism. Nevertheless this naturalism seems at present to have gained the upper hand in the social sciences, except perhaps in political economics; at least in English-speaking countries. I wish to formulate the symptoms of this victory in my eighth thesis.

Eighth thesis: Before the Second World War, sociology was regarded as a general theoretical social science, comparable, perhaps, with theoretical physics, and social anthropology was regarded as a sociology of very specific, that is to say, primitive societies. Today this relationship has been completely reversed; a fact to which attention should be drawn. Social anthropology or ethnology has become a general social science, and sociology has resigned itself more and more to becoming one element within social anthropology: that is, the social anthropology of a very specific form of society – of the highly industrialized Western European form of society. Restated more briefly, the relationship between sociology and anthropology has been completely reversed. Social anthropology has been promoted from an applied specialist discipline to a fundamental science, and the anthropologist has been elevated from a modest and somewhat short-sighted *fieldworker* to a far-seeing and profound social theorist and social depth-psychologist. The former theoretical sociologist, however, must be happy to find employment as a *fieldworker* and a specialist: his function is to observe and to describe the totems and taboos of the white natives of the Western European countries and of the United States.

But this change in the fate of the social scientist should perhaps not be taken too seriously; particularly as there is no such thing as the essence of a scientific subject. This leads me to my ninth thesis.

Ninth thesis: A so-called scientific subject is merely a conglomerate of problems and tentative solutions, demarcated in an artificial way. What really exists are problems, and scientific traditions.

Despite this ninth thesis, the complete reversal in the relations between sociology and anthropology is extremely interesting, not on account of the subjects or their titles, but because it points to the victory of a pseudo-scientific method. Thus I come to my next thesis.

Tenth thesis: The victory of anthropology is the victory of an allegedly observational, allegedly descriptive method, which purports to use inductive generalizations. Above all, it is the victory of an allegedly more objective method, and thus of what is taken to be the method of the natural sciences. It is a Pyrrhic victory: another such victory and we – that is, both anthropology and sociology – are lost.

My tenth thesis may be formulated, I readily admit, a little too pointedly. I admit of course that much of interest and importance has been discovered by social anthropology, which is one of the most successful social sciences. Moreover, I readily admit that it can be a very fascinating and interesting experience for us Europeans to see ourselves, for a change, through the spectacles of the social anthropologist. But although these spectacles are perhaps more coloured than others, this hardly makes them more objective. The anthropologist is not the observer from Mars he often thinks he is, whose social role he often attempts to play (and not without gusto); nor have we the slightest reason to suppose that an inhabitant of Mars would see us more 'objectively' than we, for instance, see ourselves.

In this context I should like to tell a story which is admittedly extreme but is in no way unique. Although it is a true story, this is immaterial in the present context: should the story seem improbable to you, please, take it as an invention, as a freely invented illustration, designed to make clear an important point by means of crass exaggeration.

Years ago, I was a participant in a four-day conference, organized by a theologian, in which philosophers, biologists, anthropologists and physicists took part – one or two representatives from each discipline; there were eight of us in all. The topic was 'Science and Humanism'. After a few teething troubles and the defeat of an attempt to impress us by sublime argument, the joint efforts of roughly four or five participants succeeded in the course of three days in raising the discussion to an uncommonly high level. Our conference had reached the stage – or so it appeared to me at least – at which we all had the happy feeling that we were learning something from one another. At any rate, we were all immersed in the subject of our debate when out of the blue the social anthropologist made his contribution.

'You will, perhaps, be surprised', he said, 'that I have said nothing so far in this conference. This is because I am an observer. As an anthropologist I came to this conference not so much in order to participate in your verbal behaviour but rather to study your verbal behaviour. That is what I have been doing. Consequently, I was not always able to follow the actual content of your discussion. But someone like myself who has studied dozens of discussion groups learns in time that the topic discussed is relatively unimportant. We anthropologists learn' – this is almost verbatim (so far as I remember) – 'to look at such social phenomena from the outside and from a more objective standpoint. What interests us is the *how*: for example, how one person or another tries to dominate the group and how his attempts are rejected by the others, either singly or through the formation of a coalition; how after various attempts of this kind a hierarchical order and hence a group equilibrium develops, along with a group ritual of verbalization; these things are always very similar no matter how varied the question appears to be which serves as the topic of the discussion.'

We listened to all that our anthropological visitor from Mars had to say; and then I put two questions to him. First, whether he had any comment to make on the actual results of our discussion; and then, whether he could not see that there were such things as impersonal reasons or arguments which could be valid or invalid. He replied that he had had to concentrate too much on the observation of our group behaviour to have been able to follow our arguments in detail; moreover, had he done so, he would have endangered (so he said) his objectivity; for he might have become involved in the argument; and had he allowed himself to be carried away by it, he would have become one of us – and that would have been the end of his objectivity. Besides, he was trained not to judge the literal content of verbal behaviour (he constantly used the terms 'verbal behaviour' and 'verbalization'), or to take it as being important. What concerned him, he said, was the social and psychological function of this verbal behaviour. And he went on: 'While argument or reasons make an impression on you, as participants in a discussion, what interests us is the fact that through such means you can mutually impress and influence each other; and especially of course the symptoms of this influence. We are concerned with concepts such as emphasis, hesitation, intervention and concession. We are never actually concerned with the factual content of the discussion but only ever with the role which the various participants are playing: with the dramatic interplay as such. As to the so-called arguments, they are of course only one aspect of verbal behaviour and no more important than any of the other aspects. The idea that one can distinguish clearly between arguments and other impressive verbalizations is a purely subjective illusion; and so is the idea of a distinction between objectively valid and objectively invalid arguments. If hard pressed, one could classify arguments according to the societies or groups within which they are, at certain times, *accepted* as valid or invalid. That the time element plays a role is also revealed by the fact that so-called arguments which are at one time accepted in a discussion group such as the present one, may nonetheless be attacked or rejected again at a later stage by one of the participants.'

I do not wish to prolong the description of this incident. I imagine that it will not be necessary to point out, in the present gathering, that the somewhat extreme position of my anthropological friend shows in its intellectual origin the influence not only of the behaviourist ideal of objectivity but also of certain ideas which have grown in German soil. I refer to the idea of philosophical relativism: historical relativism, which holds that there is no objective truth, only truths for this or that age; and sociological relativism, which teaches that there are truths or sciences for this or that group or class, such as proletarian science and bourgeois science. I also believe that the so-called sociology of knowledge played a large part in the early history of the dogmas echoed by my anthropological friend.

Admittedly, my anthropological friend adopted a somewhat extreme position at that conference. But this position, especially if one modifies it a little, is neither untypical nor unimportant.

But this position is *absurd*. Since I have criticized historical and sociological relativism and also the sociology of knowledge in detail elsewhere, I shall not do so here. I will confine myself to a brief discussion of the naive and misguided idea of scientific objectivity which underlies this position.

Eleventh thesis: It is completely erroneous to assume that the objectivity of a science depends upon the objectivity of the scientist. And it is completely erroneous to believe that the attitude of the natural scientist is more objective than that of the social scientist. The natural scientist is just as partisan as anyone else, and unless he belongs to the few who are constantly producing new ideas, he is, unfortunately, often extremely biased, favouring his own ideas in a one-sided and partisan manner. Several of the most outstanding contemporary physicists have even founded schools which set up a powerful resistance to new ideas.

However, my thesis also has a positive side and this is more important. It forms the content of my twelfth thesis.

Twelfth thesis: What may be described as scientific objectivity is based solely upon that *critical* tradition which, despite all kinds of resistance, so often makes it possible to criticize a dominant dogma. In other words, the objectivity of science is not a matter for the individual scientist but rather the social result of mutual criticism, of the friendly-hostile division of labour among scientists, of their co-operation and also of their competition. For this reason, it depends, in part, upon a whole string of social and political circumstances which make this criticism possible.

Thirteenth thesis: The so-called sociology of knowledge, which sees objectivity in the behaviour of individual scientists, and which explains lack of objectivity in terms of the social habitat of the scientists, has completely missed the following decisive point:

the fact that objectivity rests solely upon criticism. What the sociology of knowledge has overlooked is none other than the sociology of knowledge itself – the theory of scientific objectivity. Objectivity can only be explained in terms of social ideas such as competition (both of individual scientists and of various schools of thought); tradition (that is, the critical tradition); social institutions (for instance, publications in various competing journals and by various competing publishers; discussions at congresses); the power of the state (that is, its political tolerance of free discussion).

Such minor details as, for instance, the social or ideological habitat of the researcher tend to be eliminated by this process in the long run; although admittedly they always play a part in the short term.

The so-called problem of 'value *freedom*', just like the problem of objectivity, may be solved in a much *freer* way than is usually done.

Fourteenth thesis: In critical discussion we may distinguish such questions as: (1) The question of the truth of an assertion; the question of its relevance, of its interest and of its significance vis-à-vis the problems in which we are interested. (2) The question of its relevance and of its interest and of its significance vis-à-vis various *extra-scientific problems* like the problem of human welfare or the quite differently structured problem of national defence or of an aggressive nationalist policy; or of industrial expansion; or of the acquisition of personal wealth.

It is clearly impossible to eliminate such extra-scientific interests from scientific research. And it is just as impossible to eliminate them from research in the natural sciences – for example from research in physics – as from research in the social sciences.

What is possible and what is important and what gives science its special character is not the elimination of extra-scientific interests but rather the distinction between the interests which do not belong to the search for truth and the purely scientific interest in truth. But although truth is the chief scientific value, it is not the only one. Relevance, interest and the significance of statements vis-à-vis a purely scientific problem situation are also scientific values of the first order; and this is also true of values like fruitfulness, explanatory power, simplicity and precision.

In other words, there exist those positive and negative values that are *purely* scientific and those that are *extra*-scientific. And although it is impossible to separate scientific work from extra-scientific applications and evaluations, it is one of the tasks of scientific criticism and scientific discussion to fight against the confusion of value-spheres and, in particular, to eliminate extra-scientific evaluations from *questions of truth*.

This cannot, of course, be achieved once and for all, by means of a decree; rather it remains one of the enduring tasks of mutual scientific criticism. The purity of pure science is an ideal which is presumably unattainable; but it is an ideal for which we constantly fight – and should fight – by means of criticism.

In formulating this thesis I have said that it is practically impossible to banish extra-scientific values from scientific activity. The situation is similar with respect to objectivity: we cannot rob the scientist of his partisanship without also robbing him of his humanity, nor can we suppress or destroy his value judgements without destroying him as a human being *and as a scientist*. Our motives and our purely scientific ideals, like the ideal of a pure search for truth, are deeply anchored in extra-scientific and, in part, in religious value judgements. The objective and 'value-free' scientist is not the ideal scientist. Without passion we can achieve nothing – certainly not in pure science. The phrase 'the *love* of truth' is no mere metaphor.

It is, therefore, not just that objectivity and value freedom are unattainable in practice for the individual scientist, but rather that objectivity and 'value freedom' are themselves *values*. And since value freedom itself is a value, the demand for unconditional value freedom is paradoxical. This objection is not very important, but it should be noted that the paradox disappears quite of its own accord if we replace the demand for value freedom with the demand that it should be one of the tasks of scientific criticism to expose confusions of value and to separate purely scientific value questions of truth, relevance, simplicity and so forth from extra-scientific questions.

I have so far attempted to develop briefly the thesis that the method of science consists in the choice of problems and in the criticism of our ever tentative and provisional attempts to solve them. And I have attempted to show further, using as my examples two much discussed questions of method in the social sciences, that this critical approach to methods (as it might be called) leads to quite reasonable methodological results. But although I have said a few words about epistemology, about the logic of knowledge, and a few critical words about the methodology of the social sciences, I have in fact thus far made only a small positive contribution to my topic, the logic of the social sciences.

I do not wish to detain you by giving reasons or excuses why I consider it important to identify scientific method, at least in first approximation, with the critical method. Instead, I should like now to move straight to some purely logical questions and theses.

Fifteenth thesis: The most important function of pure deductive logic is as an organon of criticism.

Sixteenth thesis: Deductive logic is the theory of the validity of logical inferences or of the relation of logical consequence. A necessary and crucial condition for the validity of a logical inference is the following: if the premisses of a valid inference are *true* then the conclusion must also be *true*.

This may also be expressed as follows. Deductive logic is the theory of the transmission of truth from the premisses to the conclusion.

Seventeenth thesis: We can say: if all the premisses are true and the inference is valid, then the conclusion *must* also be true; and if, consequently, the conclusion is false in a valid inference, then it is not possible for all the premisses to be true.

This trivial but decisively important result may also be expressed in the following manner: deductive logic is not only the theory of the *transmission of truth* from the premisses to the conclusion, but it is also, at the same time, the theory of the *retransmission of falsity* from the conclusion to at least one of the premisses.

Eighteenth thesis: In this way deductive logic becomes the theory of rational criticism. For all rational criticism takes the form of an attempt to show that unacceptable conclusions can be derived from the assertion we are trying to criticize. If we are successful in deriving, logically, unacceptable conclusions from an assertion, then the assertion may be taken to be refuted.

Nineteenth thesis: In the sciences we work with theories, that is to say, with deductive systems. There are two reasons for this. First, a theory or a deductive system is an attempt at explanation, and consequently an attempt to solve a scientific problem. Second, a theory, that is, a deductive system, can be criticized rationally through its consequences. It is thus a tentative solution, which is subject to rational criticism.

So much for formal logic as the organon of criticism.

Two fundamental concepts that I have used here require a brief elucidation: the concept of truth and the concept of explanation.

Twentieth thesis: The concept of truth is indispensable for the critical approach developed here. What we are criticizing is the claim that a theory is true. What we attempt to show as critics of a theory is, clearly, that this claim is unfounded: that it is false.

The important methodological idea that we can learn from our mistakes cannot be understood without the regulative idea of truth: any mistake simply consists in a failure to live up to our goal, our standard of objective truth, which is our regulative idea.

We term a proposition 'true' if it agrees with the facts or corresponds to the facts, or if things are as described by the proposition. This is what is called the absolute or objective concept of truth, which each of us constantly uses. The successful rehabilitation of this absolute concept of truth is one of the most important results of modern logic.

This remark implies that the concept of truth had been undermined. Indeed, this was the driving force which produced the dominant relativistic ideologies of our time.

This is why I am inclined to describe the rehabilitation of the concept of truth by the logician and mathematician Alfred Tarski as the most important philosophical result of modern mathematical logic.

I cannot of course discuss this result here; I can only say quite dogmatically that *Tarski* succeeded in providing the simplest and most convincing explanation imaginable of where the agreement of a statement with the facts lies. But this was precisely the task whose hopeless difficulty led to sceptical relativism – with social consequences which I am sure I do not need to spell out here.

The second concept which I have used and which may require elucidation is the concept of explanation or, more precisely, the concept of *causal explanation*.

A purely theoretical problem – a problem of pure science – always consists in the task of finding an explanation, the explanation of a fact or of a phenomenon or of a remarkable regularity or of a remarkable exception from a rule. That which we hope to explain may be called the explicandum. The tentative solution of the problem – that is, the explanation – always consists of a theory, a deductive system, which permits us to explain the explicandum by connecting it logically with other facts (the so-called initial conditions). A fully explicit explanation always consists in pointing out the logical derivation (or the derivability) of the explicandum from the theory strengthened by some initial conditions.

Thus the basic logical schema of every explanation consists of a logical deductive inference whose premisses consist of a theory and some initial conditions, and whose conclusion is the explicandum.

This basic schema has a remarkable number of applications. For instance, it may be used to show the distinction between an *ad hoc* hypothesis and an independently testable hypothesis. Further – and this might be of more interest to you – one can analyse logically, in a simple manner, the distinction between theoretical problems, historical problems and problems of applied science. This shows that there is a complete logical justification for the famous *distinction* between theoretical or nomothetic and historical or ideographic sciences – provided that one takes the term 'science' in this context to mean a concern with a definite, logically distinguishable, set of problems.

So much for the elucidation of the logical concepts which I have employed up to now.

Both of these concepts, that of truth, and that of explanation, give rise to the logical development of further concepts which are perhaps even more important for the logic of knowledge or for methodology. The first of these concepts is that of *approximation to the truth* and the second that of the *explanatory power* or the *explanatory content* of a theory.

These two concepts are purely logical concepts in so far as they may be defined with the help of the purely logical concepts of the truth of a statement and of the content of a statement – that is, of the class of logical consequences of a theory.

Both are relative concepts. Although each statement is simply true or false, nevertheless *one* statement can represent a better approximation to the truth than *another* statement. This will be so, for example, if the first statement has 'more' true and 'fewer' false logical consequences than the second. (It is assumed here that the true and the false sub-sets of the sets of consequences of the two statements are comparable.) It can then easily be shown why we rightly assume that Newton's theory is a better approximation to the truth than Kepler's.

Similarly it can be shown that the explanatory power of Newton's theory is greater than that of Kepler's.

Thus we are obtaining logical concepts which underlie the appraisal of our theories, and permit us to speak meaningfully of progress or regress with reference to scientific theories.

So much for the general logic of knowledge. Concerning, in particular, the logic of the social sciences, I should like to introduce some additional theses.

Twenty-first thesis: There is no such thing as a purely observational science; there are only sciences in which we theorize (more or less consciously and critically). This also holds for the social sciences.

Twenty-second thesis: Psychology is a social science since our thoughts and actions largely depend upon social conditions. Ideas such as (a) imitation, (b) language, (c) the family, are obviously social ideas; and it is clear that the psychology of learning and thinking, and also, for instance, psychoanalysis, cannot exist without utilizing one or other of these social ideas. Thus psychology presupposes social concepts; which shows that it is impossible to explain society exclusively in psychological terms, or to reduce it to psychology. Therefore we cannot look upon psychology as the basis of the social sciences.

What we cannot, in principle, explain psychologically, and what we must presuppose in every psychological explanation, is man's social environment. The task of describing this social environment (that is, with the help of explanatory theories since – as stated before – theory-free descriptions do not exist) is therefore the fundamental task of social science. It might well be appropriate to allot this task to sociology. I therefore assume this in what follows.

Twenty-third thesis: Sociology is autonomous in the sense that, to a considerable extent, it can and must make itself independent of psychology. Apart from the dependence of psychology on social ideas, this is also due to the fact that sociology is constantly faced with the task of explaining unintended and often undesired social consequences of human action. An example: competition is a social phenomenon which is usually undesirable for the competitors, but which can and must be explained as a (usually inevitable) unintended consequence of (conscious and planned) actions of the competitors.

Thus even though there may be a psychological explanation for some of the actions of the competitors, the social phenomenon of competition is a psychologically inexplicable social consequence of these actions.

Twenty-fourth thesis: But sociology is also autonomous in a second sense; that is, as what has often been termed the sociology of objective understanding (*verstehende Soziologie*).

Twenty-fifth thesis: The logical investigation of the methods of economics yields a result which can be applied to all social sciences. This result shows that there is a *purely objective method* in the social sciences, which may well be called the method of *objective* understanding, or situational logic. A social science orientated towards *objective* understanding can be developed independently of all subjective or psychological ideas. Its method consists in analysing the *situation* of the acting person sufficiently to explain the action in terms of the situation without any further help from psychology. Objective 'understanding' consists in realizing that the action was objectively *appropriate to the situation*. In other words, the situation is analysed far enough for the elements which initially appeared to be psychological (such as wishes, motives, memories and associations) to be transformed into elements of the situation. The man with specific wishes therefore becomes a man whose situation may be characterized by the fact that he pursues specific objective *aims*; and a man with particular memories or associations becomes a man whose situation can be characterized by the fact that he is equipped objectively with particular theories or with specific information.

This then allows us to understand actions in an objective sense so that we can say: admittedly, I have different aims and I hold different theories (from, say, Charlemagne); but had I been placed in his situation thus analysed – where the situation includes goals and knowledge – then I, and presumably you too, would have done what he did. The method of situational analysis is certainly an individualistic method and yet it is certainly not a psychological one; for it excludes, in principle, all psychological elements and replaces them with objective situational elements. I usually call it the 'logic of the situation' or 'situational logic'.

Twenty-sixth thesis: The explanations of situational logic described here are rational, theoretical reconstructions. They are oversimplified and overschematized and consequently in general *false*. Nevertheless, they can possess a considerable truth content and they can, in the strictly logical sense, be good approximations to the truth, and even better than other testable explanations. In this sense, the logical concept of approximation to the truth is indispensable for a social science which uses the method of situational analysis. Above all, however, situational analyses are rational, empirically criticizable and capable of improvement. For we may, for instance, find a letter which shows that the knowledge at Charlemagne's disposal was completely different from what we assumed in our analysis. By contrast, psychological or characterological hypotheses are hardly ever criticizable.

Twenty-seventh thesis: In general, situational logic assumes a physical world in which we act. This world contains, for example, physical resources, which are at our disposal and about which we know something, and physical barriers about which we also know something (often not very much). Beyond this, situational logic must also assume a social world, inhabited by other people, about whose goals we know something (often not very much), and, furthermore, *social institutions*. These social institutions determine the peculiarly social character of our social environment. They consist of all the social realities of the social world, realities which correspond to the things of the physical world. A grocer's shop or a university institute or a police force or a law are, in this sense, social institutions. Church, state and marriage are also social institutions, as are certain coercive customs like, for instance, hara-kiri in Japan. But in our European society suicide is not a social institution in the sense in which I use the term and in which I assert that the category is of importance.

That was my final thesis. What follows is a suggestion and a short concluding remark.

Suggestion: We may, perhaps, adopt tentatively, as the fundamental problems of a purely theoretical sociology, first the study of the general logic of situations, and second the theory of institutions and of traditions. This would include such problems as the following:

1. Institutions do not act; rather, only individuals act, within or on behalf of institutions. The general situational logic of these actions would be the theory of the quasi-actions of institutions.

2. We might construct a theory of intended and unintended institutional consequences of purposive action. This could also lead to a theory of the creation and the development of institutions.

One final comment. I believe that epistemology is important not only for the individual sciences but also for philosophy, and that the religious and philosophical uneasiness of our time, which surely concerns us all, is largely an uneasiness about the philosophy of human knowledge. Nietzsche called it the European nihilism, and Benda the treason of the intellectuals. I should like to characterize it as a consequence of the Socratic discovery that we know nothing; that is, that we can never justify our theories rationally.

But this important discovery, which has produced, amongst many other malaises, the malaise of existentialism, is only half a discovery; and nihilism can be overcome. For although we cannot justify our theories rationally and cannot even prove that they are probable, we can criticize them rationally. And we can distinguish better from worse theories.

But this was known, even before Socrates, to Xenophanes, who told us:

> The gods did not reveal, from the beginning,
> All things to us; but in the course of time,
> Through seeking we may learn, and know things better.

6

AGAINST BIG WORDS
(A letter not originally intended for publication)

Preface. *About fourteen years ago I received a letter from a Herr Klaus Grossner, whom I had never previously heard of. He mentioned my friend Hans Albert and asked me for a written interview about the state of (German) philosophy. I agreed with a great deal of his letter, and although I disagreed with some of it, I nevertheless thought it worthy of discussion; and so I answered his questions in spite of some reservations. In a subsequent letter, Herr Grossner asked me for permission to publish the parts of the letter printed here below in a book he was planning. Despite further misgivings I gave him my permission, but only for his book: I retained all my author's rights, and stressed that my contribution to his book must not be reprinted without my express permission. Yet shortly afterwards an excerpt appeared (under the excellent title 'Against Big Words' ['Wider die großen Worte']) in the weekly newspaper* Die Zeit, *without my permission and with no mention of my rights. (In Germany and Austria copyright is often considerably abused.) Since my letter has already been printed twice in excerpts and has been misquoted on many occasions, I have decided to reprint the previously published section here without any amendments, in spite of its aggressiveness. I wrote:*

First, in answer to your four questions (or groups of questions).

1. I started out as a socialist at secondary school, but did not find school very stimulating. I left school at sixteen and only returned to take the university entrance examination (*Reifeprüfung*). At seventeen (1919) I was still a socialist, but I had become an opponent of Marx (as a result of some encounters with Communists). Further experiences (of bureaucrats) led me to the insight, even prior to fascism, that the increasing power of the machine of the state constitutes the utmost danger for personal freedom, and that we must therefore keep on fighting the machine. My social-

ism was not just a theoretical stance: I learnt cabinetmaking (by contrast with my intellectual socialist friends) and took the journeyman's examination; I worked in children's homes; I became a primary school teacher; prior to the completion of my first book ('The Two Fundamental Problems of Epistemology', unpublished [published by Mohr in Tübingen in 1979]) I had no intention of becoming a Professor of Philosophy. (*The Logic of Scientific Discovery* was published in 1934; I accepted an appointment in New Zealand at Christmas-time, 1936.)

I have retained many ideas and ideals from my socialist youth in my old age. In particular:

Every intellectual has a very special responsibility. He has the privilege and the opportunity of studying. In return, he owes it to his fellow men (or 'to society') to represent the results of his study as simply, clearly and modestly as he can. The worst thing that intellectuals can do – the cardinal sin – is to try to set themselves up as great prophets vis-à-vis their fellow men and to impress them with puzzling philosophies. Anyone who cannot speak simply and clearly should say nothing and continue to work until he can do so.

During the Philosophy Congress in Vienna (1968) I was invited to two television discussions between philosophers and was surprised to find Bloch at one of them. We had some insignificant clashes. (I said, quite truthfully, that I am too stupid to understand the way he expresses himself.) At the end of the discussion the chairman, Dr Wolfgang Kraus, said to us: 'Please tell us in *one* sentence what, in your opinion, is most needed.' I was the only one to give a brief answer. My answer was: 'Rather more intellectual modesty.'

I am an anti-Marxist and a liberal. But I admit that both Marx and Lenin wrote in a simple and direct manner. What would they have said of the pomposity of the neo-Dialecticians? They would have found harsher words than 'pomposity'. (In my opinion, Lenin's book against empirio-criticism is most excellent.)

In answer to your question about the social problems that underlie my works:

All my philosophical works are connected with non-philosophical problems. I wrote about this in 1952 (see *Conjectures and Refutations*, p. 72): 'Genuine philosophical problems are always rooted in urgent problems outside philosophy, and they die if these roots decay.'[1] And I cited examples of areas in which problems are rooted, politics, social life, religion, cosmology, mathematics, natural science, and history.

A description of these 'roots' of my 'logic of scientific discovery' may be found in chapter 1 (1957), pp. 33–8 of *Conjectures and Refutations*. (*Conjectures and Refutations* has not yet been translated into German, because I cannot find a good enough translator. A copy [for you] is in the post.)

For 'The Poverty of Historicism' please see my dedication in my book of that title (p. v), the end of my preface to the German edition (the last paragraph on p. viii to the end of p. ix).

For the 'Logic of Scientific Discovery' please see also the first page of the introduction to the third German edition (p. xxv).

2. More about this later.

3. At the moment I am working upon my contributions to a volume of the 'Library of Living Philosophers', edited by Paul Arthur Schilpp. (I think that some of these volumes have also appeared in Germany, including the Einstein volume.) The volume that I am working upon is called 'The Philosophy of Karl Popper', and it contains (a) a so-called 'intellectual autobiography', (b) critical contributions by about twenty-five people (including some scientists, as well as philosophers) and (c) my answers.

My current writings are largely dedicated to the struggle against irrationalism and subjectivism in physics and in other sciences, especially in the social sciences. My works are, as always, attempts to formulate intractable problems as precisely as possible and then to solve them. (Even my scientific, logical works – for example, on physics – are attempts to solve problems that are connected with our social and political diseases.)

I also return time and again to problems that I solved many years ago, to tighten up the solution for instance, or to pursue the new problems that arise from my suggested solution – or to follow up new connections.

Here is a list of those problems:

The problem of demarcation. Science/non-science; rationality/irrationality.

The problem of induction in all its guises; including propensities, universals and 'essence'; the problem of definition (the impossibility of the defining postulate and the non-essential nature of all definitions).

The problem of realism (against positivism). Methodology of the natural sciences and of the humanities.

The role of problems and problem situations in the social sciences and in history. The problem of general problem-solving.

Problems of objectivity. Tarski's theory of truth; content, truth content, approximation to the truth. Objectivity in logic (the theory of deduction), mathematics, probability theory. Probability in physics. The problem of time and the direction of time.

The status of Darwin's theory of natural selection. Improvement of the theory of natural selection (selective explanation of developmental trends). Human language and its development. The language of political suggestions.

Indeterminism and selection. Theory of the 'third world' and of logical and non-logical values.

The mind–body problem. A large number of historical problems, especially about the history of theories (from Hesiod and the Presocratics right up to quantum theory).

This is a long list (and will be partly incomprehensible to anyone who does not know my works). Yet I have omitted a great deal, and I am still working upon all these problems and others. See my List of Publications; although a great deal has not been published.

4. I have (I believe) never written a word about Marcuse. In my view, it is pointless to get involved in this diatribe. (See point 2 below. A swamp!) If I remember correctly, I first met Marcuse in 1966 in California (although we were at Harvard at the same time in 1950), but we did not discuss anything. I have the same opinion of Marcuse as does my friend and colleague Cranston.

I have already written about aestheticism in chapter 9 of volume 1 of *The Open Society* (of which the German translation is unfortunately poor). (See the motto by Roger Martin du Gard.) On the whole, Marcuse merely repeats what Mourlan says in du Gard. My criticism can be found in chapter 9 of *The Open Society*. Of course, I wrote this criticism, in chapter 9, long before Marcuse adopted his present stance ('negative philosophy'), and du Gard had already published his book in 1936–40.

In my view, the difference between the 'idealists' among the fascists and Marcuse is almost negligible.

I now turn to your point 2.

2. This group of questions in your letter covers a great deal of ground. I must begin with my epistemological theory.

You say that you have read my works; but please take another look at my *Second Thesis* on p. 103 of the Adorno book on *The Positivist Dispute*. The thesis that we know nothing is meant seriously. It is important never to forget our ignorance. *We should therefore never pretend to know anything, and we should never use big words.*

What I called the cardinal sin above (point 1) – the presumptuousness of the three-quarters educated – is simply talking hot air, professing a wisdom we do not possess. The recipe is: tautologies and trivialities seasoned with paradoxical nonsense. Another recipe is: write down some scarcely comprehensible pomposity and add trivialities from time to time. This will be enjoyed by the reader who is flattered to find thoughts he has already had himself in such a 'deep' book. (Anyone can see these days that the emperor's new clothes are fashionable!)

When a student comes up to university he has no idea what standards he should apply, and so he adopts the standards he finds. Since the intellectual standards in most departments of Philosophy (and particularly of Sociology) permit pomposity and presumed knowledge (all these people seem to know an awful lot), even good heads are completely turned. And those students who are irritated by the false presumptions of the 'ruling' philosophy become opponents of philosophy, and *rightly so*. They then believe, *wrongly*, that these presumptions are those of the 'ruling class', and that a philosophy influenced by Marx would be better. But modern left-wing nonsense is generally even worse than modern right-wing nonsense.

What have the neo-Dialecticians learnt? They have not learnt how hard it is to solve problems and to come nearer to the truth. They have only learnt how to drown their fellow human beings in a sea of words.

Consequently, I do not like squabbling with these people: they have no standards.

It will perhaps interest you to know that, during the entire period of student unrest, we have up to now had only a single revolutionary student in my department (of Philosophy, Logic and Scientific Method) at the London School of Economics. He had so much opportunity to put forward his view that he had no reason to complain. My departmental colleagues and I have *never* taught in an authoritarian or dogmatic fashion. Our students were *always* (since I took over the Department in 1946) asked to interrupt the lectures if they either did not understand something or did not agree; and they were never treated condescendingly. We have never set ourselves up as great thinkers. I stress repeatedly that I do not want to convert anybody: I simply set problems and trial solutions before the students. Of course I make it very clear where I stand – what I take to be correct, and what I think is false.

So I do not propound any philosophical doctrine, or any new revelation (unlike *every one* of the people you mention in your letter, with the exception of Hans Albert); rather I put forward problems and trial solutions, and these trial solutions are critically examined.

This throws a little light upon the great difference between myself and the other philosophers you mention. There are only a very few philosophers who solve problems. I hesitate to say it, but I believe that I have solved a whole string of really fundamental philosophical problems – like, for example, the problem of induction. (These trial solutions have – as always – produced new and fertile problems.)

Although I have had so much undeserved success, the fact that I have solved problems is largely ignored. (Hans Albert is the great exception in Germany.) Most philosophers are incapable of recognizing either a problem or a solution, even when they are staring them in the face: these things simply lie outside their field of interest.

I am unwilling to criticize these philosophers. To criticize them would be (as my friend Karl Menger once said) to plunge after them, sword drawn, into the swamp in which they are already sinking, only to sink with them. (Hans Albert risked it, and he has not yet sunk.) Instead of criticizing them, I try to establish new and better standards by discussing the solutions to problems. This may sound arrogant. Nevertheless, I believe that this is the only correct course of action. This explains why I have never published a single word about Marcuse nor about Habermas (until my letter in the *Times Literary Supplement* on 26 March 1970, of which I am sending you a copy).

The basic thesis of Adorno and Habermas in *The Positivist Dispute* is the *claim* (made by Mannheim) *that factual knowledge and value judgements in sociology are inextricably linked*. I have dealt with this entire topic in my criticism of Mannheim [*Open Society*, vol. II, *The Poverty of Historicism*; also *The Positivist Dispute*, from the final paragraph before the 11th thesis up to the 13th thesis[2]], in which I attempt to prove not the falsity, but rather the triviality and irrelevance of Mannheim's sociology of knowledge. My opponents merely repeat Mannheim's thesis over and over again, in old or new words, instead of providing a serious discussion of the points I have made. Clearly, this does not answer my criticisms.

I now turn to a new point, which is connected with *your philosophical dictionary* (in your article), and in which I criticize this dictionary.

5. I never quarrel over words. But the expressions '*Positivism*' and '*Neo-Positivism*', which have been brought into this debate by Habermas, have an almost laughable history.

(a) *Positivism*. The expression was introduced by Comte. It originally denoted the following epistemological position. There is positive, that is to say, non-hypothetical, knowledge. This positive knowledge must be retained as a starting point and a foundation.

(b) *Moral and juridical positivism*. Critics of Hegel (including, for example, myself in *The Open Society*) have argued that the Hegelian theory 'Anything that is reasonable is real' is a form of positivism: moral and legal values (for example: justice) are replaced by *positive facts* (the prevailing custom and the prevailing law). (It is precisely this Hegelian conflation of values and facts which still haunts Habermas: it is the remains of this positivism that prevent him from distinguishing the normative from the factual.)

This positivist mixture of values (norms) and facts is a consequence of Hegelian epistemology; moreover, a consistent epistemological positivist must also be a moral and juridical positivist. This means, as I explained in *The Open Society*, that

Right = Might

or that:

Today's might = Right;

a position I resist just as strongly is moral futurism:

Tomorrow's might = Right.

(c) *Ernst Mach's Positivism*. Mach and later Bertrand Russell accepted Berkeley's sensationalism in some of their works:

esse = percipi,

that is, roughly speaking: nothing exists other than sensations. They combined this with Comte's positivism: Knowledge consists of *descriptions of facts (and not of explanations and hypotheses)*.

(d) *The 'Logical Positivism'* of the Vienna Circle combined the positivism of Mach and Russell with Russell's 'logistic' philosophy of mathematics. (This was then and is now often called 'New Positivism'.)

(e) Now it is my turn.

I have argued against all forms of positivism both in Vienna, 1930–7, and in England, 1935–6.

In 1934 I published my book *The Logic of Scientific Discovery*. This was a criticism of positivism. But Schlick and Frank, the leaders of the Vienna Circle, were so tolerant that they accepted the book for a series they were editing.

One result of this tolerance was that *everyone who just glanced at the book took me for a positivist*.

This resulted in the widely believed myth of Popper the positivist. The myth was perpetrated in countless discourses, in footnotes or in subordinate clauses. Once someone has 'learnt' in this fashion that I am a positivist, and once he has publicly committed himself to this view, he then generally tries to alter the concept of positivism afterwards so that it applies to me. This has already happened from time to time, especially with people who have either not read my books at all, or have read them only very superficially. *This is all relatively unimportant*, since it is only a question of words ('positivism'); and I do not quarrel over words.

Nevertheless, my position could not be more different from positivism. (The only similarity is that I am very interested in physics and biology, whilst the hermeneutists have not the slightest interest in any of the natural sciences.)

In particular I am:

an anti-inductivist;
an anti-sensationalist;
a champion of the primacy of the theoretical and the hypothetical;
a *realist*.

My epistemology implies that the natural sciences do not begin with 'measurements', but with great ideas; and that scientific progress does *not* consist in the accumulation or clarification of facts, but in bold and revolutionary ideas, which are then sharply criticized and examined.

As far as social matters are concerned, I stress a practical approach: the combating of evils, of avoidable suffering and of avoidable lack of freedom (by contrast with promises of a heaven on earth), and in the social sciences I fight against the habit of counterfeiting.

In reality my position is as far removed from positivism as is (for example) that of Gadamer.

You see, I have discovered – and this is the basis for my criticism of positivism – that natural science does *not* proceed in a positivist fashion, but in the main employs a method which works with 'prejudices'. But, wherever possible, it uses new prejudices and *prejudices that can be criticized* and subjects them to severe criticism. (This can all be found in *The Logic of Scientific Discovery*, 1934 [first published in English 1959].) I have even used the word 'prejudice' in this sense and shown that Bacon, who denounced prejudices, misunderstood the method of natural science; see my little booklet *On the Sources of Knowledge and of Ignorance*, 1960, reprinted in my anthology *Conjectures and Refutations*, especially p. 14.[3]

Therefore: what separates me from Gadamer is a better understanding of the 'method' of the natural sciences, a logical theory of truth and the *critical* attitude. But my theory is just as anti-positivistic as his, and I have shown that textual interpretation (hermeneutics) employs genuinely scientific methods. Furthermore, my criticism of positivism was astonishingly successful. After many years, it was largely accepted by the surviving members of the Vienna Circle; thus John Passmore, the historian of philosophy, was able to write that: 'Positivism is as dead as a philosophical movement ever can be.'

I do not think much of words and names. But the name ('Neo-)Positivism' is just a symptom of the widespread habit of criticizing before reading. I must make this clear because of your philosophical dictionary. I do not have discussions with those people who discuss things in terms of such catchwords. See Karl Menger's remark, above. This way can lead only into the infinite mire of scholastic quarrels about words. I hope to make better use of my time: in studying more pressing problems.

(The task of reading – and refuting – *The Logic of Scientific Discovery* fell to Herr Wellmer as the other members of the Frankfurt School did not have the time. In his hands, Gadamer's *Truth and Method* becomes the antithesis of epistemology and methodology. But nothing fits together.)

Adorno and Habermas are anything but clear in their criticism of my position. In brief: they believe that, because my epistemology is (they think) positivist, it forces me to defend the social *status quo*. In other words: my (supposed) epistemological positivism forces me to accept a moral and juridical positivism. (That was my criticism of Hegel.) They have unfortunately overlooked the fact that, although I am indeed a (non-revolutionary) liberal, my epistemological theory is a *theory of the growth of knowledge through intellectual and scientific revolutions*. [Through new and great ideas.]

Adorno and Habermas do not know what they are criticizing; and they do not know that their own theory of the analytically indissoluble connection between values and facts is a moral and juridical positivism that derives from Hegel.

Résumé of the book about the so-called 'Positivist Dispute'. This book is sailing under the wrong flag. Besides: my contribution, which was both temporally and logically the *first* and which really gave rise to all the others, was meant to be a basis for discussion. It consisted of twenty-seven clearly and precisely formulated theses, which should and could have been discussed. Yet my theses are hardly ever mentioned in the course of this long book, and my contribution, in the middle of the book, is drowned in a sea of words. No review has mentioned that my theses and arguments are never answered. The method (where arguments are lacking, replace them by a torrent of words) succeeded, and my drowned theses and arguments have been forgotten.

But all this (that is to say, the entire 'Positivist Dispute') is simply walking upon eggshells and is almost grotesque in its insignificance.

Résumé of the whole. Although I almost always work upon sharply defined scientific problems, a common thread runs through all my work: *in favour of* critical argument – *against* empty words and against intellectual immodesty and presumptuousness – against the *betrayal* of the intellectuals, as Julien Benda called it (see the 4th and 5th English editions of *The Open Society*, vol. II, p. 393). I am convinced (see *The Open Society*) that we, the intellectuals, are to blame for almost all misery, because we do not strive hard enough to achieve intellectual honesty. (Consequently, the most pig-headed anti-intellectualism will probably triumph in the end.) In *The Open Society* I say this in a hundred different attacks upon false prophets, and I do not mince my words. For example, I have made a couple of *very harsh* brief remarks about Jaspers and Heidegger (see the Index of Names to *The Open Society*, vol. II, English or German editions).

It seems that you would like to know my reasons for refusing to have any discussions with Professor Habermas.

Here are my reasons. They consist (1) of quotations of Professor Habermas from the beginning of his postscript to the controversy between Popper and Adorno, in the '*Positivist Dispute*' (nota bene, I never published a word about either Adorno or Habermas until 26 March 1970), and (2) of my translations. Many readers will think that I have failed to provide an adequate translation of the original. They may well be right. I am a reasonably experienced translator, but I am perhaps too stupid for this task. Be this as it may, I have done my best:

> To the original I feel
> I must appeal,
> And render faithfully the holy text
> In my beloved German next.[4]

It is not the aim of my translation to avoid foreign words, provided that their meaning is clear (co-operation = team work; antagonism = opposition), rather my *sole* concern is to make the – somewhat meagre – informational content of every sentence as clear as possible, even if this should make the translation longer than the original.

Habermas begins with a quotation from Adorno, whom he applauds (page 155).

[Quotations from Habermas's Essay][5]	*[My 'translation']*
Social totality does not lead any life of its own over and above that which it unites and of which it is, itself, composed.	Society consists of social connections.

It produces and reproduces itself through its individual elements.	These different connections *somehow* produce society.
It is no more possible to separate this totality from the life, the co-operation, and the antagonism of the individual,	Co-operation and antagonism may be found between these connections; and since (as stated previously) society consists in these connections, it cannot be separated from them;
than it is to understand any element merely in terms of its functions without an insight into the whole, the essence of which inheres in the motion of the individual entity itself.	but the converse is also true: none of the connections can be understood without the others.
System and individual entity are reciprocal and can only be understood in their reciprocity.	(Repetition of the above.)

(Note: The doctrine of unity given here has been expressed countless times, and very often better; but the words become more impressive every time.)

Now Professor Habermas himself writes:

Adorno comprehends society in terms of categories, which do not deny their descent from Hegel's logic.	Adorno uses a terminology reminiscent of Hegel.
He sees society as a totality in the strictly dialectical sense, which forbids the organic comprehension of the whole in terms of the statement that it is more than the sum of its parts;	This is why (sic) he does not say that the whole is more than the sum of its parts;

<table>
<tr><td>nor is the totality a class whose logical parameters could be determined by amalgamating all the elements within it.</td><td>nor is (sic) the whole a class of elements.</td></tr>
</table>

And so on. For example, further down the same page we find

<table>
<tr><td>the totality of the social interrelations of life . . .</td><td>we are all somehow related to each other . . .</td></tr>
</table>

or on page 157

<table>
<tr><td>Theories are ordering schemata which we may construct as we wish within a syntactically binding framework.</td><td>Theories should not be formulated ungrammatically; apart from that, you can say anything you like.</td></tr>
<tr><td>These theories prove usable in a particular object domain if they satisfy its real diversity.</td><td>They can be applied to a specific field, if they are applicable.</td></tr>
</table>

Unfortunately many sociologists, philosophers, *et al.*, traditionally regard the dreadful game of making the simple appear complex and the trivial seem difficult as their legitimate task. That is what they have learnt to do and they teach others to do the same. There is absolutely nothing that can be done about it. Even Faust could not change things. Our very ears have been deformed by now so that they can only hear very big words.

> Men do believe, if they hear words,
> There must be thoughts to go with them.[6]

This is why Goethe goes on to say of the great hidden power of this magical knowledge:

> But if you can't think,
> Just give me a wink,
> And I give it to you for nothing.[7]

As you already know, I am an opponent of Marx; but among the many of his remarks that I admire is the following: 'Dialectic in its mysticized form became the German fashion . . .'.

It still is.

This is my excuse for not entering this debate, but preferring to work upon formulating my ideas as simply as possible. This is often not easy.

NOTE (1984)

The quotation from Marx (at the end of my letter) comes from *Das Kapital*, 2nd edition, 1872, p. 822. Earlier on the same page Marx had written: 'I criticized the mysticizing side of the Hegelian dialectic almost 30 years ago, at a time when it was still fashionable.'

Marx did not suspect that it might remain so, perhaps for ever.

NOTES

1 Translator's note: The quotation is given directly from *Conjectures and Refutations*, 5th edn, Routledge, London and New York, 1989, p. 72.

2 Translator's note: This paper also appears in the present volume, chapter 5. See pp. 72 f.

3 Translator's note: Chapter 3 of this volume is an abbreviated version of this booklet as reprinted in *Conjectures and Refutations*.

4 Translator's note: This passage (from Goethe's *Faust*) was translated by the author from the German text below:

> Mich drängt's, den Grundtext aufzuschlagen,
> Mit redlichem Gefühl einmal
> Das heilige Original
> In mein geliebtes Deutsch zu übertragen.

5 Translator's note: The original German texts of both the Habermas quotations and the author's translations are given in the Appendix (pp. 233–5 below).

6 Translator's note: This passage was translated by the author from the German text below.

> Gewöhnlich glaubt der Mensch, wenn er nur Worte hört,
> Es müsse sich dabei doch auch was denken lassen.

7 Translator's note: This passage was translated by the author from the German text below.

> Und wer nicht denkt,
> Dem wird sie geschenkt,
> Er hat sie ohne Sorgen.

Part II
ON HISTORY

7

BOOKS AND THOUGHTS

Europe's first publication

I am grateful for the invitation to give a lecture about books. This is not only because I think that books, and therefore libraries, are the most characteristic and the most important physical things in our European civilization, and perhaps in human civilization as a whole, but also because of the dominating role books have played – and still play – in my own life. When I was five years old, the first volume of Selma Lagerlöf's book *The Wonderful Adventures of Nils* (*Wunderbare Reise des kleinen Nils Holgersson mit den Wildgänsen*) was read to me. The work had just been published in three green volumes. No other book had such a decisive influence not only on my own character, but also on that of my childhood friend Konrad Lorenz. Konrad fell in love with the wild geese, whilst I fell in love with Selma Lagerlöf and her books. Like her I became a school teacher. Both Konrad and I remained true to our loves.

Since those early years, books have played an important role in my life, more important even than music. No other human achievement, not even the greatest creations of literature and of art, seem to me as transcendent of all human powers and at the same time so moving, so miraculous as the great works of classical music. Yet books, I think, are culturally still more important.

I do not wish to speak here about the great European revolution that we owe to Johann Gutenberg (or perhaps to Lauren Janszoon Coster?), whose invention of the printed book was most probably the main force of the humanistic movement and of the Reformation, of the rise of science and, eventually, of democracy.

A lecture delivered on 2 November 1982 in the old Imperial Palace (Hofburg) in Vienna to celebrate the opening of an exhibition of books by Rudolf Kirchschläger, then the President of the Federal Republic of Austria. Translation by Melitta Mew.

I shall speak instead about a very similar, although more localized, process that began in Greece two thousand years before Gutenberg and, I conjecture, was the origin of our specifically European civilization.

It was a time that is rightly called the Greek miracle or, more specifically, the Athenian miracle: the sixth and fifth centuries BC, the time of the repulsion of the Persians; the time when the Greek world, by defending freedom, became aware of the idea of freedom; the time that produced Pericles and led to the building of the Parthenon.

A miracle like this can never be fully explained. I have thought about it for many years, and also written about it, and I suggest that a part, certainly only a small part, of the explanation lies in the collision, the clash, of the Greek and the eastern cultures, in what has been termed 'culture clash'. In any case, Homer's epics (whose topic was culture clash) and almost all the great new ideas emerged in the eastern Greek colonies on the coast of Asia Minor where the culture clash was most strongly felt. And all this was brought to the West, at least in part, by political and other refugees who were fleeing from the Persians. Pythagoras, Xenophanes and Anaxagoras were such refugees.

But for some time I have had the idea that the Greek miracle, and especially the Athenian miracle, might perhaps be partially explained – and surely only *very* partially – by the invention of the written book, of book publishing and of the book market.

Writing in various forms had existed for a very long time, and here and there something like a book could be found, especially in the East, although written records on wax, clay and similar materials were not very convenient. There were of course religious scripts. Indeed, for a long time writing was used (apart from letters) mainly for official documents, for religious documents, and perhaps by merchants for making notes, as shown by the lists of goods and other possessions in Pylos and Knossos. It also was sometimes used to record the deeds of great Kings.

According to a hypothesis that I am communicating here for the first time, the specifically European culture began with the publication of the works of Homer in book form.

Homer's epics had existed for about three hundred years. But they were collected and for the first time written down, and offered for sale to the public, around the year 550 BC. They had been well known as a whole only to professional reciters, the

Homerids, the Homeric rhapsodists. Reproduced in many handwritten copies by literate slaves, on papyrus imported from Egypt, they were sold to the public. This was the first publication of a book. It happened in Athens, and as tradition has it, on the initiative of the ruler of Athens, the tyrant Pisistratus.

Pisistratus' main occupation was to rule Athens – an exceedingly troublesome and arduous task. As a hobby he seems to have adopted book publishing, and thus become the founder and director of a state enterprise comparable, to some extent, to Her Majesty's Stationery Office. The enterprise did not outlive its founder, but its cultural consequences endured and proved to be of immeasurable significance.

In Athens, with the advent of the first European book, the first European book market came into being. Everybody read Homer, whose works became the first primer and the first bible of Europe. Hesiod, Pindar, Aeschylus and other poets followed. Athenians learnt to read (for a long time, all reading meant reading aloud) and to write, especially prepared speeches and letters, and Athens became a democracy. Books were written, and eager Athenians rushed to buy them. Already by the year 466 BC there followed, apparently in a large edition, the first scientific publication: Anaxagoras' great work *On Nature*. (Anaximander's work apparently was never published, although it seems that the Lyceum had a copy, or perhaps a summary, and that Apollodorus later discovered a copy – perhaps the same one – in an Athenian library. Heraclitus did not publish his work, which was deposited in the Temple of Artemis.) Anaxagoras was a political refugee from Clazomenae, near Smyrna in Ionia, and wrote his work in Athens. We know that copies of the book were sold off cheaply in Athens, sixty-seven years after it was first published; yet it survived for a thousand years. It was, I conjecture, the first book written with the intention of having it published.

Some thirty-seven years after Anaxagoras' *On Nature*, the great historical work of Herodotus was published in Athens, accompanied by a public recitation of a part of it by the author himself. This proved that Pericles had been right when, two years earlier, he had referred to Athens as the 'School of Hellas'.

My hypothesis is that, by making books available for sale in Athens, Pisistratus had put in train a cultural revolution comparable in its importance to that started by Gutenberg two thousand years later; but my hypothesis is of course not testable. The printed book set new values and standards for the whole of Western Europe. Although historical parallels should never be taken too seriously, they are at times astonishingly close. For example, after the publication of his book, Anaxagoras was accused of impiety, as was Galileo two thousand years later. Both were in danger of their lives. Neither was executed, thanks to their personal relations with some unusual men of power: Pericles and the Pope. Owing to the intervention of Pericles (who had been his pupil), Anaxagoras was not executed but was banned from Athens after paying a heavy fine. Themistocles, a great Athenian, who also had been banned from the city, invited Anaxagoras, his former teacher, to Lampsakos. There Anaxagoras died a few years later. In the case of Galileo, his personal relations with the Pope saved him from execution; he too had to spend the rest of his life in banishment.

As yet, nobody seems to have hit upon the idea of burning or banning a dangerous book like Anaxagoras' treatise *On Nature*. Books were still too much of a novelty to have become objects of juridical intervention. Thus, owing to the sensational trial of its author, Anaxagoras' book became a local bestseller; and those parts of the book that were not too abstract became the talk of the town. All the same, by 399 BC interest in the book had waned, and it could be bought on the market for next to nothing (whereas Galileo's book, which was put on the Index, soon attained scarcity value and shot up in price).

Plato was undoubtedly the first to recognize the powerful influence of the book and its potential political significance (and, in particular, the influence and significance of Homer). This prompted him to suggest that the poets – and especially Homer, whom he admired – should be banned from the city on account of their undesirable political influence.

Part of my information about the fate of Anaxagoras' book stems from Plato's book *The Apology of Socrates*, the most beautiful philosophical work I know. There we can read that only the illiterate are unfamiliar with the content of Anaxagoras' book, and that the young who are eagerly searching for knowledge 'can buy copies any time for a drachma, if as much, on the book market'. I doubt whether there were specialized booksellers to be found at the place that Plato indicates – 'near the orchestra' ('ek tēs orchēstras'). More likely there were merchants who, besides selling other goods (snacks or suchlike), also sold books in the form of handwritten papyrus rolls. Historians before the First World War estimated that a drachma was the equivalent of a little less than 10 pence of sterling silver – let's say perhaps one or two pounds sterling in 1984 – the price of a paperback.

Anaxagoras' work consisted of at least two, probably three, handwritten rolls of papyrus ('books'). As Plato suggests, one drachma was an astonishingly low price for a book of this size, and moreover a book that had been the talk of the town.

Perhaps the low price may be explained by the local history. After twenty-seven years of war with Sparta, Athens had come under the puppet government known as the Thirty Tyrants who, within eight months, had murdered one-twelfth of the full citizens of Athens and confiscated their possessions. Many citizens fled; but they returned and conquered the Thirty Tyrants in a battle at the Piraeus, restoring the democracy. Plato's *Apology* describes a scene that happened shortly after this. It is possible that, in those bad days, some of the impoverished families were compelled to sell their books.

Nevertheless, more books were written and brought to the market. The great work of Thucydides, describing in eight books twenty-one years of war, the work of Isocrates, and the colossal work of Plato, all are proof of this.

Anaxagoras' book continued to be read, for at least one copy existed and was still being read in Athens in AD 529, almost exactly a thousand years after it was published. In that year the pagan philosophical schools in Athens were closed by an edict of the Christian Emperor Justinian, and Anaxagoras' great book disappeared.

But in our time scholars have made efforts to reconstruct its intellectual content. Passages that were quoted or discussed in other books could be thus reconstructed, although the fragments were not sufficient to reassemble into a whole. It is of interest that the man whom I regard as the outstanding expert and restorer of the contents of this book and of Anaxagoras' thought as a whole, Professor Felix M. Cleve, in 1940 had to flee from Vienna to the West – to New York – just as in 492 BC Anaxagoras had to flee to the West – to Athens.

We see here that a book can outlive its author by a thousand years. In the case of Anaxagoras, the thoughts expressed in his book, its intellectual content, outlived the book by a further fifteen hundred years.

Therein lies part of the immense cultural significance of a book. The *thought content* that has been reconstructed in our time is something objective. This *objective thought content* should be clearly distinguished from the *subjective thought processes* that went on in Anaxagoras' head and in the heads of his interpreters: from the thought processes that go on in the head of every author.

The objective thought content that is found in a book is what makes it valuable. It is not, as is often believed, the expression of subjective thought, of what goes on in the author's head. More accurately described, it is the objective product of the human mind, the result of hard mental effort, of mental activity, of an activity that time and again consists in rejecting or improving what has just been written down. Whenever this happens, there is a kind of feedback between the subjective thought processes, the mental activity and the objective thought content. The author creates the written work, but he also learns much from his own work, from his own attempts to formulate his ideas, and especially from his mistakes. And above all, he can learn from the work of others.

Of course there are authors who work in a different way, but as a rule thoughts can be criticized and improved most effectively when one attempts to write them down for the purpose of publication, so that they may be understood by others.

The superficial and misleading theory that a spoken or written sentence is the *expression* of a subjective thought has had disastrous consequences: it has led to expressionism. Even today it is almost universally accepted that a work of art is the expression of the personality or of the emotions of the artist. Many composers and artists believe in this theory; and this belief has debased and almost destroyed art.

No doubt, everything one does, including brushing one's teeth or yawning, is an expression of one's personality and of one's emotions. But this renders the theory trivial and insignificant.

In reality the great artist is a keen learner who keeps an open mind so that he may learn not only from the work of others but also from his own labours, including the mistakes and failures that neither he nor any other artist can avoid. Almost all great artists have been self-critical and regarded their work as something objective. It is not widely enough known that Haydn, on hearing the first performance of his *Creation* in the Aula of the old University of Vienna, broke out in tears saying 'It is not I who wrote this.'

You will understand that I have touched here on an inexhaustible theme. The theme is closely related to the development of Greek art – drawing, painting, sculpture – which, long before Pisistratus, had been influenced by Homer. Yet after the publication of Homer, and especially in Athens, art took a distinct turn, first in the direction of the representational and illustrative art form, and later towards a kind of idealized naturalism.

All this clearly illustrates the immense significance of thought content, of thoughts in the objective sense. They form a world which I have called world 3. I call world 1 the world of material things, the world described by physics and by astronomy, by chemistry and by biology. I call world 2 the world of our personal subjective experiences, of our hopes and aims, of our joys and sorrows, and of our elations, of our thought processes – in the subjective sense; the world that psychology tries to describe and to explain. And I call world 3 the world of the products of the human mind, the products of our mental activity and, above all, the world of our specifically human language, of our objective thought contents, whether spoken or written; and also the world of technology and of art. In thus distinguishing three worlds, I have introduced nothing but a terminology. It is not even a new terminology since it stems from Gottlob Frege. The only new thing is the thesis that our mind, our thinking, our feeling, our world 2, our mental world, develops through interaction with both of the other worlds, and especially by interaction and feedback with that world 3 which man has created himself: the world of language, the world of writing and the world of the objective content of our thoughts; the world of books, and also the world of art; the world of our social institutions, the world of culture.

This thesis of the powerful role of feedback, especially the feedback between the world 3 of books and the world of our mental experiences, is important. That there are such objective contents we owe almost entirely to the invention of our specifically human language. For the first time in the history of the evolution of life on our wonderful planet, the invention of language made it possible for objective thought contents to exist; and by making it possible for us to look upon our thought contents as objects, it became possible for us to criticize them – and so to become critical of ourselves.

The discovery of writing was the next step. But the most momentous step was the invention of the book and of the critical competition between books.

It is not improbable that Pisistratus intended to establish a kind of state monopoly for Homer, as there had been in the East monopolies for books before. Perhaps he did not fully comprehend the situation, and he probably did not anticipate competition from private publishers. But most likely it was his lack of foresight that played the crucial part in starting the evolution of our European science and our European culture.

Note: The lecture following here as an Appendix, and the notes following that lecture, develop the same topic and take it somewhat further.

APPENDIX TO CHAPTER 7
ON A LITTLE-KNOWN CHAPTER OF MEDITERRANEAN HISTORY

Mr President, ladies and gentlemen, it is a great honour, and a great experience, to have been chosen to be the first person to receive the Catalonia International Prize: a newly founded prize whose foundation is of clear historical and symbolic significance for Catalonia. I am now standing before you with two tasks to perform. The first is to thank the Generalitat of Catalonia, the Catalan Institute for Mediterranean Studies, its President and Officers, its Advisory Council, and all others concerned, for having conferred on me so great an honour by judging me, and my work, worthy of this honour. The task of giving thanks is easy to perform; for since I feel abundantly grateful, it is easy for me to say: Thank you very much indeed, thank you for your appreciation of my work, thank you for your good will, and thank you all for your generosity. Thank you also for all the work and all the effort and all the time you have spent in preparing for this solemn ceremony. And I want to thank also all of you who have come here to participate in this great occasion. And finally, let me express my thanks to the people of Catalonia.

My second task is far more difficult. It is my task to address you. But it is obviously impossible for me to make, in a short address, anything like an adequate return to you, much as I wish to do so. When I was preparing this address, I felt this inadequacy as a heavy weight; and I found it very difficult to decide on a topic. Should I talk to you on an abstract subject like the theory of scientific knowledge? Or on democracy? But democracy is something whose value you may appreciate quite as much as I do, so that you may not need me to tell you anything about it. If possible, I should say something interesting about the Mediterranean, I thought, to honour your Institute of Mediterranean Studies; but I know nothing, or very little, about the Mediterranean. So in my mind's eye I saw myself standing here before you, an old man of eighty-

Translator's note: This lecture was presented on 24 May 1989 at the Palace of the Generalitat de Catalunya, when the author received the Catalonia International Prize. The English text is by the author.

seven before his stern judges, and not a good speaker – rather like Socrates before the 501 stern Athenian judges who condemned him to death.

When I had come so far in my considerations, I suddenly knew what was to be the topic of my address: 'The Miracle of Athens and the Origin of Athenian Democracy'. This was an appropriate theme, for it was to become the Miracle of Greece, and later, the Miracle of the Mediterranean, of the Mediterranean civilization. It is a topic that combines the themes of democracy and Mediterranean civilization, and it gives me the opportunity of addressing you on a topic to which I myself have made a contribution – a contribution that I have not fully developed before.

Our civilization, which is, essentially, the Mediterranean civilization, derives from the Greeks. This civilization was born in the period from the sixth century before Christ to the fourth century, and it was born in Athens.

The Athenian miracle is staggering. Here we have, in a short period, beginning with Solon at about 600 BC, a peaceful revolution. Solon saved the city by shaking off the burden of debt from the exploited Athenian citizens, and by forbidding that any Athenian citizen could be made a slave because of his debts. It was the first constitution ever designed to preserve the freedom of the citizens, and it was never forgotten, although the history of Athens shows abundantly clearly that freedom is never secure but always threatened.

Solon was not only a great statesman; he was the first Athenian poet of whom we have knowledge, and he explained his aims in his poetry. He spoke of '*eunomia*' or 'good government', and he explained this as balancing the conflicting interests of the citizens. It was, no doubt, the first time, at least the first time in the Mediterranean region, that a constitution had been shaped with an ethical and humanitarian aim. And what was here at work was the universally valid ethical imperative that Schopenhauer brought into the simple form: *Neminem laede imo omnes, quantum potes, juva!* That is: Hurt no one, but help all, as well as you can!

Like the American Revolution, which came over two thousand years later, Solon's revolution had in mind the freedom of the citizens only: the slavery of the bought barbarian slaves was in both cases overlooked.

After Solon, Athenian politics were far from stable. Several leading families were contesting for power, and after some unsuccessful attempts, Pisistratus, a relation of Solon's, established himself as a monarch or tyrant in Athens. His great wealth derived from silver mines situated outside Attica, and he used his wealth largely for cultural purposes and for stabilizing the Solonian reforms in Athens. He built a lot of beautiful buildings and instituted festivals, especially the theatrical festivals; to him is due the founding of the performances of tragedies in Athens. And, as we know from Cicero, he organized the writing down of the works of Homer, the *Iliad* and *Odyssey*, which previously seem to have existed only as oral traditions.

It is the main thesis of my address that this was an act that had the most far-reaching consequences; that it was an event of focal significance in the history of our civilization.

For many years, ever since I wrote my *Open Society and its Enemies*, the Athenian miracle has been a problem that has fascinated me. It is a problem that follows me around and does not let me go. What was it that created our civilization in Athens? What made Athens invent art and literature, tragedy, philosophy, science and democracy, all in a short period of time of less than one hundred years?

I had one answer to this problem, an answer that was undoubtedly true but, I felt, quite insufficient. The answer was: *culture clash*. When two or more different cultures come into contact, people realize that their ways and manners, so long taken for granted, are not 'natural', not the only possible ones, neither decreed by the gods nor part of human nature. They discover that their culture is the work of men and their history. It thus opens a world of new possibilities: it opens the windows and it lets in fresh air. This is a kind of sociological law, and it explains a lot. And it certainly played an important role in Greek history.

Indeed, one of Homer's main themes in the *Iliad*, and even more in the *Odyssey*, is, precisely, this topic of culture clash. And culture clash is of course a main topic also of Herodotus' *History*. Its significance for Greek civilization is very great.

And yet this explanation did not satisfy me. And for a long time I felt that I had to give up. A miracle like the Athenian miracle, I felt, *cannot* be explained, and I still think so, that it cannot be fully explained. Least of all can it be explained by the writing down of the works of Homer, although this certainly had great influence. Books, indeed great books, had been written down before, and at other places, and nothing comparable to the Athenian miracle had happened.

But one day I read again Plato's *Apology of Socrates Before His Judges* – the most beautiful philosophical work I know. And re-reading a much discussed passage, I had a new idea. The passage [26 D–E] implies that there was a flourishing book market in Athens in the year 399 BC, a market, at any rate, where old books (like Anaxagoras' book *On Nature*) were regularly sold, and where they could be bought very cheaply. Eupolis, the great master of the old comedy, even speaks [in a fragment cited by Pollux, *Onomasticon* IX, 47; cf. VII, 211] of a book market fifty years earlier. Now, when could such a market have arisen and how could it have arisen? It was clear: only after Pisistratus had the works of Homer written down.

Slowly, the whole significance of this event dawned on me: the picture began to unfold. Before Homer had been written down, there were books, but no popular books freely for sale at a market: books were, even where they existed, a great rarity, not commercially copied and distributed, but (like the book written by Heraclitus) kept in a holy place, under the surveillance of priests. But we know that in Athens Homer quickly became popular: everybody read Homer, most knew him by heart, or at least passages of Homer by heart. Homer was the first public entertainment ever! And this was the case mainly in Athens, as we can learn again from Plato, who in his *Republic* complains about the dangerous entertainment, while in his *Laws* he satirizes Sparta and Crete for their lack of literary interest: in Sparta, he indicates, Homer's name was known – just known; and in Crete, he indicates, Homer had hardly been heard of.

The great success of Homer in Athens led to something like commercial book publishing: books, we know, were dictated to groups of literate slaves, who wrote them down on papyrus; the sheets were collected in scrolls or 'books', and they were sold in the market, at a place called the 'Orchestra'.

How did all this start? The simplest hypothesis is that Pisistratus himself, who was a rich man, not only had Homer edited, but had him copied and distributed. By a strange coincidence I stumbled about six years ago across a report saying that the first and very considerable export of papyrus from Egypt to Athens began in a year in which Pisistratus was still ruling at Athens.

Since Pisistratus had been interested in having public recitals of Homer, it is very plausible that he started distributing the newly edited books; and their popularity led to the emergence of other publishers.

Collections of poems written by other poets, and tragedies and comedies followed. None of these had been written deliberately for publication; but books written with that intention followed as soon as publishing became an established practice in Athens, and the book market (*biblionia*) in the Agora became an established institution. I conjecture that the first book written deliberately for publication was Anaxagoras' great work *On Nature*. Anaximander's work appears never to have been published, although it seems that the Lyceum had a copy – perhaps a summary – and that Apollodorus later discovered a copy – perhaps the same one – in an Athenian library. So I suggest that the publication of the works of Homer was the first publication ever, actually the invention of publication, at least in the Mediterranean region. It not only made Homer the bible (*biblion*) of Athens – it made him the first instrument of education, the first primer, the first spelling book, the first novel. And it made the Athenians literate.

That this was highly significant for the establishment of the Athenian democratic revolution – the expulsion of Pisistratus' son Hippias from Athens, and the establishment of a constitution – may be seen from one of the characteristic institutions of the democracy that was established about fifty years after this first publication. I mean the institution of ostracism. For on the one hand, this institution assumed silently that the citizen could write – that he could write on a potsherd the name of the citizen he thought dangerously popular or otherwise prominent. These were the citizens that the Athenians thought could create a tyranny. On the other hand, the institution of ostracism shows that the Athenians, at least during the first century after expelling the tyrant Hippias, regarded as the central problem of their democracy the prevention of a tyranny.

This idea comes out very clearly when we realize that the institution of ostracism did not regard the banishment as a punishment. By being ostracized, a citizen retained his honour unblemished, he retained his property and indeed all rights except his right to remain in the city. This right he lost, first for ten years and later for five, though he could be recalled. In a sense, ostracism was a tribute, since it recognized that a citizen was outstanding; and some of the most outstanding leaders were ostracized. Thus the idea was: nobody is irreplaceable in a democracy, and much as we admire leadership, we must be able to do without any particular leader; otherwise he may make himself our master, and it is the main task of our democracy to avoid this. It should be noted that ostracism was not long in use. The first known case was in 488 BC, and the last in 417. All the cases were tragic for the great men who were banished. The period almost coincides with the period of the greatest works of Athenian tragedy, with the period of Aeschylus, Sophocles and Euripides, who later banished himself.

So it is my hypothesis that the first publication in Europe was the publication of Homer, and this fortunate fact led to the Greek love of Homer and of the Homeric heroes, to popular literacy and to the Athenian democracy. But I think it did more. Homer was of course popular before; and almost all the vase paintings had been for some time illustrations of his work. So had many sculptures. Homer himself had been a detailed and realistic painter in words of so many vivid and interesting scenes, and as Ernst Gombrich has pointed out, this challenged sculptors and painters to emulate him in their own different media. And the challenge became even greater as detailed knowledge of the Homeric text became more widespread. So the influence upon the arts of the power to read cannot be denied. The influence of Homeric themes upon the Athenian tragedians is evident; and even in the few cases when they used non-Homeric themes, they still continued to choose themes which their audience could be assumed to be familiar with. So I can indeed claim that the cultural influence of the book market was incalculable. All the components of the Athenian cultural miracle were undoubtedly greatly influenced by this market.

But to crown all these arguments, we have a kind of historical experiment. The great invention that, as it were, repeated on a far larger scale the invention of the publication of books was the invention of book printing by Gutenberg, two thousand years after Pisistratus' invention of book publishing. It is interesting that, even though the invention was made in the North of Europe, the majority of printers who acquired the skill brought it quickly south to the Mediterranean – to Italy. And there they played a decisive role in that great new movement called the Renaissance, which included the development of the new humanist scholarship and the new science that ultimately transformed our whole civilization.

This was a movement on a much larger scale than the movement that I dubbed 'The Athenian Miracle'. It was, first of all, a movement based on a very much larger edition of books. In 1500, Aldus printed editions of one thousand copies. It was, obviously, the size of the printed editions that was the salient point of this new revolution. But otherwise there is an astonishing analogy, or similarity, between what had started in Athens in, say, 500 BC and had spread from there over the Mediterranean, and what happened in Florence or Venice in, say, 1500 of our era. And the new humanist scholars were aware of this: they wanted to renew the spirit of Athens, and they were proud of their ability to do so, and of their success in doing so.

As in Athens and later in Graecia Magna – and especially in Alexandria, but indeed all over the Mediterranean – scientific and, in particular, cosmological speculation played an important role in these movements. Renaissance mathematicians, such as Commandino, successfully recaptured the lost works of Euclid, Archimedes, Apollonius, Pappus and Ptolemy, but also of Aristarchus, which led to the Copernican Revolution and so to Galileo, to Kepler, to Newton and to Einstein. If our own civilization is correctly described as the first scientific civilization, then it all comes from the Mediterranean and, I suggest, from Athenian book publishing, and the Athenian book market.

In all this I have badly neglected the contribution of the Arabs, who brought an Indian number system to the Mediterranean. They gave much, but they received as much as they gave, if not more, when they reached the Mediterranean.

Ladies and gentlemen, I have briefly retold a well-known story – well known except for one small yet, I think, significant contribution: the decisive role played by books, and especially by published books, from the very beginning. Our civilization is, indeed, a bookish one: its traditionality and its originality, its seriousness and sense of intellectual responsibility, its unprecedented power of imagination and its creativity, its understanding of freedom and its watchfulness for it – all these rest on our love of books. May short-term fashions, the media and the computers never spoil or even loosen this close personal attachment to books!

But I do not wish to end with books, however important they are for our civilization. It is most important not to forget that a civilization consists of civilized individual men and women, of individuals who wish to live good lives and civilized lives. It is to this end that books and our civilization must make their contributions. I believe that they are doing so with great success.

I thank you for having come, and I thank you for your attention.

BIBLIOGRAPHICAL NOTES

On Anaxagoras and the controversial problem of his dating, see Felix M. Cleve, *The Giants of Pre-Sophistic Greek Philosophy*, 2nd edition, Martinus Nijhoff, The Hague, 1969, especially pp. 170 ff.; also D. O'Brien, *Journal of Hellenic Studies*, 1968, pp. 93–113. For a different dating see Charles H. Kahn, *Anaximander*, 2nd edition, Columbia University Press, New York, 1964, especially pp. 164 ff. For Anaximander's book see Kahn, op. cit., and Olof Gigon, *Der Ursprung der griechischen Philosophie*, Basel, 1945; also W. K. C. Guthrie, *A History of Greek Philosophy*, volume I, Cambridge University Press, 1962. On Anaxagoras' book see the passages collected in Diels–Kranz, *Die Fragmente der Vorsokratiker*, 5th edition, 1964; especially Plato, *Apology*, 26 D–E. Concerning Plato's suggestion for censorship of literature and music, see my *Open Society and Its Enemies*, 9th reprint of the 5th edition, Routledge, London, 1991, volume I, chapter 4, notes 39–41, and text. For Homer's influence on art, see E. H. Gombrich, *Art and Illusion*, 4th reprint of the 5th edition, Phaidon Press, London, 1986, chapter IV, 4. On world 1, world 2 and world 3 see K. R. Popper, *Unended Quest*, Routledge, London, 1992, sections 38–44; K. R. Popper, *Objective Knowledge*, 7th edition, Oxford University Press, 1991; and K. R. Popper and J. C. Eccles, *The Self and Its Brain*, Springer International; also Routledge, 1984. For predecessors of my theory of world 3, see Bernard Bolzano, *Wissenschaftslehre*, Sulzbach 1837 (English extract ed. by Rolf George, *Theory of Science*, Blackwell, Oxford, 1972); Heinrich Gomperz, *Weltanschauungslehre*, Bd. II, first half, Eugen Diederichs, Jena 1908; Karl Bühler, *Sprachtheorie*, Gustav Fischer, Jena 1934; Gottlob Frege, 'Der Gedanke', *Beiträge zur Philosophie des deutschen Idealismus*, Bd. I, 1918.

ADDITIONAL COMMENTS (1992)

1. Cicero's report about Pisistratus' edition of Homer fits well with all we seem to know about Pisistratus and his cultural activities; and it is corroborated by the Egyptian export of papyrus to Athens.

2. At the time of Pisistratus and of the first publication of Homer (550 BC), and from this time on, considerable amounts of papyrus were imported into Athens from Egypt. (Egyptian exports of papyrus had been

since the eleventh century BC a carefully controlled monopoly of the Pharaohs. This is why Egyptologists know of these exports.)

3. For many centuries after the first publication of Homer, written material, including books, was usually read aloud. Letters were so read (as emerges from Isocrates), and the reading was not always adequate. Speeches were classified into those prepared by writing and those that were produced extempore: for the first type Isocrates is one of the main authorities; for the second, Alcidamas. (Cf. also Plato's *Phaedrus*.) Books were read aloud, or even publicly recited (as in the case of the publication of Herodotus). All these were called *logoi*. St Augustine was deeply impressed when, nine hundred years after the first publication of Homer, he first saw St Ambrose reading silently. It prevented him, he explains, from asking St Ambrose for help in his religious perplexities. (See Book VI of the *Confessions*.)

4. *Biblos* and *byblos* seem to have been for some time used as synonyms of *papyros*. Herodotus uses *byblos* a few times for 'book', that is, for *a roll of papyrus that forms part* of a greater work; but this usage seems to have taken time to be accepted. Although a book market existed in Athens at least since 450 BC, the concept of *a book as a saleable unit* was not easily established. Written texts were generally read aloud for centuries before silent reading became a universally practised art (see point 3 above). Early written texts were poems (Solon, Homer), juridical laws, dramatic plays, dialogues, letters. The written communication was often regarded as an inferior substitute for an oral communication. All this has a bearing on my hypothesis that Anaxagoras' book was the first to be written with the intention to have it published. Even Plato thought not only that the best he could say was not in his writings, but that it was impossible fully to communicate one's ideas by writing; and that written legislation was inferior to legislation that lived by oral tradition. The slow acceptance of a book as a saleable property helps us to understand why Plato, who realizes the political danger of books such as Homer's (which he considers banning from his ideal city), does not speak of burning them; and it explains the fact that Anaxagoras' book was not burned.

5. Diogenes Laertius IX, 52 reports that the works of Protagoras were confiscated in Athens and publicly burned. This somewhat late report seems to me to be irreconcilable not only with Plato's *Apology* but with many passages in Plato and other early sources. Moreover, the event reported by Diogenes would have happened in approximately 411 BC, when Plato was sixteen. It would have left traces on his proposals for censorship.

6. Some scholars have tried to conclude from the low price of one drachma that Anaxagoras' book (which had definitely been published far more than thirty years previous to Plato's *Apology*) was a *short* book. But such a conclusion is unjustifiable in the case of an antiquarian book; and what we know of its content is incompatible with its being a short book. It contained, among other things, an astronomy and meteorology; a theory of the origin of the world and of the origin and structure of matter; above all a non-atomic theory of molecules and of the infinite divisibility of matter; and of the various more or less homogeneous substances (such as water, metals; substances in living creatures like hair, flesh, bones, etc.).

The theory of infinite divisibility, which was extremely subtle, contained remarks (which have, I suspect, not been understood until now) about the equivalence of infinite numbers (brought about by division, that is to say 'enumerable', as we now call them); a result that was probably not rediscovered until the nineteenth century (Bolzano, Cantor). It was obviously a long book and, as Plato suggests, it went for a song. The most likely explanation for this is that the original edition was large.

7. Only a book market allows anything like publication. But facilities for publication would explain the great attraction of Athens for writers, and the beginning of what we now call *literature*.

8. I was too old when I started these researches into the beginning of a book market in Athens and, with it, the beginning of publishing and of 'literature', to do more than scratch the surface of a whole range of problems. When some years ago I mentioned my ideas to Gregory Vlastos – the only classical scholar whom I told about them – he was fascinated and said that everything was completely new to him. But I had so many quite different problems on my hands that in spite of his encouragement I could not even find any of the existing books related to the subject. I believe that there is much work to be done; and I hope that the hypotheses I have been able to propose here may provoke some classical scholars both to criticism and to further developments.

8

ON CULTURE CLASH

I was very pleased to be invited to Vienna to see old friends again and to make new friends; and it was a great honour to be invited here today by the President of the Society of Expatriate Austrians (*Auslandsösterreicherwerk)* to give a short lecture. His invitation stressed that the subject of my lecture was completely up to me. Consequently, he very kindly left me spoilt for choice.

I had considerable difficulty in making a decision. I was obviously expected to choose a subject that interests me. On the other hand it should also have some relevance to this occasion – to the meeting of expatriate Austrians in Vienna on the occasion of the Silver Jubilee of the Austrian State Treaty (*Staatsvertrag*) – the unique event that terminated the occupation of Austria after the Second World War.

I doubt if the subject I have chosen fulfils these expectations. Remembering the Austrian State Treaty and the Russian occupation of Austria that followed the Second World War, my talk is dedicated to the problem of culture clash.

My interest in culture clash is connected with my interest in a major problem: the problem of the characteristics and the origin of our European civilization. In my opinion, a partial answer to this question seems to lie in the fact that our western civilization is derived from Greek civilization. And Greek civilization – an unparalleled phenomenon – originated in a culture clash, between the cultures of the eastern Mediterranean. It was the first major clash between western and eastern cultures, and its effects

A lecture written for the 25th anniversary celebrations of the Austrian State Treaty. The lecture was read by Dr Elisabeth Herz in the presence of the Austrian (Federal) President. Published in *25 Jahre Staatsvertrag*, Österreichischer Bundesverlag, Vienna, 1981.

were deeply felt. Homer made it into a *leitmotif* of Greek literature and of the literature of the western world.

The title of my lecture, 'On Culture Clash', refers to a hypothesis, to a historical conjecture. This is the conjecture that a clash of this kind need not always result in bloody battles and destructive wars, but may also be the cause of a fruitful and life-promoting development. It may even lead to the development of a unique culture like that of the Greeks, which was then taken over by the Romans when it clashed with theirs. After many more clashes, particularly with Arab culture, it was deliberately revived during the Renaissance; and so it became that culture of the West, that civilization of Europe and of America, which eventually transformed all the other cultures of the world in the course of further clashes.

But is this western civilization a good and desirable thing? This question has been raised over and over again since at least the time of Rousseau, and particularly by young people, who are quite rightly always on the lookout for something better. It is a question typical of today's western civilization, which is more self-critical and kindly disposed towards reform than any other civilization in the world. Before I go on with my subject of culture clash, I should like to answer this question.

I believe that our western civilization is, in spite of all the faults that can quite justifiably be found with it, the most free, the most just, the most humanitarian and the best of all those we have ever known throughout the history of mankind. It is the best because it has the greatest capacity for improvement.

All over the world men have created new and often very different cultural worlds: the worlds of myth, of poetry, of art, of music; the worlds of production methods, of tools, of technology, of business; the worlds of morality, of justice, of protection and of help for children, for invalids, the weak and for others in need. But it is only in our western civilization that the moral demand for personal freedom is widely acknowledged and even widely realized, along with the demand for equality before the law, for peace, and for the minimum use of force.

This is why I regard our western civilization as the best to date. Of course it is in need of improvement. But, when all is said and done, it is the only civilization in which almost everyone is working together to improve it as much as possible.

I admit that even our civilization is very imperfect. But this almost goes without saying. It is easy to see that a perfect society is impossible. For practically all the values that a society should embody, there are other, conflicting values. Even freedom, perhaps the highest of all social and personal values, must be limited, since, of course, Hans's freedom may conflict only too easily with Peter's freedom. As an American judge once told a defendant who made reference to his freedom: 'The freedom of the movement of your fists is limited by the position of your neighbour's nose.' This brings us to Immanuel Kant's formulation that the task of legislation is to allow the greatest possible freedom of every individual to exist side by side with the greatest possible freedom of everyone else. In other words, freedom must, unfortunately, be limited by the law, that is, by order. Order is a necessary – an almost logically necessary – counterbalance of freedom. And there is such a counterbalance for all, or at least almost all the values, that we should like to see realized.

For instance, we are learning at this very moment that the great idea of the welfare state has its limitations. It appears that it is dangerous to relieve a person of his responsibility for himself and his dependants; and in many cases it is perhaps even dubious whether we ought to make the struggle for life very much easier for young people. It seems that, for many people, life may be robbed of its meaning by the withdrawal of direct personal responsibility.

Another example is peace, which we all desire more strongly nowadays than ever before. We want to, indeed we must do everything in our power to avoid conflicts, or at least to limit them. On the other hand, a society without conflict would be inhuman. It would not be a human society, but an ant colony. Nor should we overlook the fact that the great pacifists were also great fighters. Even Mahatma Gandhi was a fighter: a fighter for non-violence.

Human society needs peace, but it also needs serious ideational conflicts: values, ideas, that we can fight for. Our western society has learned – from the Greeks – that words have a much greater and more lasting effect in these conflicts than the sword; most effective of all, however, are rational arguments.

A perfect society is therefore impossible. But some social orders are better than others. Our western society has opted for democracy as a social system that can be changed by words and in places – if only rarely – even by means of rational arguments; by rational, that is to say, by objective criticism: by non-personal critical considerations, just like those typically used in science, particularly in natural science since the Greeks. I therefore declare my support for western civilization; for science; and for democracy. They give us the chance to prevent avoidable tragedy and to try out reforms, such as the welfare state, to assess them critically and to make any further necessary improvements. I also declare my support for science, so often maligned these days, which employs self-criticism in its search for truth and which discovers afresh with each new discovery just how little we know: how infinitely great our ignorance really is. All the great natural scientists were conscious of their infinite ignorance and of their fallibility. They were intellectually modest. If Goethe says: 'Only rogues are modest', then I should like to reply: 'Only intellectual rogues are immodest.'

Now that I have declared my support for western civilization and for science, particularly for natural science, I shall soon return to my subject of culture clash. But first I should like to make a very brief reference to a dreadful heresy that is unfortunately still an important element of this western civilization. I am referring to the dreadful heresy of nationalism – or more precisely, the ideology of the national state: the doctrine that is still so often upheld and is apparently a moral demand, that the boundaries of the state should coincide with the boundaries of the area inhabited by the nation. The fundamental error in this doctrine or demand is the assumption that peoples or nations exist prior to the states – rather like roots – as natural units, which should be occupied accordingly by the states. In reality they are created by the states.

This completely unworkable demand must be contrasted with the important moral demand for the protection of minorities: the demand that the linguistic, religious and cultural minorities of each state should be protected against attacks by the majority; including, of course, those minorities that differ from the majority because of the colour of their skin, or the colour of their eyes, or the colour of their hair.

Unlike the principle of the national state, which is totally impracticable, the principle of minority protection, though not of course easy to implement, nevertheless seems to be more or less workable. The advances that I have witnessed in this area on numerous visits to the United States since 1950 are far greater than

I would ever have thought possible. And, unlike the principle of nationality, the principle of the protection is quite clearly a moral principle, just like, for example, the principle of child protection.

Why is the principle of the national state unworkable anywhere in the world, and nothing short of insane, especially in Europe? This question brings me back to the subject of culture clash. The population of Europe is, as we all know, the result of mass migrations. From time immemorial wave after wave of people have surged from the steppes of Central Asia and encountered earlier immigrants on the southern, south-eastern and particularly on the fissured western peninsulas of Asia, which we call Europe, and dispersed. The result is a linguistic, ethnic and cultural mosaic: a chaotic jumble, which cannot possibly be disentangled.

Languages are, comparatively speaking, the best guides through this chaos. But then there are some more or less native or natural dialects and overlapping written languages, which themselves originate from glorified dialects, as Dutch, for instance, clearly illustrates. Other languages, such as French, Spanish, Portuguese and Romanian, are products of violent Roman conquests. So it is crystal-clear that the linguistic chaos cannot be a genuinely reliable guide through the ethnic chaos. An examination of surnames also makes this point. Although many Slavonic surnames were replaced by German ones in Austria and Germany, so that many traces were covered over – thus I knew a Bohuschalek, who, if I remember rightly, became a Bollinger – the traces of Slavonic-German assimilation are still everywhere. In particular, the numerous noble families in Germany whose names end in -off or -ow are obviously descended in some way from Slavs. However, this does not give us any further clues as to their ethnic origin, particularly where noble families are concerned, for whom it was natural to marry across greater distances; in contrast to, for example, the peasant serfs.

But now the crazy idea of the principle of nationalism has sprung up amid this European chaos, primarily under the influence of the philosophers Rousseau, Fichte and Hegel, and no doubt also as a result of reaction to the Napoleonic wars.

There were of course precursors of nationalism. But neither Roman culture nor Ancient Greek culture was nationalistic. Every one of these ancient cultures emerged as a result of the clash of the different cultures on the Mediterranean and in the Near East. This is also true of Greek culture, which probably made the most important contributions to our present-day western culture: I mean the idea of freedom, the discovery of democracy, and the critical, rational attitude which ultimately resulted in modern natural science.

Even the oldest of the Greek literary works to come down to us, the *Iliad* and the *Odyssey*, are eloquent testimonies of culture clash; indeed, this clash is their actual theme. Yet at the same time they bear witness to an attitude both rational and explanatory. In fact, the precise function of the Homeric gods is to explain the otherwise unintelligible, the irrational (such as the quarrel between Achilles and Agamemnon) using a comprehensible psychological theory: that is, in terms of the interests and petty jealousies of these all too human divine forms – divine forms, whose human weaknesses are apparent and who are also sometimes judged critically. Aries, the God of War, comes off particularly badly. And it is important that the non-Greeks in both the *Iliad* and the *Odyssey* are at the very least treated just as sympathetically as the Greeks, the Achaeans.

This critical and enlightened attitude recurs in those works in which, under the influence of the Greek struggle for freedom against Persian attacks, the idea of freedom was first celebrated; especially in the works of Aeschylus and Herodotus. It is not national freedom, but rather personal freedom, above all the freedom of the democratic Athenians, which is contrasted with the lack of freedom endured by the subjects of the great Persian kings. In this context, freedom is no mere ideology but a way of life which makes life better and more worth living. Both Aeschylus and Herodotus make this clear. They both write as witnesses of the clash of these western and eastern cultures, the cultures of freedom and of despotism; and both testify to the enlightening effect of this clash, which led to a conscious and critically distanced evaluation of one's own culture, and hence to a rational and critical evaluation of traditional myths. In Ionia (a part of Asia Minor), this resulted in critical cosmology, in critical speculative theories about the architecture of the cosmic system and ultimately in natural science, the search for the true explanation of natural phenomena. One might say that natural science comes about as a result of the influence of a rational and critical attitude to the mythical explanation of nature. When I speak of rational criticism, I mean a criticism from the standpoint of truth: of the questions 'Is this true?' and 'Can this be true?'

By questioning the truth of these mythical explanations of natural phenomena, the Greeks created the theories that led to the birth of the natural sciences. And by questioning the truth of mythical reports about prehistoric times, they brought about the beginning of the study of history.

But Herodotus, who is rightly called the father of historiography, was not just a predecessor of the study of history. It was he who actually discovered the critical and illuminating nature of culture clash, especially the clash between the Greek, the Egyptian and the Median-Persian cultures.

At this point I should like to quote an anecdote from Herodotus' historical work, which is in fact the history of the military and cultural clash of the Greeks with the inhabitants of the Near East, particularly with the Persians. In this anecdote Herodotus uses an extreme and rather gruesome example to show that a rational person must learn that even those things which at first he takes for granted may be called into question.

Herodotus writes (III, 38): 'Once, while Darius was King, he summoned the Greeks who were at his court and asked them at what price they would be prepared to eat their dead fathers' corpses. They replied that nothing, but absolutely nothing at all, could induce them to do so. Then Darius summoned the Kallatier, an Indian people accustomed to eating their fathers, and asked them in the presence of the Greeks, who had an interpreter at their disposal, at what price they would agree to cremate their deceased fathers. At this the Kallatier gave loud screams of horror and implored him not even to utter such blasphemy. That is the way of the world.'

In relating this anecdote to his Greek contemporaries, Herodotus not only intended to teach them to respect foreign customs, but also to make them capable of criticizing things that they took for granted. He had obviously learnt a great deal himself through cultural confrontations of this kind; and he wanted to share this experience with the reader.

Similarities and differences among customs and traditional myths fascinated him. My hypothesis, my conjecture is that these very differences accounted for that critical and rational attitude which became crucially important for his and for subsequent generations and, I conjecture, ultimately had such a decisive influence upon European culture – together, of course, with many other important influences.

In England and America I am repeatedly asked for the most likely explanation for the singular creativity and cultural wealth of Austria and of Vienna in particular: of the unrivalled heights of the great Austrian symphonists, of our Baroque architecture, and our achievements in science and in the philosophy of nature.

Ludwig Boltzmann and Ernst Mach were not only great physicists, but also pioneering philosophers of nature. They were the predecessors of the Vienna Circle. Josef Popper-Lynkeus, the social philosopher, who might be described as a philosophical founder of the modern welfare state, also lived here. But here in Vienna concern with social matters was not simply confined to philosophical debate, but resulted in some remarkable practical achievements even in the time of the monarchy. There were the truly marvellous 'People's Universities' (*Volkshochschulen*), there was the 'Free School' club, which became one of the most important seeds of the school reform movement, there were social relief organizations, such as the Society for the Protection and Salvation of Children, the Emergency Service, the Home for the Homeless and many others.

There is probably no real explanation for this extraordinary cultural and social activity and productivity. But I should like to put forward a tentative hypothesis here. Perhaps this Austrian cultural productivity is related to my topic, that is to say, to culture clash. The old Austria was a reflection of Europe: it contained almost innumerable linguistic and cultural minorities. And many of these people who found it hard to eke out an existence in the provinces came to Vienna where most of them had to learn German as best they could. Many came here under the influence of a great cultural tradition, and a few were able to make fresh contributions to it. We know that Haydn and Mozart were influenced not only by German, Italian and French composers, but also by Hungarian folk music and even by Turkish music. Haydn and Mozart were newcomers to Vienna, and Beethoven, Brahms, Bruckner and Mahler also came to Vienna from elsewhere. The genius of the musicians remains unexplained. It was Beethoven who acknowledged the 'divine spark in Schubert', who may well have been the greatest genius to be born in Vienna.

A consideration of Viennese music might even lead us into drawing a comparison between Vienna from Haydn to Bruckner and Athens in Pericles' time. And the circumstances were perhaps more similar than we might at first suppose. It seems that both, situated as they were in an extremely vital location between the East and the West, were immensely enriched by culture clash.

9

IMMANUEL KANT: THE PHILOSOPHER OF THE ENLIGHTENMENT

A lecture to commemorate the 150th anniversary of Kant's death

One hundred and fifty years ago Immanuel Kant died, having spent the eighty years of his life in the Prussian provincial town of Königsberg. For years his retirement had been complete,[1] and his friends intended a quiet burial. But this son of an artisan was buried like a king. When the rumour of his death spread through the town the people flocked to his house demanding to see him. On the day of the funeral the life of the town was at a standstill. The coffin was followed by thousands, while the bells of all the churches were tolling. Nothing like this had ever before happened in Königsberg, say the chroniclers.[2]

It is difficult to account for this astonishing upsurge of popular feeling. Was it due solely to Kant's reputation as a great philosopher and a good man? It seems to me that there was more in it than this; and I suggest that in the year 1804, under the absolute monarchy of Frederick William, those bells tolling for Kant carried an echo of the American and French revolutions – of the ideas of 1776 and 1789. I suggest that to his countrymen Kant had become an embodiment of these ideas.[3] They came to show their gratitude to a teacher of the Rights of Man, of equality before the law, of world citizenship, of peace on earth, and, perhaps most important, of emancipation through knowledge.[4]

English text by the author. See *Conjectures and Refutations,* 5th edn, Routledge, London, 1989.

I. KANT AND THE ENLIGHTENMENT

Most of these ideas had reached the Continent from England through a book published in 1733, Voltaire's *Letters Concerning the English Nation*. In this book Voltaire contrasts English constitutional government with Continental absolute monarchy; English religious toleration with the attitude of the Roman Church; and the explanatory power of Newton's cosmology and of Locke's analytic empiricism with the dogmatism of Descartes. Voltaire's book was burnt; but its publication marks the beginning of a philosophical movement – a movement whose peculiar mood of intellectual aggressiveness was little understood in England, where there was no occasion for it.

Sixty years after Kant's death these same English ideas were being presented to the English as a 'shallow and pretentious intellectualism': and ironically enough the English word 'Enlightenment', which was then used to name the movement started by Voltaire, is still beset by this connotation of shallowness and pretentiousness; this, at least, is what the *Oxford English Dictionary* tells us.[5] I need hardly add that no such connotation is intended when I use the word 'Enlightenment'.

Kant believed in the Enlightenment. He was its last great defender. I realize that this is not the usual view. While I see Kant as the defender of the Enlightenment, he is more often taken as the founder of the school which destroyed it – of the Romantic School of Fichte, Schelling and Hegel. I contend that these two interpretations are incompatible.

Fichte, and later Hegel, tried to appropriate Kant as the founder of their school. But Kant lived long enough to reject the persistent advances of Fichte, who proclaimed himself Kant's successor and heir. In *A Public Declaration Concerning Fichte*, which is too little known, Kant wrote: 'May God protect us from our friends . . . . For there are fraudulent and perfidious so-called friends who are scheming for our ruin while speaking the language of good will.'[6] It was only after Kant's death, when he could no longer protest, that this world-citizen was successfully pressed into the service of the nationalistic Romantic School, in spite of all his warnings against Romanticism, sentimental enthusiasm and *Schwärmerei*. But let us see how Kant himself describes the idea of the Enlightenment:

> Enlightenment is the emancipation of man from a state of self-imposed tutelage . . . of incapacity to use his own intelligence without external guidance. Such a state of tutelage I call 'self-imposed' if it is due, not to lack of intelligence, but to lack of courage or determination to use one's own intelligence without the help of a leader. *Sapere aude!* Dare to use your own intelligence! This is the battle-cry of the Enlightenment.[7]

Kant is saying something very personal here. It is part of his own history. Brought up in near poverty, in the narrow outlook of Pietism – a severe German version of Puritanism – his own life was a story of emancipation through knowledge. In later years he used to look back with horror to what he called 'the slavery of childhood',[8] his period of tutelage. One might well say that the dominant theme of his whole life was the struggle for spiritual freedom.

II. KANT'S NEWTONIAN COSMOLOGY

A decisive role in this struggle was played by Newton's theory, which had been made known on the Continent by Voltaire. The cosmology of Copernicus and Newton became the powerful and exciting inspiration of Kant's intellectual life. His first important book, *The Theory of the Heavens*, has the interesting sub-title: *An Essay on the Constitution and the Mechanical Origin of the Universe, Treated According to Newtonian Principles.*[9] It is one of the greatest contributions ever made to cosmology and cosmogony. It contains the first formulation not only of what is now called the 'Kant–Laplace hypothesis' of the origin of the solar system, but also, anticipating Jeans, an application of this idea to the 'Milky Way' (which Thomas Wright had interpreted as a stellar system five years earlier). But all this is excelled by Kant's identification of the nebulae as other 'Milky Ways' – distant stellar systems similar to our own.

It was the cosmological problem, as Kant explains in one of his letters,[10] which led him to his theory of knowledge, and to his *Critique of Pure Reason*. He was concerned with the knotty problem (which has to be faced by every cosmologist) of the finitude or infinity of the universe, with respect to both space and time. As far as space is concerned a fascinating solution has been suggested since, by Einstein, in the form of a world which is both finite and without limits. This solution cuts right through the Kantian knot, but it uses more powerful means than those available to Kant and his contemporaries. As far as time is concerned no equally promising solution of Kant's difficulties has been offered up to now.

III. THE *CRITIQUE* AND THE COSMOLOGICAL PROBLEM

Kant tells us that he came upon the central problem of his *Critique* when considering whether the universe had a beginning in time or not.[11] He found to his dismay that he could produce seemingly valid proofs for both of these possibilities. The two proofs are interesting; it needs concentration to follow them, but they are not long, and not hard to understand.[12]

For the first proof we start by analysing the idea of an infinite sequence of years (or days, or any other equal and finite intervals of time). Such an infinite sequence of years must be a sequence which goes on and on and never comes to an end. It can never be completed: a completed or an elapsed infinity of years is a contradiction in terms. Now in his first proof Kant simply argues that the world must have a beginning in time since otherwise, at this present moment, an infinite number of years must have elapsed; which is impossible. This concludes the first proof.

For the second proof we start by analysing the idea of a completely empty time – the time before there was a world. Such an empty time, in which there is nothing whatever, must be a time none of whose time-intervals is differentiated from any other by its temporal relation to things and events, since things and events simply do not exist at all. Now take the last interval of the empty time – the one immediately before the world begins. Clearly, this interval is differentiated from all earlier intervals since it is characterized by its close temporal relation to an event – the beginning of the world; yet the same interval is supposed to be empty, which is a contradiction in terms. Now in his second proof Kant simply argues that the world cannot have a beginning in time since otherwise there would be a time-interval – the moment immediately before the world began – which is empty and yet characterized by its immediate temporal relation to an event in the world; which is impossible.

We have here a clash between two proofs. Such a clash Kant called an 'antinomy'. I shall not trouble you with the other antinomies in which Kant found himself entangled, such as those concerning the limits of the universe in space.

IV. SPACE AND TIME

What lesson did Kant draw from these bewildering antinomies? He concluded that our ideas of space and time are inapplicable to the universe as a whole.[13] We can, of course, apply the ideas of space and time to ordinary physical things and physical events. But space and time themselves are neither things nor events: they cannot even be observed: they are more elusive. They are a kind of framework for things and events: something like a system of pigeon-holes, or a filing system, for observations. Space and time are not part of the real empirical world of things and events, but rather part of our mental outfit, our apparatus for grasping this world. Their proper use is as instruments of observation: in observing any event we locate it, as a rule, immediately and intuitively in an order of space and time. Thus space and time may be described as a frame of reference which is not based upon experience but intuitively used in experience, and properly applicable to experience. This is why we get into trouble if we misapply the ideas of space and time by using them in a field which transcends all possible experience – as we did in our two proofs about the universe as a whole.

To the view which I have just outlined Kant chose to give the ugly and doubly misleading name 'Transcendental Idealism'. He soon regretted this choice,[14] for it made people believe that he was an idealist in the sense of denying the reality of physical things: that he declared physical things to be mere ideas. Kant hastened to explain that he had only denied that space and time are empirical and real – empirical and real in the sense in which physical things and events are empirical and real. But in vain did he protest. His difficult style sealed his fate: he was to be revered as the father of German Idealism. I suggest that it is time to put this right. Kant always insisted that the physical things in space and time are real.[15] And as to the wild and obscure metaphysical speculations of the German Idealists, the very title of Kant's *Critique* was chosen to announce a critical attack upon all such speculative reasoning. For what the *Critique* criticizes is pure reason; it criticizes and attacks all reasoning about the world that is 'pure' in the sense of being untainted by sense experience. Kant attacked pure reason by showing that pure reasoning about the world must always entangle us in antinomies. Stimulated by Hume, Kant wrote his *Critique* in order to establish that the limits of sense experience are the limits of all sound reasoning about the world.[16]

V. KANT'S COPERNICAN REVOLUTION

Kant's faith in his theory of space and time as an intuitive frame of reference was confirmed when he found in it a key to the solution of a second problem. This was the problem of the validity of Newtonian theory, in whose absolute and unquestionable truth he believed,[17] in common with all contemporary physicists. It was inconceivable, he felt, that this exact mathematical theory should be nothing but the result of accumulated observations. But what else could be its basis? Kant approached this problem by first considering the status of geometry. Euclid's geometry is not based upon observation, he said, but upon our intuition of spatial relations. Newtonian science is in a similar position. Although confirmed by observations it is the result not of these observations but of our own ways of thinking, of our attempts to order our sense-data, to understand them, and to digest them intellectually. It is not these sense-data but our own intellect, the organization of the digestive system of our mind, which is responsible for our theories. Nature as we know it, with its order and with its laws, is thus largely a product of the assimilating and ordering activities of our mind. In Kant's own striking formulation of this view, 'Our intellect does not draw its laws from nature, but imposes its laws upon nature.'[18]

This formula sums up an idea which Kant himself proudly calls his 'Copernican Revolution'. As Kant puts it, Copernicus, finding that no progress was being made with the theory of the revolving heavens, broke the deadlock by turning the tables, as it were: he assumed that it is not the heavens which revolve while we the observers stand still, but that we the observers revolve while the heavens stand still.[19] In a similar way, Kant says, the problem of scientific knowledge is to be solved – the problem how an exact science, such as Newtonian theory, is possible, and how it could ever have been found. We must give up the view that we are passive observers, waiting for nature to impress its regularity upon us. Instead we must adopt the view that in digesting our sense-data we actively impress the order and the laws of our intellect upon them. Our cosmos bears the imprint of our minds.

By emphasizing the role played by the observer, the investigator, the theorist, Kant made an indelible impression not only upon philosophy but also upon physics and cosmology. There is a Kantian climate of thought without which Einstein's theories or Bohr's are hardly conceivable; and Eddington might be said to be more of a Kantian, in some respects, than Kant himself. Even those who, like myself, cannot follow Kant all the way can accept his view that the experimenter must not wait till it pleases nature to reveal her secrets, but that he must question her.[20] He must cross-examine nature in the light of his doubts, his conjectures, his theories, his ideas, and his inspirations. Here, I believe, is a wonderful philosophical find. It makes it possible to look upon science, whether theoretical or experimental, as a human creation, and to look upon its history as part of the history of ideas, on a level with the history of art or of literature.

There is a second and even more interesting meaning inherent in Kant's version of the Copernican Revolution, a meaning which may perhaps indicate an ambivalence in his attitude towards it. For Kant's Copernican Revolution solves a human problem to which Copernicus's own revolution gave rise. Copernicus deprived man of his central position in the physical universe. Kant's Copernican Revolution takes the sting out of this. He shows us not only that our location in the physical universe is irrelevant, but also that in a sense our universe may well be said to turn about us; for it is we who produce, at least in part, the order we find in it; it is we who create our knowledge of it. We are discoverers: and discovery is a creative art.

VI. THE DOCTRINE OF AUTONOMY

From Kant the cosmologist, the philosopher of knowledge and of science, I now turn to Kant the moralist. I do not know whether it has been noticed before that the fundamental idea of Kant's ethics amounts to another Copernican Revolution, analogous in every respect to the one I have described. For Kant makes man the law-giver of morality just as he makes him the law-giver of nature. And in doing so he gives back to man his central place both in his moral and in his physical universe. Kant humanized ethics, as he had humanized science.

Kant's Copernican Revolution in the field of ethics is contained in his doctrine of autonomy[21] – the doctrine that we cannot accept the command of an authority, however exalted, as the ultimate basis of ethics. For whenever we are faced with a command by an authority, it is our responsibility to judge whether this command is moral or immoral. The authority may have power to enforce its commands, and we may be powerless to resist. But unless we are physically prevented from choosing, the responsibility remains ours. It is our decision whether to obey a command, whether to accept authority.

Kant boldly carries this revolution into the field of religion. Here is a striking passage:

> Much as my words may startle you, you must not condemn me for saying: every man creates his God. From the moral point of view . . . you even *have* to create your God, in order to worship in Him your creator. For in whatever way . . . the Deity should be made known to you, and even . . . if He should reveal Himself to you: it is you . . . who must judge whether you are permitted [by your conscience] to believe in Him, and to worship Him.[22]

Kant's ethical theory is not confined to the statement that a man's conscience is his moral authority. He also tries to tell us what our conscience may demand from us. Of this, the moral law, he gives several formulations. One of them is: 'Always regard every man as an end in himself, and never use him merely as a means to your ends.'[23] The spirit of Kant's ethics may well be summed up in these words: dare to be free; and respect the freedom of others.

Upon the basis of these ethics Kant erected his most important theory of the state,[24] and his theory of international law. He demanded a league of nations, or a federal union of states, which ultimately was to proclaim and to maintain eternal peace on earth.[25]

I have tried to sketch in broad outline Kant's philosophy of man and his world, and its two main inspirations – Newtonian cosmology, and the ethics of freedom; the two inspirations to which Kant referred when he spoke of the starry heavens above us and the moral law within us.[26]

Stepping back further to get a still more distant view of Kant's historical role, we may compare him with Socrates. Both were accused of perverting the state religion, and of corrupting the minds of the young. Both denied the charge; and both stood up for freedom of thought. Freedom meant more to them than absence of constraint; it was for both a way of life.

From Socrates' apology and from his death there sprang a new idea of a free man: the idea of a man whose spirit cannot be subdued; of a man who is free because he is self-sufficient; who is not in need of constraint because he is able to rule himself, and to accept freely the rule of law.

To this Socratic idea of self-sufficiency, which forms part of our western heritage, Kant has given a new meaning in the fields of both knowledge and morals. And he has added to it further the idea of a community of free men – of all men. For he has shown that every man is free; not because he is born free, but because he is born with the burden of responsibility for free decision.

NOTES

1 Six years before Kant's death, Pörschke reports (see his letter to Fichte of 2 July 1798) that owing to Kant's retired way of life, he was being forgotten even in Königsberg.

2 C. E. A. Ch. Wasianski, *Immanuel Kant in seinen letzten Lebensjahren* (from *Ueber Immanuel Kant, Dritter Band,* Königsberg, bei Nicolovius, 1804); 'The public newspapers, and a special publication have made Kant's funeral known in all its circumstances.'

3 Kant's sympathies with the ideas of 1776 and 1789 were well known, for he used to express them in public. Cf. Motherby's eye-witness report on Kant's first meeting with Green in R. B. Jachmann, *Immanuel Kant geschildert in Briefen – Ueber Immanuel Kant, Zweiter Band,* Königsberg, bei Nicolovius, 1804; eighth letter: pp. 77 ff. (or pp. 54 ff. of the edition of 1902.)

4 I say 'most important' because events like Kant's well-deserved rise from near poverty to fame and comparatively easy circumstances helped to create on the Continent the idea of emancipation through self-education, in this form hardly known in England where the 'self-made man' was the uncultured upstart. The significance of this idea is connected with the fact that on the Continent, the educated had been for a long time the middle classes, while in England they were – of course with exceptions – the upper classes.

5 The *OED* says (some of the italics are mine): 'Enlightenment . . . 2. Sometimes used [after the German *Aufklärung, Aufklärerei*] to designate the spirit and the aims of the French philosophers of the 18th century, or of *others whom it is intended to associate with them in the implied charge of shallow and pretentious intellectualism,* unreasonable contempt for tradition and authority, etc.' The *OED* does not mention that '*Aufklärung*' is a translation of the French *éclaircissement*, and that it does

not have these connotations in German, while *Aufklärerei* (or *Aufkläricht*) are disparaging neologisms invented and exclusively used by the Romantics, the enemies of the Enlightenment. The *OED* quotes J. H. Stirling, *The Secret of Hegel*, 1865, and Caird, *The Philosophy of Kant*, 1889, as users of the word in sense 2.

6 The date of this Declaration is 1799. Cf. *WWC* (i.e. *Immanuel Kant's Werke*, ed. Ernst Cassirer *et al.*), vol. VIII, pp. 515 ff., and my *Open Society*, note 58 to ch. 12 (4th edn, 1962, vol. II, p. 313).

7 *What is Enlightenment?* (1785); *WWC*, vol. IV, p. 169.

8 See T. G. von Hippel's Biography (Gotha, 1801, pp. 78 ff.). See also the letter to Kant from D. Ruhnken (one of Kant's schoolfellows in the Pietist Frederickan College), in Latin, of 10 March 1771, in which he speaks of the 'stern yet not regrettable discipline *of the fanatics*' who had educated them.

9 Published in 1755. The full principal title might be translated: *General Natural History [of the Heavens] and Theory of the Heavens.* The words 'General Natural History' are used to indicate that the work is a contribution to the theory of the *evolution* of stellar systems.

10 To C. Garve, 21 September 1798: 'My starting point was not an investigation into the existence of God, but the antinomy of pure reason: 'The world has a beginning: it has no beginning', etc. down to the fourth . . . (Here comes a place where Kant, apparently, mixes up his own third and fourth antinomies.) 'It was these [antinomies] which first stirred me from my dogmatic slumber and drove me to the critique of reason . . . , in order to resolve the scandal of the apparent contradiction of reason with itself.'

11 See the foregoing note. See also *A Collection of Papers which passed between the late Learned Mr. LEIBNITZ, and Dr. CLARKE, In the Years* 1715 *and* 1716 . . . by Samuel Clarke, D.D. (London 1717); and Kant's *Reflexionen zur Kritischen Philosophie*, edited by B. Erdmann; esp. no. 4.

12 See *Critique of Pure Reason* trans. Norman Kemp Smith, 2nd edn, Macmillan, London, 1933 (reprinted 1990), pp. 454 ff.

13 ibid., pp. 518 ff. 'The Doctrine of Transcendental Idealism as the Key to the Solution of the Cosmological Dialectic.'

14 *Prolegomena* (1783), Appendix: 'Specimen of a Judgement on the *Critique* Anticipating its Investigation.' See also the *Critique*, 2nd edn (1787; the first edition had been published in 1781), pp. 274–9, 'The Refutation of Idealism', and the last footnote to the Preface of the *Critique of Practical Reason.*

15 See the passages mentioned in the foregoing note.

16 See Kant's letter to M. Herz, of 21st February 1772, in which he gives, as a tentative title of what became the first *Critique*, 'The Limits of Sense Experience and of Reason'. See also the *Critique of Pure Reason* (2nd edn), pp. 738 ff. (italics mine): '*There is no need for a critique of reason* in its empirical use; for its principles are continuously submitted to tests, being tested by the touchstone of experience. Similarly, there is no need for it within the field of mathematics, where its conceptions must be presented at once in pure intuition [of space and time] . . . But in a field in which reason is constrained neither by sense-experience nor by pure intuition to follow a visible track – namely, in the field of

its transcendental use . . . – *there is much need to discipline reason, so that its tendency to overstep the narrow limits of possible experience may be subdued . . .*'

17 See, for example, Kant's *Metaphysical Foundations of Natural Science* (1786), containing the *a priori* demonstration of Newtonian mechanics. See also the end of the penultimate paragraph of the *Critique of Practical Reason.* I have tried to show elsewhere (chapter 2 of *Conjectures and Refutations*) that some of the greatest difficulties in Kant are due to the tacit assumption that Newtonian Science is demonstrably true (that it is *epistēmē*), and that, with the realization that this is not so, one of the most fundamental problems of the *Critique* dissolves. See also chapter 8 of *Conjectures and Refutations.*

18 See *Prolegomena*, end of section 37. Kant's footnote referring to Crusius is interesting: it suggests that Kant had more than an inkling of the analogy between what he called his 'Copernican Revolution' and his principle of autonomy in ethics.

19 My text here is a free translation from the *Critique of Pure Reason,* 2nd edn, pp. xvi ff.

20 ibid., pp. xii ff.; cf. especially the passage: 'The physicists . . . realized that they . . . had to coerce Nature to reply to their questions, rather than let themselves be tied to her apron-strings, as it were.'

21 See the *Grundlegung zur Met. d. Sitten,* 2nd section (*WWC,* pp. 291 ff., especially 299 ff.): 'The Autonomy of the Will as the Highest Principle of Morality', and the 3rd section (*WWC*, pp. 305 ff.).

22 This is a free translation (although as close as is compatible with lucidity, I believe) from a passage contained in the footnote to chapter 4, part II, 1, of *Religion within the Limits of Pure Reason* (2nd edn, 1794 = *WWC*, vol. VI, p. 318; the passage is *not* in the 1st edn, 1793. See also the Introduction to *Conjectures and Refutations*, note 9). The passage is foreshadowed by the following: 'We ourselves judge revelation by the moral law' (*Lectures on Ethics by Immanuel Kant*, translated by L. Infield, 1930; the translation of the passage is corrected by P. A. Schilpp, *Kant's Pre-Critical Ethics,* 1938, p. 166, note 63). Just before, Kant says of the moral law that 'our own reason is capable of revealing it to us'.

23 See the *Grundlegung*, 2nd section (*WWC*, vol. IV, p. 287). My translation is, again, free.

24 See, especially, Kant's various formulations to the effect that the principle of the just state is to establish equality in those limitations of the freedom of its citizens that are unavoidable if *the freedom of each should coexist with the freedom of all* (e.g. *Critique of Pure Reason,* 2nd edn, p. 373).

25 *On Peace Eternal* (1795).

26 At the Conclusion of the *Critique of Practical Reason;* see especially the end of the penultimate paragraph, referred to in note 17 above.

10

EMANCIPATION THROUGH KNOWLEDGE

The philosophy of Immanuel Kant, and with it his philosophy of history, is often looked upon in Germany as antiquated, and as superseded by Hegel and his followers. This may well be due to the surpassing intellectual and moral stature of Kant, Germany's greatest philosopher; for the very greatness of his achievement was a thorn in the flesh of his lesser successors, so that Fichte, and later Hegel, tried to solve this irritating problem by persuading the world that Kant had been merely one of their forerunners. But Kant was nothing of the sort. On the contrary he was a determined opponent of the whole Romantic Movement and especially of Fichte: Kant was in fact the last great exponent of that much reviled movement, the Enlightenment. In an important essay entitled 'What is Enlightenment?' (1785) Kant wrote:

> Enlightenment is the emancipation of man from a state of self-imposed tutelage. This state is due to his incapacity to use his own intelligence without external guidance. Such a state of tutelage I call 'self-imposed' [or 'culpable'] if it is due not to lack of intelligence but to lack of courage or determination to use one's own intelligence without the help of a leader. *Sapere aude!* Dare to use your own intelligence! This is the battle-cry of the Enlightenment.

This passage from Kant's essay explains what was for him the central idea of the Enlightenment. It was the idea of *self-liberation through knowledge*.

A broadcast delivered in German on the Bavarian Broadcasting Network in February 1961, in a series of broadcasts 'On the Meaning of History'. English text by the author.

This idea of self-liberation or self-emancipation through knowledge remained for Kant a task as well as a guide throughout his life; and although he was convinced that this idea might serve as an inspiration for every man possessed of the necessary intelligence, Kant did not make the mistake of proposing that we adopt self-emancipation through knowledge, or any other mainly intellectual exercise, as the whole meaning or purpose of human life. Indeed, Kant did not need the assistance of the Romantics for criticizing pure reason, nor did he need their reminders to realize that man is not purely rational; and he knew that mere intellectual knowledge is neither the best thing in human life, nor the most sublime. He was a pluralist who believed in the variety of human experience and in the diversity of human aims; and being a pluralist, he believed in an open society – a pluralist society that would live up to his own maxim: 'Dare to be free, and respect the freedom and the autonomy of others; for the dignity of man lies in his freedom, and in his respect for other people's autonomous and responsible beliefs, especially if these differ widely from his own.' Yet in spite of his pluralism he saw in intellectual self-education, or self-emancipation through knowledge, a task which is indispensable from a philosophical point of view; a task demanding of every man immediate action here and now and always. For only through the growth of knowledge can the mind be liberated from its spiritual enslavement: enslavement by prejudices, idols and avoidable errors. Thus the task of self-education, though certainly not exhausting the meaning of life, could, he thought, make a decisive contribution towards it.

The analogy between the expressions '*the meaning of life*' and '*the meaning of history*' is worthy of examination; but I shall first examine the ambiguity of the word 'meaning' in the expression 'the meaning of life'. This expression is sometimes used in the sense of a deeper, a hidden meaning – something like the hidden meaning of an epigram, or of a poem, or of the *Chorus Mysticus* in Goethe's *Faust*. But the wisdom of some poets and perhaps also of some philosophers has taught us that the phrase 'the meaning of life' can be understood in a different way; that the meaning of life may not be so much something hidden and perhaps discoverable but, rather, something with which we ourselves can endow our lives. We can bestow a meaning upon our lives through our work, through our active conduct, through our whole way of life, and through the attitude we adopt towards our friends and our fellow men and towards the world. (Of course, that we can endow our lives in this way may strike us as an important discovery.)

In this way the quest for the meaning of life turns into an ethical question – the question 'What tasks can I set myself in order to make my life meaningful?' Or as Kant puts it: 'What should I do?' A partial answer to this question is given in Kant's ideas of freedom and autonomy, and of a pluralism which is limited only by the idea of equality before the law and of mutual respect for the freedom of others; ideas which, like the idea of self-emancipation through knowledge, can contribute meaning to our lives.

We can understand the expression 'the meaning of history' in a similar way. This, too, has been often interpreted in the sense of a secret or hidden meaning, underlying the course of world history; or perhaps of a hidden direction or evolutionary tendency which is inherent in history; or of a goal towards which the world is striving. Yet I believe that the quest for the hidden 'meaning of history' is misconceived, as is the quest for the hidden meaning of life: instead of searching for a hidden meaning of history, we can make it our task to *give* it a meaning. We can try to give an aim to political history – and thereby to ourselves. Instead of looking for a deeper, a hidden meaning in political history, we can ask ourselves what could be worthy and humane aims of political history: aims both feasible and beneficial to mankind.

My *first thesis* is, therefore, that we should refuse to speak of the meaning of history in the sense of something concealed in it, or of a moral lesson hidden in the divine tragedy of history, or in the sense of some evolutionary tendencies or laws of history, or of some other meaning which might perhaps be discovered by some great historian or philosopher or religious leader.

Thus my first thesis is negative. I contend that there is no hidden meaning in history, and that those historians and philosophers who believe they have discovered one are deceiving themselves (and others).

My *second thesis*, however, is very positive. I believe that we ourselves can try to give a meaning to political history – or rather a plurality of meanings; meanings that are feasible for, and worthy of, human beings.

But I go even further than that. For my *third thesis* is that we can learn from history that the attempt to give history an ethical meaning, or to set ourselves up as modest ethical reformers, need not be vain. On the contrary, we shall never understand history if we underrate the historical power of ethical aims. No doubt they often have led to terrible results, unforeseen by those who first conceived them. Yet in some respects we have approached more closely than any previous generation to the aims and ideals of the Enlightenment, as represented by the American Revolution, or by Kant. More especially the idea of self-emancipation or self-liberation through knowledge, the idea of a pluralist or open society, and the idea of ending the frightful history of wars by the establishment of eternal peace, though perhaps still far distant ideals, have become the aim and the hope of almost all of us.

By saying that we have got nearer to these aims I am not, of course, venturing to prophesy that we shall soon, or ever, attain them. Certainly we may fail. But I think that at least the idea of peace which Erasmus of Rotterdam, Immanuel Kant, Friedrich Schiller, Bentham, the Mills and Spencer, and in Germany Berta von Suttner and Friedrich Wilhelm Förster, have fought for, is nowadays openly acknowledged by the diplomats and politicians of all civilized states as the aim of international politics. This is more than those great fighters for the idea of peace expected, and it is more than we could have expected even twenty-five years ago.

Admittedly, this great success is only a very partial one, and it has been brought about not so much by the ideas of Erasmus or of Kant as by the realization that a nuclear war would put an end to mankind. But that does not alter the fact that peace is now generally and openly recognized as our political aim, and that our difficulties are mainly due to the failure, so far, of diplomats and politicians to find the means to its realization. I cannot discuss those difficulties here; yet a more detailed explanation and discussion of my three theses might make it possible to understand the difficulties and to see them in perspective.

My *first thesis*, the negative assertion that there is no hidden meaning in political history – no meaning that we might look for and discover – nor anything like a hidden tendency, contradicts the various *theories of progress* of the nineteenth century – for example the theories of Comte, Hegel and Marx. But it also contradicts Oswald Spengler's twentieth-century theory of the *Decline of the West* as well as the classical theories of *cycles* propounded for example by Plato, Giovanni Battista Vico, Nietzsche, and others.

I regard all these theories as wrong-headed, and even, in a way, pointless. For they answer a question that is wrongly put. Ideas such as 'progress', 'retrogression', 'decline', etc., imply judgements of value; and thus all these theories, whether they predict historical progress or retrogression, or a cycle consisting of progress and retrogression, must necessarily refer to some scale of values. Such a scale of values can be moral, or economic, or perhaps aesthetic or artistic; and within the realm of the latter values it can refer to music or painting or architecture or literature. It may also refer to the realms of science, or of technology. Another scale of values may be based upon the statistics of our health or mortality, and another on our morality. Obviously, we can progress in one or several of these fields and, *at the same time*, retrogress and reach rock-bottom in others. (Thus we find in Germany at the time of the greatest works of Bach, 1720–50, no very outstanding works in literature or in painting.) And progress in some fields – say in the fields of economics or of education – must often be paid for with retrogression in others; just as progress in the speed, spread and frequency of motor traffic is paid for at the expense of safety.

Now what is true of the realization of technological or economic values also holds, of course, for the realization of certain moral values and especially for the fundamental postulates of freedom and human dignity. Thus many citizens of the United States felt that the continuation of slavery in the Southern States was intolerable, and incompatible with the demands of their conscience; but they had to pay for the freeing of the slaves with a most terrible civil war, and with the destruction of a flourishing and unique civilization.

Similarly, the progress of science – itself partly a consequence of the ideal of self-emancipation through knowledge – is contributing to the lengthening and to the enrichment of our lives; yet it has led us to spend those lives under the threat of an atomic war, and it is doubtful whether it has on balance contributed to the happiness and contentment of man.

The fact that we can progress and simultaneously retrogress shows that the historical theories of progress, the theories of retrogression, the theories of cycles, and even the prophecies of doom, are all equally untenable, since they are clearly wrong in the way they pose their questions. They all are in the grip of pseudo-scientific theories (as I have tried to show elsewhere).[1] These pseudo-scientific theories of history, which I have called '*historicist*' theories, have a rather interesting history of their own.

Homer's theory of history – like that in Genesis – interprets historical events as the immediate expression of the erratic will of some highly capricious man-like deities. This type of theory was incompatible with the conception of God prevailing in later Judaism and Christianity. And indeed, to view political history – the history of robbery, war, plunder, pillage and of ever-increasing means of destruction – as the direct work of God is nothing short of blasphemy. If history is the work of a merciful God, it can be so only if His will is for us inscrutable, incomprehensible and unfathomable. This makes it impossible for us to understand the meaning of history, if we try to see in history the direct action of a merciful God. Thus a religion that tries to make the meaning of history really comprehensible to us (rather than leave it inscrutable) must try to understand it not as a direct revelation of the divine will of an omnipotent God but as a struggle between some good and some evil powers – powers that act in us and through us. This is what St Augustine tried to do in his book *De Civitate Dei*. He was influenced not only by the Old Testament but also by Plato, who interpreted political history as the history of the fall from grace of an originally divine, perfect, harmonious and communist city state, whose moral decline was caused by racial degeneration and its consequences: the worldly ambition and selfishness of the leading aristocracy. Another important influence on the work of St Augustine derives from his own Manichean period: from the Persian-Manichean heresy which interpreted this world as an arena for the struggle between the good and the evil principles, personified by Ormuzd and Ahriman.

These influences led St Augustine to describe the political history of mankind as the struggle between the good principle of the *civitas dei*, and the evil principle of the *civitas diaboli* – that is, between heaven and hell. And almost all later theories of history – possibly with the exception of some of the more naive theories of progress – can be traced back to this almost Manichean theory of St Augustine. Most of the modern historicist theories simply translate his metaphysical and religious categories into the language of natural or social science. Thus they may merely replace God and the Devil by morally or biologically good races, or races fit to rule, and morally or biologically bad, or unfit, races; or by good classes and bad classes – proletarians and capitalists. ('We Communists believe', writes Khrushchev in about 1970, 'that

Capitalism is a hell in which labouring people are condemned to slavery."[2]). This hardly alters the character of Augustine's theory.

The little that may be allowed to be correct in these theories is their inherent assumption that our own ideas and ideals are powers that influence our history. But it is important to realize that good and noble ideas may sometimes have a disastrous influence on history; and that, conversely, we can sometimes find an idea, a historical power, which wills the Bad and works the Good (as Bernard de Mandeville was perhaps the first to see); just as we can often find that an error leads to the discovery of truth.

So we must guard carefully against viewing our highly pluralist history as a drawing in black and white, or as a picture painted in a few contrasting colours. And we must be even more careful not to read into it historical laws that can be used for the prediction of progress, cycles, or doom, or for any similar historical prediction.

Yet unfortunately the general public expects and demands, especially since Hegel, and still more since Spengler, that a real scholar – a sage or a philosopher or a historian – should be able to play the role of an augur or soothsayer: that he should be able to predict the future. And what is even worse, this demand creates its own supply. In fact, the insistent demand has produced quite a glut of prophets. Without much exaggeration one could say that nowadays every intellectual of repute feels an irresistible obligation to become an expert in the art of historical prophecy. And the abysmal depth of his pessimism (for not to be a pessimist would be almost a breach of professional etiquette) is matched by the abysmal profundity and the general impressiveness of his oracular revelations.

I think it is high time to make an attempt to keep soothsaying where it belongs – in the fairground. I do not of course mean to say that soothsayers never predict the truth: if their predictions are sufficiently vague, the number of their true predictions will even exceed that of their false ones. All I assert is that there does not exist a scientific or historical or philosophical method which might help us to produce anything like those ambitious historical predictions for which Spengler created so great a demand.

Whether a historical prediction will come true or not is neither a matter of method, nor of wisdom or intuition: it is purely a matter of chance. These predictions are arbitrary, accidental, and unscientific. But any of them may well achieve a powerful propagandist effect. Provided a sufficient number of people believe in the decline of the West, the West will decline; even if, without that propaganda for its decline, it would have continued to flourish. Prophets, even false prophets, can move mountains; and so can ideas, even wrong ones. Fortunately there may be occasions when it is possible to fight wrong ideas with right ones.

In what follows I shall express some rather optimistic ideas; but they are, most emphatically, not to be taken as predictions of the future, for I do not know what the future holds, and I do not believe in those who believe they do. I am optimistic only about our ability to learn from the past and the present; we can learn that many things, both good and bad, have been and still are possible, and that we have no reason to give up hoping, striving and working for a better world.

My *second thesis* was that we can give a meaning and set an aim to political history; a meaning and an aim or several meanings and aims, which are beneficent and humane.

Giving a meaning to history can be understood in two different ways: the more important and fundamental one is *proposing an aim* based on our ethical ideas. In another and less fundamental sense of the expression 'giving a meaning', a Kantian philosopher, Theodor Lessing, has described the writing of history as '*The Giving of Meaning to the Meaningless' (Geschichte als Sinngebung des Sinnlosen)*. Theodor Lessing's thesis (with which I am inclined to agree even though it differs from mine) is this: we may read a meaning into the written, traditional books of history, even though history is meaningless in itself; for example, by asking how our ideas – say, the idea of freedom and the idea of self-emancipation through knowledge – have fared throughout history's tortuous course. If we are careful not to use the word 'progress' in the sense of a 'law of progress', we may even give a meaning to traditional history by asking what 'progress' we have made, or what setbacks we have suffered, and especially what price we had to pay for making progress in certain directions. Part of the price we have paid is revealed by the history of our many tragic errors – errors in our aims and errors in our choice of means.

A similar idea has been beautifully expressed by H. A. L. Fisher, the great English historian who rejected historicism and with it all the alleged laws of historical evolution, yet who did not shrink from judging events in history from a critical point of view, applying to them the yardstick of ethical, economic and political progress. Fisher wrote[3]:

> Men wiser and more learned than I have discerned in history a plot, a rhythm, a predetermined pattern . . . I can see only one emergency following upon another as wave follows wave, only one great fact with respect to which, since it is unique, there can be no generalizations, only one safe rule for the historian: that he should recognize . . . the play of the contingent and the unforeseen.

Here Fisher states that there are no intrinsic developmental tendencies. Yet he continues as follows:

> This is not a doctrine of cynicism and despair. The fact of progress is written plain and large on the pages of history; but progress is not a law of nature. The ground gained by one generation may be lost by the next.

Thus some progress – by progress Fisher means here social betterment in the fields of freedom and justice, and also economic progress – may occur in spite of the senseless and cruel emergencies of war or power-political strife. But since there are no historical laws that might ensure the continuation of this progress, the future fate of progress – and with it our own fate – will largely depend on ourselves.

I have quoted Fisher not only because I believe that he is right, but also because I want to show how his idea that history depends, in part, on ourselves, is much more 'meaningful' and 'noble' than the idea that history has its inherent, and inexorable, laws – whether mechanical, dialectical, or organic; or that we are puppets in a historical puppet-show; or victims of superhuman historical powers, such as the powers of Good and Evil; or perhaps victims of the collective forces of proletarians and capitalists.

Thus in writing and reading history, or books of history, we can give a meaning to it. But now I turn to the other and more important sense of 'giving a meaning to history': I mean the idea that we can set ourselves tasks; not only as individuals living personal lives, but also as citizens and, particularly, as citizens of the world, who regard the senseless tragedy of history as intolerable and see in it a challenge to do our best to make future history meaningful. The task is immensely difficult, mainly because good intentions and good faith can lead us tragically astray. And because I support the ideas of the Enlightenment, of self-emancipation through knowledge, and of a critical rationalism, I feel it all the more necessary to emphasize the point that even the ideas of the Enlightenment and of rationalism have led to the most terrible consequences.

It was Robespierre's rule of terror that taught Kant, who had welcomed the French Revolution, that the most heinous crimes can be committed in the name of liberty, equality and fraternity: crimes just as heinous as those committed in the name of Christianity during the Crusades, the various eras of witch hunting, and the Thirty Years' War. And with Kant we may learn a lesson from the terror of the French Revolution, a lesson which cannot be repeated too often: that fanaticism is always evil and incompatible with the aim of a pluralist society, and that it is our duty to oppose it in any form – even when its aims, though fanatically pursued, are in themselves ethically unobjectionable, and still more so when its aims coincide with our own personal aims. The dangers of fanaticism, and our duty to oppose it under all circumstances, are two of the most important lessons we can learn from history.

But is it possible to avoid fanaticism and its excesses? Does not history teach us that all attempts to be guided by ethical aims must be futile, just because those aims can play a historical role only when they are believed in and upheld fanatically? And does not the history of all religions and all revolutions show that the fanatical belief in an ethical idea will not only pervert it, but again and again transform it into its very opposite? That it will make us open all prison doors in the name of liberty, only to close them almost at once behind the new enemies of our new liberty? That it makes us proclaim the equality of all men, and also, that some of them 'are more equal than others'? And is not this equality a jealous god who commands us to visit the inequity of some of the less equal fathers upon the children unto the third and fourth generation? Does it not make us proclaim the brotherhood of all men; and also, that we are the keepers of our brother – as if to remind us that our wish to rule over him may be fratricidal? Does not history teach us that all ethical ideas are pernicious, and the best of them often the most pernicious? Can we not learn from the French and Russian and more recently from some African revolutions that the ideas of the Enlightenment and the dreams of a better world are not merely nonsense, but criminal nonsense?

My answer to these questions is contained in my *third thesis*: we can learn from the history of Western Europe and the United States that the attempt to give to our history an ethical meaning or aim need not always be futile. That is not to say that we ever have realized, or ever will fully realize, our ethical aims. My assertion is very modest. All I say is that an ethically inspired social criticism has been successful in some places, and that it has been able to eliminate, at least for the time being, some of the worst shortcomings of social and public life.

This then is my *third thesis*. It is optimistic in that it is a denial of all pessimistic views of history. For all theories of cyclical evolution, and of decline, are clearly refuted if it is possible that we ourselves impose successfully an ethical aim, an ethical meaning, upon history.

But there are certain very definite prerequisites for the imposition of ethical aims, for the successful betterment of social relations. Social ideals and social criticism were crowned by success only where people had learnt to respect opinions that differ from their own, and to be sober and realistic in their political aims: where they had learnt that the attempt to create the Kingdom of Heaven on earth may easily succeed in turning our earth into a hell for our fellow men.

The first countries to learn this lesson were Switzerland and England, where some Utopian attempts to create a Kingdom of Heaven on earth soon led to disenchantment.

The English Revolution, the first of the great modern revolutions, did not bring about the Kingdom of Heaven but the execution of Charles I and the dictatorship of Cromwell. Thoroughly disenchanted, England learnt its lesson: it was converted to believe in the need for a rule of law. The attempt of James II to re-introduce Roman Catholicism in England by force foundered on the rock of that attitude. Tired of religious and civil strife, England was ready to listen to the arguments for religious tolerance of John Locke and other pioneers of the Enlightenment, and to accept the principle that an enforced religion can have no value; that one may *guide* people into church, but must not try to *force* them into it against their convictions (as Pope Innocent XI expressed it).

The American Revolution managed to avoid the trap of fanaticism and intolerance.

It can hardly be accidental that Switzerland, England and America, which all had to go through some disenchanting political experiences, are the countries which have succeeded in achieving, by democratic reforms, ethical-political aims which would have been unattainable by means of revolution, fanaticism, dictatorship and the use of force.

At any rate we can learn not only from the history of the English-speaking democracies but also from the history of Switzerland and Scandinavia that we can set ourselves aims, and that we can sometimes achieve them – provided that these aims are neither too wide, nor too narrow, but conceived in a pluralist spirit – that is, that they embody respect for the freedom and convictions of all sorts of people with widely differing ideas and beliefs. This shows that it is not impossible to give meaning to our political history; which is, precisely, my *third thesis*.

In my view it is the Romantic School and its criticism of the Enlightenment that were superficial, and not the Enlightenment, even though its name has become a synonym for superficiality. Kant and the Enlightenment were ridiculed as superficial and naive for taking seriously the ideals of liberty, and for believing that the idea of democracy was more than a transient historical phenomenon. And nowadays we can hear again a lot about the necessary transience of these ideas. But instead of explaining their necessary transience and prophesying their impending decline, it would be better to fight for their survival. For these ideas have not only shown their vitality, and their power to survive terrible attacks: they also have turned out to provide, as Kant thought they would, the necessary framework for a pluralist society; and *vice versa*: the pluralist society is the necessary framework for the working out of political meanings and aims; for any policy which transcends the immediate present; for any policy which reads a meaning into our past history, and tries to give our present and future history a meaning.

Enlightenment and Romanticism have one important point in common: both see the history of mankind mainly as a history of contending ideas and beliefs; as a history of ideological struggles. In this respect they agree. But it is in their attitude towards these ideas that Enlightenment and Romanticism diverge so widely. Romanticism values the power of faith as such: it values its vigour and depth, independently of the question of its *truth*. This it seems is the real reason why the Romantic School is so contemptuous of the Enlightenment. For the Enlightenment views faith and the power of faith with a measure of distrust. Although it teaches tolerance and even respect for other people's faith, its greatest value is not faith, but truth. And it teaches that there is something like absolute truth, even though it may be unknown to us; and that we can get nearer to it through correcting our errors. This, in fact, is the fundamental thesis of the philosophy of the Enlightenment; and in this lies its greatest contrast with the historical relativism of the Romantics.

But the approach to truth is not easy. There is only one way towards it, the way through error. Only through our errors can we learn; and only he will learn who is ready to appreciate and even to cherish the errors of others as stepping stones towards truth, and who searches for his own errors: who tries to find them, since only when he has become aware of them can he free himself from them.

The idea of our self-emancipation through knowledge is therefore not the same as the idea of our mastery over nature. The former is, rather, the idea of a spiritual self-liberation from error, from superstition and from false idols. It is the idea of one's own spiritual self-emancipation and growth, through one's own criticism of one's own ideas – though the help of others will always be needed.

Thus we see that the Enlightenment does not reject fanaticism and fanatical forms of belief for purely utilitarian reasons, nor because it has found that better things can be achieved in politics and in practical affairs by a more sober attitude. Its rejection of fanatical belief is, rather, the natural corollary of the idea that we should search for truth by criticizing our errors. This self-criticism and this self-emancipation are possible only in a pluralist society, that is, in an open society which tolerates our errors as well as the errors of others.

The idea of self-emancipation through knowledge, which was the basic idea of the Enlightenment, is in itself a powerful enemy of fanaticism; for it makes us try hard to detach ourselves or even to dissociate ourselves from our own ideas (in order to look at them critically) instead of identifying ourselves with them. And the recognition of the sometimes overwhelming historical power of ideas should teach us how important it is to free ourselves from the overpowering influence of false or wrong ideas. In the interests of the quest for truth and of our liberation from errors we have to train ourselves to view our own favourite ideas just as critically as those we oppose.

This is not a concession to relativism. In fact, the very idea of error presupposes the idea of truth. Admitting that the other man may be right and that I may be wrong obviously does not and cannot mean that each man's personal point of view is equally true or equally tenable and that, as the relativists say, everybody is right within his own frame of reference, though he may be wrong within that of somebody else. In the western democracies many of us have learned that at times we are wrong and our opponents are right; but too many who have digested this important truth have slipped into relativism. In our great historical task of creating a free pluralist society, and with it a social framework for the growth of knowledge and for self-emancipation through knowledge, nothing is more vital than to be able to view our own ideas critically; without however becoming relativists or sceptics, and without losing the courage and the determination to fight for our convictions, even though we realize that these convictions should always be open to correction, and that only through correcting them may we free ourselves from error, thus making it possible for us to grow in knowledge.

NOTES

1 See *The Open Society and Its Enemies*, 9th reprint of the 5th edition, vol. I, 1991, vol. II, 1992, Routledge, London; also *The Poverty of Historicism*, 14th impression, Routledge, London, 1991.

2 See *Khrushchev Remembers, with an Introduction, Commentary and Notes by Edward Crankshaw. Translated and Edited by Strobe Talbott.* Book Club Associates, London, 1971. Copyright 1971 by Little, Brown and Company (Inc.); see especially pp. 521–2.

3 H. A. L. Fisher, *History of Europe*, 1936, vol. I, p. vii.

11

PUBLIC OPINION AND LIBERAL PRINCIPLES

The following remarks were designed to provide material for debate at an international conference of liberals (in the English sense of the term[1]). My purpose was simply to lay the foundations for a good general discussion. Because I could assume liberal views in my audience I was largely concerned to challenge, rather than to endorse, popular assumptions favourable to these views.

I. THE MYTH OF PUBLIC OPINION

We should beware of a number of myths concerning 'public opinion' which are often accepted uncritically.

There is, first, the classical myth, *vox populi vox dei,* which attributes to the voice of the people a kind of final authority and unlimited wisdom. Its modern equivalent is faith in the ultimate commonsense rightness of that mythical figure, 'the man in the street', his vote, and his voice. The avoidance of the plural in both cases is characteristic. Yet people are, thank God, seldom univocal; and the various men in the various streets are as different as any collection of VIPs in a conference-room. And if, on occasion, they do speak more or less in unison, what they say is not necessarily wise. They may be right, or they may be wrong. 'The voice' may be very firm on very doubtful issues. (Example: the nearly unanimous and unquestioning acceptance of the demand for 'unconditional surrender'.) And it may waver on issues over which there is hardly room for doubt. (Example: the question

This paper was read before the 6th meeting of the Mont Pèlerin Society at their Conference in Venice, September 1954; it was published (in Italian) in *Il Politico*, 20, 1955, and (in German) in *Ordo*, 8, 1956. English text by the author.

whether to condone political blackmail, and mass-murder.) It may be well-intentioned but imprudent. (Example: the public reaction which destroyed the Hoare–Laval plan.) Or it may be neither well-intentioned nor very prudent. (Example: the approval of the Runciman mission; the approval of the Munich agreement of 1938.)

I believe nevertheless that there is a kernel of truth hidden in the *vox populi* myth. One might put it in this way: In spite of the limited information at their disposal, many simple men are often wiser than their governments; and if not wiser, then inspired by better or more generous intentions. (Examples: the readiness of the people of Czechoslovakia to fight, on the eve of Munich; the Hoare–Laval reaction again.)

One form of the myth – or perhaps of the philosophy behind the myth – which seems to me of particular interest and importance is the doctrine that *truth is manifest.* By this I mean the doctrine that, though error is something that needs to be explained (by lack of good will or by bias or by prejudice), truth will always make itself known, as long as it is not suppressed. Thus arises the belief that liberty, by sweeping away oppression and other obstacles, must of necessity lead to a Reign of Truth and Goodness – to 'an Elysium created by reason and graced by the purest pleasures known to the love of mankind', in the words of the concluding sentence of Condorcet's *Sketch for a Historical Picture of the Progress of the Human Mind.*

I have consciously oversimplified this important myth, which also may be formulated: 'Nobody, if presented with the truth, can fail to recognize it.' I propose to call this 'the theory of rationalist optimism'. It is a theory, indeed, which the Enlightenment shares with most of its political offspring and its intellectual forebears. Like the *vox populi* myth, it is another myth of the univocal voice. If humanity is a Being we ought to worship, then the unanimous voice of mankind ought to be our final authority. But we have learned that this is a myth, and we have learned to distrust unanimity.

A reaction to this rationalist and optimistic myth is the romantic version of the *vox populi* theory – the doctrine of the authority and uniqueness of the popular will, of the *'volonté générale'*, of the spirit of the people, of the genius of the nation, of the group mind or of the instinct of the blood. I need hardly repeat here the criticism which Kant and others – among them myself – have levelled against these doctrines of the irrational grasp of truth, which culminate in the Hegelian doctrine of the cunning of reason which uses our passions as instruments for the instinctive or intuitive grasp of truth; and which makes it impossible for the people to be wrong, especially if they follow their passions rather than their reason.

An important and still very influential variant of the myth may be described as the myth of the progress of public opinion, which is the myth of public opinion of the nineteenth-century liberal. It may be illustrated by quoting a passage from Anthony Trollope's *Phineas Finn*, to which Professor E. H. Gombrich has drawn my attention. Trollope describes the fate of a parliamentary motion for Irish tenant rights. The division comes, and the Ministry is beaten by a majority of twenty-three. 'And now', says Mr Monk, MP, 'the pity is that we are not a bit nearer tenant-rights than we were before.'

> 'But we are nearer to it.'
>
> 'In one sense, yes. Such a debate and such a majority will make men think. But no; – think is too high a word; as a rule men don't think. But it will make them believe that there is something in it. Many who before regarded legislation on the subject as chimerical, will now fancy that it is only dangerous, or perhaps not more than difficult. And so in time it will come to be looked on as among the things possible, then among the things probable; – and so at last it will be ranged in the list of those few measures which the country requires as being absolutely needed. That is the way in which public opinion is made.'
>
> 'It is not loss of time,' said Phineas, 'to have taken the first great step in making it.'
>
> 'The first great step was taken long ago,' said Mr Monk, – 'taken by men who were looked upon as revolutionary demagogues, almost as traitors, because they took it. But it is a great thing to take any step that leads us onwards.'

The theory here expounded by the radical-liberal Member of Parliament, Mr Monk, may be perhaps called the *'avant-garde theory of public opinion'*, or the theory of the leadership of the advanced. It is the theory that there are some leaders or creators of public opinion who, by books and pamphlets and letters to *The Times*, or by parliamentary speeches and motions, manage to get some ideas first rejected and later debated and finally accepted. Public opinion is here conceived as a kind of public response to the thoughts and efforts of those aristocrats of the mind who produce new thoughts, new ideas, new arguments. It is conceived as slow, as somewhat passive and by nature conservative, but nevertheless as capable, in the end, of intuitively discerning the truth of the claims of the reformers – as the slow-moving but final and authoritative umpire of the debates of the elite. This, no doubt, is again another form of our myth, however much of the English reality may at first sight appear to conform to it. No doubt, the claims of reformers have often succeeded in exactly this way. But did only the valid claims succeed? I am inclined to believe that, in Great Britain, it is not so much the truth of an assertion or the wisdom of a proposal that is likely to win for a policy the support of public opinion, as the feeling that injustice is being done which can and must be rectified. It is the characteristic *moral sensitivity* of public opinion, and the way in which it has often been roused, at least in the past, which is described by Trollope; its intuition of injustice rather than its intuition of factual truth. It is debatable how far Trollope's description is applicable to other countries; and it would be dangerous to assume that even in Great Britain public opinion will remain as sensitive as in the past.

II. THE DANGERS OF PUBLIC OPINION

Public opinion (whatever it may be) is very powerful. It may change governments, even non-democratic governments. Liberals ought to regard any such power with some degree of suspicion.

Owing to its anonymity, public opinion is an *irresponsible form of power,* and therefore particularly dangerous from the liberal point of view. (Example: colour bars and other racial questions.) The remedy in *one* direction is obvious: by minimizing the power of the state, the danger of the influence of public opinion, exerted through the agency of the state, will be reduced. But this does not secure the freedom of the individual's behaviour and thought from the direct pressure of public opinion. Here, the individual needs the powerful protection of the state. These conflicting requirements can be at least partly met by a certain kind of tradition.

The doctrine that public opinion is not irresponsible, but somehow 'responsible to itself' – in the sense that its mistakes will rebound upon the public who held the mistaken opinion – is another form of the collectivist myth of public opinion: the mistaken propaganda of one group of citizens may easily harm a very different group.

III. LIBERAL PRINCIPLES: A GROUP OF THESES

1. The state is a necessary evil: its powers are not to be multiplied beyond what is necessary. One might call this principle the *'Liberal Razor'*. (In analogy to Ockham's Razor, i.e. the famous principle that entities or essences must not be multiplied beyond what is necessary.)

In order to show the necessity of the state I do not appeal to Hobbes's *homo-homini-lupus* view of man. On the contrary, its necessity can be shown even if we assume that *homo homini felis,* or even that *homo homini angelus* – in other words, even if we assume that, because of their gentleness, or angelic goodness, nobody ever harms anybody else. In such a world there would still be weaker and stronger men, and the weaker ones would have *no legal right* to be tolerated by the stronger ones, but would owe them gratitude for their being so kind as to tolerate them. Those (whether strong or weak) who think this an unsatisfactory state of affairs, and who think that every person should have a *right* to live, and that every person should have a *legal claim* to be protected against the power of the strong, will agree that we need a state that protects the rights of all.

It is easy to see that the state must be a constant danger, or (as I have ventured to call it) an evil, though a necessary one. For if the state is to fulfil its function, it must have more power at any rate than any single private citizen or public corporation; and although we might design institutions to minimize the danger that these powers will be misused, we can never eliminate the danger completely. On the contrary, it seems that most men will always have to pay for the protection of the state, not only in the form of taxes but even in the form of humiliation suffered, for example, at the hands of bullying officials. The thing is not to pay too heavily for it.

2. The difference between a democracy and a tyranny is that under a democracy the government can be got rid of without bloodshed; under a tyranny it cannot.

3. Democracy as such cannot confer any benefits upon the citizen and it should not be expected to do so. In fact democracy can do nothing – only the citizens of the democracy can act (including, of course, those citizens who comprise the government). Democracy provides no more than a framework within which the citizens may act in a more or less organized and coherent way.

4. We are democrats, not because the majority is always right, but because democratic traditions are the least evil ones of which we know. If the majority (or 'public opinion') decides in favour of tyranny, a democrat need not therefore suppose that some fatal inconsistency in his views has been revealed. He will realize, rather, that the democratic tradition in his country was not strong enough.

5. Institutions alone are never sufficient if not tempered by traditions. Institutions are always ambivalent in the sense that, in the absence of a strong tradition, they also may serve the opposite purpose to the one intended. For example, a parliamentary opposition is, roughly speaking, supposed to prevent the majority from stealing the taxpayer's money. But I well remember an affair in a south-eastern European country which illustrates the ambivalence of this institution. There, the opposition shared the spoils with the majority.

To sum up: Traditions are needed to form a kind of link between institutions and the intentions and valuations of individual men.

6. A liberal Utopia – that is, a state rationally designed on a traditionless *tabula rasa* – is an impossibility. For the liberal principle demands that the limitations to the freedom of each which are made necessary by social life should be minimized and equalized as much as possible (Kant). But how can we apply such an *a priori* principle in real life? Should we prevent a pianist from practising, or prevent his neighbour from enjoying a quiet afternoon? All such problems can be solved in practice only by an appeal to existing traditions and customs and to a traditional sense of justice; to common law, as it is called in Britain, and to an impartial judge's appreciation of equity. All laws, being universal principles, have to be interpreted in order to be applied; and an

interpretation needs some principles of concrete practice, which can be supplied only by a living tradition. And this holds more especially for the highly abstract and universal principles of Liberalism.

7. Principles of Liberalism may be described (at least today) as principles of assessing, and if necessary of modifying or changing, existing institutions, rather than of replacing existing institutions. One can express this also by saying that Liberalism is an evolutionary rather than a revolutionary creed (unless it is confronted by a tyrannical regime).

8. Among the traditions we must count as the most important is what we may call the 'moral framework' (corresponding to the institutional 'legal framework') of a society. This incorporates the society's traditional sense of justice or fairness, or the degree of moral sensitivity it has reached. This moral framework serves as the basis which makes it possible to reach a fair or equitable compromise between conflicting interests where this is necessary. It is, of course, itself not unchangeable, but it changes comparatively slowly. Nothing is more dangerous than the destruction of this traditional framework, as it was consciously aimed at by Nazism. In the end its destruction will lead to cynicism and nihilism, i.e. to the disregard and the dissolution of all human values.

IV. THE LIBERAL THEORY OF FREE DISCUSSION

Freedom of thought, and free discussion, are ultimate liberal values, which do not really need any further justification. Nevertheless, they can also be justified pragmatically in terms of the part they play in the search for truth.

Truth is not manifest; and it is not easy to come by. The search for truth demands at least

(a) imagination
(b) trial and error
(c) the gradual discovery of our prejudices by way of (a), of (b) and of critical discussion.

The western rationalist tradition, which derives from the Greeks, is the tradition of critical discussion – of examining and testing propositions or theories by attempting to refute them. This critical rational method must not be mistaken for a method of proof, that is to say, for a method of finally establishing truth; nor is it a method which always secures agreement. Its value lies, rather, in the fact that participants in a discussion will, to some extent, change their minds, and part as wiser men.

It is often asserted that discussion is only possible between people who have a common language and accept common basic assumptions. I think that this is a mistake. All that is needed is a readiness to learn from one's partner in the discussion, which includes a genuine wish to understand what he intends to say. If this readiness is there, the discussion will be the more fruitful the more the partners' backgrounds differ. Thus the value of a discussion depends largely upon the variety of the competing views. Had there been no Tower of Babel, we should invent it. The liberal does not dream of a perfect consensus of opinion; he only hopes for the mutual fertilization of opinions, and the consequent growth of ideas. Even when we solve a problem to universal satisfaction, we create, in solving it, many new problems over which we are bound to disagree. This is not to be regretted.

Although the search for truth through free rational discussion is a public affair, it is not public opinion (whatever this may be) which results from it. Though public opinion may be influenced by science and may judge science, it is not the product of scientific discussion.

But the tradition of rational discussion creates, in the political field, the tradition of government by discussion, and with it the habit of listening to another point of view; the growth of a sense of justice; and the readiness to compromise.

Our hope is thus that traditions, changing and developing under the influence of critical discussion and in response to the challenge of new problems, may replace much of what is usually called 'public opinion', and take over the functions which public opinion is supposed to fulfil.

V. THE FORMS OF PUBLIC OPINION

There are two main forms of public opinion; institutionalized and non-institutionalized.

Examples of institutions serving or influencing public opinion: the press (including Letters to the Editor); political parties; societies like the Mont Pèlerin Society; universities; book-publishing; broadcasting; theatre; cinema; television.

Examples of non-institutionalized public opinion: what people say in railway carriages and other public places about the latest news, or about foreigners, or about 'coloured men'; or what they say about one another across the dinner table. (This may even become institutionalized.)

VI. SOME PRACTICAL PROBLEMS: CENSORSHIP AND MONOPOLIES OF PUBLICITY

No theses are offered in this section – only problems.

How far does the case against censorship depend upon a tradition of self-imposed censorship?

How far do publishers' monopolies establish a kind of censorship? How far are thinkers free to publish their ideas? Can there be complete freedom to publish? And ought there to be complete freedom to publish anything?

The influence and responsibility of the intelligentsia: (a) upon the spread of ideas (example: socialism); (b) upon the acceptance of often tyrannical fashions (example: abstract art).

The freedom of the universities: (a) state interference; (b) private interference; (c) interference in the name of public opinion.

The management of (or planning for) public opinion. 'Public relations officers'.

The problem of the propaganda for cruelty in newspapers (especially in 'comics'), cinema, etc.

The problem of *taste*. Standardization and levelling.

The problem of propaganda and advertisement *versus* the spread of information.

VII. A SHORT LIST OF POLITICAL ILLUSTRATIONS

This is a list containing cases which should be worthy of careful analysis.

1. The Hoare–Laval plan and its defeat by the unreasonable moral enthusiasm of public opinion.
2. The Abdication of Edward VIII.
3. Munich.
4. Unconditional surrender.
5. The Crichel Down case.

6. The British habit of accepting hardship without grumbling.

VIII. SUMMARY

That intangible and vague entity called public opinion sometimes reveals an unsophisticated shrewdness or, more typically, a moral sensitivity superior to that of the government in power. Nevertheless, it is a danger to freedom if it is not moderated by a strong liberal tradition. It is dangerous as an arbiter of taste, and unacceptable as an arbiter of Truth. But it may sometimes assume the role of an enlightened arbiter of justice. (Example: the liberation of slaves in the British colonies.) Unfortunately it can be 'managed'. These dangers can be counteracted only by strengthening the liberal tradition.

Public opinion should be distinguished from the publicity of free and critical discussion, which is (or should be) the rule in science, and which includes the discussion of questions of justice and other moral issues. Public opinion is influenced by, but neither the result of, nor under the control of, discussions of this kind. Their beneficial influence will be the greater the more honestly, simply and clearly, these discussions are conducted.

NOTE

1 To avoid misunderstandings I wish to make it quite clear that I use the terms 'liberal', 'liberalism', etc., always in a sense in which they are still generally used in England (though perhaps not in America): by a liberal I do not mean a sympathizer with any one political party but simply a man who values individual freedom and who is alive to the dangers inherent in all forms of power and authority.

12

AN OBJECTIVE THEORY OF HISTORICAL UNDERSTANDING

The different western philosophies are very largely variations on the theme of body–mind dualism. The main departures from this dualistic theme were attempts to replace it by some kind of monism. It seems to me that these attempts were unsuccessful. We find time and again that behind the veil of monistic protestations there still lurks the dualism of body and mind.

PLURALISM AND WORLD 3

There were, however, not only monistic deviations, but also some pluralistic ones. This is obvious in polytheism, and even in its monotheistic and atheistic variants. Yet it may seem doubtful whether the various religious interpretations of the world offer an alternative to the dualism of body and mind, for the gods, whether many or few, are either minds endowed with immortal bodies, or else pure minds, in contrast to ourselves.

However, some philosophers have put forward a genuine pluralism, by maintaining the existence of a *third* world over and above mind and body, physical objects and conscious processes. These philosophers included Plato, the Stoics, and some modern thinkers such as Leibniz, Bolzano and Frege (but not Hegel, who embodied strong monistic tendencies, although he often speaks of an 'objective mind' or 'spirit').

Plato's world of Forms or Ideas was not a world of consciousness nor of the contents of consciousness, but rather an objective,

An extended version of a lecture given on 3 September 1968 in the plenary session of the XIV International Congress for Philosophy in Vienna (see also my essay 'On the Theory of the Objective Mind', reprinted as chapter 4 of *Objective Knowledge*, Oxford University Press, 1972, 1979).

autonomous third world of logical contents. It existed alongside the physical world and the world of consciousness as a third, objective and autonomous world. I wish to defend this pluralistic philosophy here, even though I am neither a Platonist nor a Hegelian.

In this philosophy our world consists of at least three distinct sub-worlds; or, as I shall say, there are three worlds. The first is the physical world or the world of physical states; the second is the world of consciousness or the world of mental states; and the third is the world of ideas in the objective sense. It is the world of theories in themselves, and their logical relations; the world of arguments in themselves; and of problems in themselves, and problem situations in themselves. On the advice of Sir John Eccles, I have called the three worlds 'world 1', 'world 2', and 'world 3'.

One of the fundamental problems of this pluralistic philosophy concerns the relationship between these three worlds.

The three worlds are so related that world 1 and world 2 can interact and so can world 2 and world 3. This means that world 2, the world of subjective or personal experiences, can interact with each of the other two worlds. It appears that world 1 and world 3 cannot interact, save through the intervention of world 2, the world of subjective or personal experiences.

It seems to me important that the relationship of the three worlds can be described in this way – that is, with world 2 as the mediator between world 1 and world 3.

It was the Stoics who first made the important distinction between the world 3 and objective *logical content* of what we are saying, and the objects about which we are speaking. These objects, in their turn, can belong to any of the three worlds: we can speak first about the physical world (either about physical objects or about physical states) or second about psychological states (including our grasp of theories) or third about the logical content of theories, such as some arithmetical propositions, and especially about their truth or falsity.

It is important that the Stoics extended the theory of world 3 from Platonic ideas to theories and propositions. However, they also included still other world 3 linguistic entities such as problems, arguments and investigations; and they made further distinctions between such objects as commands, admonitions, prayers, treaties and narratives. They also drew a very clear distinction between a personal state of sincerity or truth and the objective truth of theories or propositions; that is to say, theories or propositions to which the world 3 predicate 'objectively true' applies.

I wish now to distinguish between two groups of philosophers. The first consists of those who, like Plato, accept an autonomous world 3 and look upon it as superhuman and consequently as divine and eternal.

The second group consists of those who, like Locke or Mill or Dilthey, point out that *language*, and what it 'expresses' or 'communicates', is man-made. For this reason, they see language and everything linguistic as a part of the first two worlds and reject the suggestion of a world 3. It is very interesting that most students of the humanities, especially historians of culture, belong to this second group, which rejects world 3.

The first group, the Platonists, are supported by the fact that there are eternal verities: an unambiguously formulated proposition is, timelessly, true or false. This seems to be decisive: eternal verities must have been true before man existed. Thus they cannot be of our making.

The philosophers of the second group agree that such eternal verities cannot be of our own making; yet they conclude from this that there are no eternal verities.

I think that it is possible to adopt a position which differs from that of both these groups. I suggest that we should accept the reality and especially the autonomy of world 3, that is to say, its independence from human whim, whilst at the same time admitting that world 3 originated as a product of human activity. One can admit that world 3 is man-made and, in a very clear sense, superhuman at the same time.

That world 3 is not a fiction but exists 'in reality' will become clear as soon as we consider its tremendous effect on world 1, mediated through world 2. One need only think of the impact of the theory of electrical power transmission or atomic theory on our inorganic and organic physical environment, of the effect of economic theories on decisions such as whether to build a boat or an aeroplane.

According to the position which I am adopting here, world 3, like human language, is the product of men, just as honey is the product of bees. Like language (and, I presume, like honey), world

3 is also an *unintended and unplanned* by-product of human (or animal) actions.

Let us look, for instance, at the theory of numbers. I believe (unlike Kronecker) that the series of natural numbers is the work of men, the product of human language and of human thought. Yet there is an infinity of such numbers, and therefore more, infinitely more, than will ever be pronounced by men, or used by a computer. And there is an infinite number of true equations between such numbers, and of false equations; more than we can ever pronounce as 'true' or 'false'. They are all inhabitants, objects, of world 3.

But what is even more interesting, new and unexpected problems arise as unintended by-products of the sequence of natural numbers; for instance the unsolved problems of the theory of prime numbers (Goldbach's conjecture, say). These problems are clearly *autonomous*. They are independent of us; rather, they are *discovered* by us. They exist, undiscovered, before their discovery. Moreover, at least some of these unsolved problems may be insoluble.

In our attempts to solve these or other *problems* we may invent new *theories*. These theories are produced by us: they are the product of our critical and creative thinking. But the truth or falsity of these theories (of Goldbach's conjecture, for instance) is not of our making. And each new theory creates new, unintended and unexpected problems, autonomous problems, problems to be discovered.

This explains how it is possible for world 3 to be our product by origin, although it is in another sense at least partly autonomous. It explains why we can act upon it, and add to it or help its growth, even though there is no man who can master even a small corner of this world. All of us contribute to its growth, but almost all our individual contributions are extremely small. All of us try to grasp it, and none of us could live without interacting with it, for all of us make use of language.

Yet world 3 has grown far beyond the grasp not only of any man, but even of all men, in a readily comprehensible manner.[1] Its action upon our spiritual growth and at the same time upon its own growth is even greater and more important than our very important creative action upon it. For almost all spiritual growth in mankind is due to a feedback effect: our own intellectual growth and the growth of world 3 result from the fact that unsolved problems require us to attempt solutions; and since many problems will always remain unsolved and undiscovered, there will always be scope for original and creative work, although – or precisely because – world 3 is autonomous.

THE PROBLEM OF UNDERSTANDING, ESPECIALLY IN HISTORY

I have given here some grounds which support and explain the theory of the existence of an autonomous world 3 because I hope to bring all this to bear upon the so-called problem of understanding. This problem has long been regarded by students of the humanities as one of their central problems.

I want to make brief reference here to the theory that it is the understanding of objects belonging to world 3 which constitutes the chief task of the humanities. This, it appears, is a radical departure from the fundamental dogma accepted by almost all students of the humanities and particularly by most historians, and especially by those who are interested in the problem of understanding. I mean the dogma that the objects of our understanding belong to world 2 as the products of human actions and that, consequently, they are mainly to be understood and explained in psychological (including social psychological) terms.

Admittedly, the act or process of understanding contains a subjective or personal or psychological element. But the *act* must be distinguished from its more or less successful *outcome*: from its (perhaps only provisional) result, the obtained understanding, the *interpretation*, with which we must work on a trial basis, and which we can try to improve further. The interpretation may in its turn be regarded as a world 3 product of a world 2 act, but also as a subjective act. But even if we regard it as a subjective act, there is in any case still a world 3 object which corresponds to that act. In my opinion this is important. Regarded as a world 3 object, the interpretation will always be a theory: take, for example, a historical interpretation, a historical explanation. This may be supported by a chain of arguments as well as by documents, inscriptions and additional historical pieces of evidence. So the interpretation proves to be a theory and, like every theory, it is anchored in other theories, and in other world 3 objects. And in this way the world 3 problem of the merits of the interpretation can be raised, and especially its value for our understanding.

But even the subjective act of understanding can be understood, in its turn, only through its connections with world 3 objects. For I assert the following three theses concerning the subjective act of understanding:

1. that every such act is anchored in world 3;
2. that almost all important remarks which can be made about such an act consist in pointing out its relations to world 3 objects; and
3. that such an act consists in nothing other than the fact that the way in which we operate with world 3 objects closely resembles the way in which we operate with physical objects.

A CASE OF OBJECTIVE HISTORICAL UNDERSTANDING

All this is especially true for the problem of historical understanding. The main aim of historical understanding is the hypothetical reconstruction of a historical *problem situation*.

I will try to illustrate this theory with the help of a few (necessarily brief) historical remarks upon Galileo's theory of the tides. This theory has turned out to be 'unsuccessful' (because it denies that the moon has any effect on the tides), and even in our own time Galileo has been severely and personally attacked (by Arthur Koestler) for sticking obstinately to such an obviously false theory.

In brief, Galileo's theory says that the tides are a result of accelerations which, in their turn, are a result of the movements of the earth. When, more precisely, the regularly rotating earth is moving round the sun, then the velocity of any surface point located on the side opposite the sun will be greater than the velocity of the same point when it faces the sun. (For if B is the orbital velocity of the earth and R is the rotational velocity of a point on the equator, then B + R is the velocity of this point at midnight and B − R its velocity at midday.) These changes in velocity mean that there must arise periodic accelerations and retardations. But any periodic retardations and accelerations of a basin of water result, says Galileo, in appearances resembling those of the tides. (Galileo's theory is plausible but incorrect in this form: apart from the constant acceleration due to the rotation of the earth – that is, the centripetal acceleration – which also arises if B is zero, there does not arise any further acceleration and therefore especially no periodic acceleration.[2]

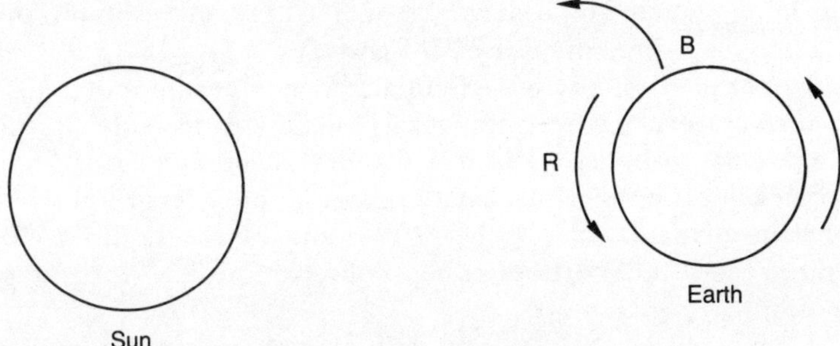

What can we do to improve our historical understanding of this theory, which has so often been misinterpreted? I claim that the first and all-important step is to ask ourselves: what was the third-world *problem* to which Galileo's theory was a tentative solution? And what was the situation – the logical *problem situation* – in which this problem arose?

Galileo's problem was, quite simply, to explain the tides. Yet his problem situation was far less simple.

It is clear that Galileo was not even immediately interested in what I have just called his problem. It was another problem which led him to the problem of the tides: the problem of the movement of the earth, the problem of the truth or falsity of the Copernican theory. It was Galileo's hope that he would be able to use a successful theory of the tides as a decisive argument in favour of the Copernican theory.

What I call Galileo's *problem situation* turns out to be a complex affair. The problem situation entails the problem of the tides, but in the specific role of a touchstone of the Copernican theory. Yet even this does not suffice for an understanding of Galileo's problem situation.

As a true cosmologist and theoretician Galileo was first attracted by the incredible daring and simplicity of Copernicus' main idea, the idea that the earth and the other planets are, so to speak, moons of the sun.

The explanatory power of this bold idea was very great; and when Galileo discovered the moons of Jupiter through his telescope and recognized in them a small model of the Copernican solar system, he saw in this an empirical corroboration of this bold and almost *a priori* idea. In addition, he succeeded in testing a prediction derivable from Copernicus' theory: it predicted that the inner planets would show phases, like those of the moon; and Galileo discovered the phases of Venus.

Copernicus' theory was essentially a geometric-cosmological model, constructed by geometrical (and kinematical) means. But Galileo was a physicist. He knew that the real problem was to find a mechanical physical explanation; and he discovered some important elements of such an explanation, especially the law of inertia and the corresponding conservation law for rotary motions.

Galileo tried to base his physics on just these two laws (which he probably took to be *one* law), although he was aware that there must be great gaps in his physical knowledge. From the point of view of method Galileo was perfectly right; for only if we try to exploit our fallible theories to the limit can we hope to learn from their weaknesses.

This explains why Galileo, in spite of his acquaintance with the work of Kepler, stuck to the *hypothesis of circular motion*; and he was quite justified in doing so. It is often said that he tried to cover up the difficulties of the Copernican cycles, and that he oversimplified the Copernican theory in an unjustifiable manner; also that he ought to have accepted Kepler's laws. But all this shows a failure of historical understanding – an error in the analysis of the third-world problem situation. Galileo was quite right to work with bold oversimplifications; and Kepler's ellipses were equally bold oversimplifications. But Kepler was lucky because his oversimplifications were later used, and thereby explained, by Newton, and so became a test of his solution of the two-body problem.

But why did Galileo deny the influence of the moon in his theory of the tides? This question opens up a highly important aspect of the problem situation. First, Galileo was an opponent of astrology, which identified the planets with the gods; in this sense he was a forerunner of the Enlightenment and an opponent of Kepler, although he admired him.[3] Second, he worked with a mechanical conservation principle for rotary motions, and this appeared to exclude interplanetary influences. Galileo's method in making a serious attempt to explain the tides on this narrow basis was perfectly correct, for without this attempt we could never have known that this basis was too narrow to provide an explanation, and that a further idea was needed – Newton's idea of attraction and long-distance effect; an idea which had an almost astrological character and which was felt to be occult by proponents of and adherents to the Enlightenment (including Newton himself).

Thus we are led by the analysis of Galileo's problem situation to a rational explanation of Galileo's method in several points in which he has been criticized by various historians; and thus we are led to a better understanding of Galileo. Psychological explanations, such as ambition, jealousy, the wish to create a stir, aggressive disposition and 'obsession' with a fixed idea, become superfluous.

Similarly it becomes superfluous to criticize Galileo for 'dogmatism' when he adhered to the circular movement, or to introduce the 'mysterious circular movement' (Dilthey) as an archetypical idea, or perhaps to try to explain this idea by psychologal means. For Galileo's method was correct when he tried to proceed as far as possible with the help of a rational conservation law for rotary motions. (No dynamic theory existed as yet.)

GENERALIZATION

In place of psychological explanatory principles we make use of third-world considerations mainly of a logical character; and this is the cause of the growth in our historical understanding.

This third-world method of historical understanding and explanation may be applied to all historical problems; I have called it the 'method of situational analysis' (or of 'situational logic').[4] It is a method which, wherever possible, replaces psychological explanations by third-world relations of an essentially logical nature as the basis of historical understanding and explanation, including the theories and hypotheses that were assumed by the acting persons.

The thesis I wanted to present here can be summarized as follows: historical understanding should abandon its psychologizing methods and adopt a method built upon a theory of world 3.[5]

NOTES

1 For it can be shown (A. Tarski, A. Mostowski, R. M. Robinson, *Undecidable Theories*, Amsterdam, 1953; see especially note 13 on pp. 60 ff.), that the (complete) system of all true propositions in the arithmetic of integers is not axiomatizable and is (essentially) undecidable. It follows that there will always be infinitely many unsolved problems in arithmetic. It is interesting that we are able to make such unexpected discoveries about world 3, completely independent of our state of mind. (This result essentially goes back to the pioneer work of Kurt Gödel.)

2 One might say that Galileo's kinematic theory of the tides contradicts the so-called Galilean relativity principle. But this criticism would be false, historically as well as theoretically, since this principle does not refer to rotational motion. Galileo's physical intuition – that the rotation of the earth has non-relativistic mechanical consequences – was right; and although these consequences (the motion of a spinning top, Foucault's pendulum, etc.) do not explain the tides, the Coriolis force at least is not quite without influence upon them. Also, we get periodic kinematical accelerations as soon as we take into account the curvature of the earth's movement round the sun.

3 See my *Conjectures and Refutations*, 1963 (12th impression, Routledge, London, 1990), p. 188, in which I show that Newton's gravitational theory – the theory of the 'influence' of the planets upon each other and of the moon upon the earth – was taken from astrology.

4 See my books *The Poverty of Historicism*, 1957 (14th impression, Routledge, London, 1991), and *The Open Society and Its Enemies* (14th impression, Routledge, London, 1991–2), 1945.

5 This makes so-called 'hermeneutics' superfluous, or at least simplifies them.

Part III

VON DEN NEUESTEN . . . ZUSAMMENGESTOHLEN AUS VERSCHIEDENEM, DIESEM UND JENEN*

* This title is stolen. It comes from a remark that Beethoven wrote on the manuscript of a string quartet: 'viertes Quartett, von den Neuesten, für 2 Violinen, Bratsche und Violincell. Zusammengestohlen aus Verschiedenem, Diesem und Jenen.' An approximate translation of Beethoven's untranslatable playful remark would be: 'Fourth quartet, for 2 violins, viola and cello, pinched from the latest compositions – from the most various, from these and from those . . . .'

13

HOW I SEE PHILOSOPHY
(Stolen from Fritz Waismann and from one of the first men to land on the moon)

I

A famous and spirited paper by my late friend Friedrich Waismann bears the title 'How I See Philosophy'.[1] There is much in this paper that I admire; and there are a number of points in it with which I can agree, even though my approach is totally different from his.

Fritz Waismann and many of his colleagues take it for granted that philosophers are a special kind of people and that philosophy can be looked upon as their peculiar activity. And what he tries to do in his paper is to show, with the help of examples, what constitutes the distinctive character of a philosopher, and the distinctive character of philosophy, if compared with other academic subjects such as mathematics or physics. Thus he tries, especially, to give a description of the interests and activities of contemporary academic philosophers, and of the sense in which they can be said to carry on what philosophers did in the past.

Not only is all this very interesting, but Waismann's paper exhibits a considerable degree of personal engagement in these academic activities, and even of excitement. Clearly, he himself is a philosopher, body and soul, in the sense of this special group of philosophers, and clearly, he wishes to convey to us something of the excitement which is shared by the members of this somewhat exclusive community.

Translator's note: This text was first published by the author in *Philosophers on Their Own Work*, vol. 3, ed. André Mercier and Maja Svilar, Peter Lang, Berne, Frankfurt am Main and Las Vegas, pp. 125–48. This is a revised version of the English text first published in *The Owl of Minerva*, ed. C. J. Bontempo and S. J. Odell, McGraw Hill, New York, 1975, pp. 41–55.

II

The way I see philosophy is totally different. I think that all men and all women are philosophers, though some are more so than others. I agree of course that there is such a thing as a distinctive and exclusive group of people, the academic philosophers, but I am far from sharing Waismann's enthusiasm for their activities and for their approach. On the contrary, I feel that there is much to be said for those (they are, in my view, philosophers of a kind) who mistrust academic philosophy. At any rate, I am strongly opposed to an idea (a philosophical idea) whose influence, unexamined and never mentioned, pervades Waismann's brilliant essay: I mean the idea of an intellectual and philosophical *elite*.[2]

I admit, of course, that there have been a few truly great philosophers, and also a small number of philosophers who, though admirable in many ways, just missed being great. But although what they have produced ought to be of major importance for any academic philosopher, philosophy does not depend on them in the sense in which painting depends upon the great painters or music upon the great composers. Besides, great philosophy – for example, that of the Presocratics – antedates all academic and professional philosophy.

III

In my own view, professional philosophy has not done too well. It is in urgent need of an *apologia pro vita sua*, of a defence of its existence.

I even feel that the fact that I am a professional philosopher myself establishes a serious case against me: I feel it as an accusation. I must plead guilty, and offer, like Socrates, my apology.

I refer to Plato's *Apology* because of all works on philosophy ever written I like it best. I conjecture that it is historically true – that it tells us, by and large, what Socrates said before the Athenian Court. I like it because here speaks a man, modest and fearless. And his apology is very simple: he insists that he is aware of his limitations, not wise, except possibly in his awareness of the fact that he is not wise; and that he is a critic, especially of all high-sounding jargon, yet a friend of his fellow men, and a good citizen.

This is not only the apology of Socrates, but in my view it is an impressive apology for philosophy.

IV

But let us look at the case for the prosecution against philosophy. Many philosophers, and among them some of the greatest, have not done too well. I will refer to four of the greatest – Plato, Hume, Spinoza and Kant.

Plato, the greatest, profoundest and most gifted of all philosophers, had an outlook on human life which I find repulsive and indeed horrifying. Yet he was not only a great philosopher and the founder of the greatest professional school of philosophy, but a great inspired poet; and he wrote, among other beautiful works, *The Apology of Socrates*.

What ailed him, and so many professional philosophers after him, was that, in stark contrast to Socrates, he believed in the *elite*: in the Kingdom of Philosophy. While Socrates demanded that the statesman should be wise, that is, aware of how little he knows, Plato demanded that the wise, the learned philosophers, should be absolute rulers. (Ever since Plato, megalomania has been the philosophers' most widespread occupational disease.) Moreover, in the tenth book of *The Laws* Plato invented an institution that inspired the Inquisition, and he came close to recommending concentration camps for the cure of the souls of dissenters.

David Hume, who was not a professional philosopher, and who was, next to Socrates, perhaps the most candid and well-balanced of all the great philosophers and a thoroughly modest, rational and reasonably dispassionate man, was led, by an unfortunate and mistaken psychological theory (and by a theory of knowledge which taught him to distrust his own very remarkable powers of reason), to the horrifying doctrine, 'Reason is, and ought only to be, the slave of the passions, and can never pretend to any other office than to serve and obey them.'[3] I am ready to admit that nothing great has ever been achieved without passion, but I believe in the very opposite of Hume's statement. The taming of our passions by that limited reasonableness of which we may be capable is, in my view, the only hope for mankind.

Spinoza, the saint among the great philosophers and like Socrates and like Hume not a philosopher by profession, taught almost exactly the opposite to Hume, but in a way which I, for one, hold to be not only mistaken but also ethically unacceptable. He was a determinist (as was Hume), and human freedom consisted for him solely in having a clear, distinct, and adequate understanding of the true compelling causes of our actions: 'An affect, which is a passion, ceases to be a passion as soon as we form a clear and distinct idea of it.'[4] As long as it is a passion, we are in its clutches and unfree; once we have a clear and distinct idea of it, we are still determined by it, but we have transformed it into part of our reason. And this alone is freedom, Spinoza teaches.

I regard this teaching as an untenable and dangerous form of rationalism, even though I am a rationalist of sorts myself. First of all, I do not believe in determinism, and I do not think that Spinoza or anybody else has produced strong arguments in its support, or in support of a reconciliation of determinism with human freedom (and thus with common sense). It seems to me that Spinoza's determinism is a typical philosopher's mistake, even though it is of course true that much of what we are doing (*but not all*) is determined and even predictable. Second, though it may be true in some sense that an excess of what Spinoza means by 'passion' makes us unfree, his formula which I have quoted would discharge us from responsibility for our actions whenever we cannot form a clear, distinct and adequate rational idea of the motives of our actions. But, I assert, we never can do that; and although to be reasonable in our actions and in our dealings with our fellow creatures is, I think, a most important aim (and Spinoza certainly thought so too), I do not think it an aim which we can ever say that we have reached.

Kant, one of the few admirable and highly original thinkers among professional philosophers, tried to solve Hume's problem of the rejection of reason, and Spinoza's problem of determinism; yet he failed in both attempts.

These are some of the greatest philosophers, philosophers whom I admire much. You will understand why I feel apologetic about philosophy.

V

I never was a member of the Vienna Circle of logical positivists, like my friends Fritz Waismann, Herbert Feigl and Victor Kraft; in fact, Otto Neurath called me 'the official opposition'. I was never invited to any of the meetings of the Circle, perhaps owing to my well-known opposition to positivism. (I would have been delighted to accept an invitation, for not only were some of the members of the Circle personal friends of mine, but I also had the greatest admiration for some of the other members.) Under the influence of Ludwig Wittgenstein's *Tractatus Logico-Philosophicus*, the Circle had become not only antimetaphysical, but antiphilosophical. Schlick, the leader of the Circle,[5] formulated this by way of the prophecy that philosophy, 'which never talks sense but utters only meaningless words', will soon disappear, because philosophers will find that 'their audience', tired of empty tirades, has gone away.

Waismann agreed with Wittgenstein and Schlick for many years. I think I can detect in his enthusiasm for philosophy the enthusiasm of the convert.

I always defended philosophy and even metaphysics against the Circle, even though I had to admit that philosophers had not been doing too well. For I believed that many people, and I among them, had genuine philosophical problems of various degrees of seriousness and difficulty, and that these problems were not all insoluble.

Indeed the existence of urgent and serious philosophical problems and the need to discuss them critically is, in my view, the only apology for what may be called professional or academic philosophy.

Wittgenstein and the Vienna Circle denied the existence of serious philosophical problems.

According to the end of the *Tractatus*, the apparent problems of philosophy (including those of the *Tractatus* itself) are pseudo-problems which arise from speaking without having given meaning to all one's words. This theory may be regarded as inspired by Russell's solution of the logical paradoxes as pseudo-propositions which are neither true nor false but meaningless. This led to the modern philosophical technique of branding all sorts of inconvenient propositions or problems as 'meaningless'. The later Wittgenstein used to speak of 'puzzles', caused by the philosophical misuse of language. I can only say that if I had no serious philosophical problems and no hope of solving them, I should have no excuse for being a philosopher: to my mind, there would be no apology for philosophy.

VI

In this section I will list certain views of philosophy and certain activities that are often taken to be characteristic of philosophy which I, for one, find unsatisfactory. The section could be entitled 'How I Do Not See Philosophy'.

1. I do not see philosophy as the solving of linguistic puzzles; although the elimination of misunderstandings is sometimes a necessary preliminary task.

2. I do not see philosophy as a series of works of art, as striking and original pictures of the world, or as clever and unusual ways of describing the world. I think that if we look upon philosophy in this way, we do a real injustice to the great philosophers. The great philosophers were not engaged in an aesthetic endeavour. They did not try to be architects of clever systems; but like the great scientists they were, first of all, seekers after truth – after true solutions of genuine problems. No, I see the history of philosophy essentially as part of the history of the search for truth, and I reject the *purely* aesthetic view of it, even though beauty is important in philosophy as well as in science.

I am all for intellectual boldness. We cannot be intellectual cowards and seekers for truth at the same time. A seeker for truth must dare to be wise – he must dare to be a revolutionary in the field of thought.

3. I do not see the long history of philosophical systems as one of intellectual edifices in which all possible ideas are tried out, and in which truth may perhaps come to light as a by-product. I believe that we are doing an injustice to the truly great philosophers of the past if we doubt for a moment that every one of them would have discarded his system (as he should have done) had he become convinced that, although perhaps brilliant, it was not a step on the way to truth. (This, incidentally, is the reason why I do not regard Fichte or Hegel as real philosophers: I mistrust their devotion to truth.)

4. I do not see philosophy as an attempt either to clarify or to analyse or to 'explicate' concepts, or words, or languages.

Concepts or words are mere tools for formulating propositions, conjectures and theories. Concepts or words cannot be true in themselves; they merely serve human descriptive and argumentative language. Our aim should not be to analyse *meanings*, but to seek for interesting and important *truths*; that is, for true *theories*.

5. I do not see philosophy as a way of being clever.

6. I do not see philosophy as a kind of intellectual therapy (Wittgenstein), an activity of helping people out of philosophical perplexities. To my mind, Wittgenstein (in his later work) did not

show the fly the way out of the bottle. Rather, I see in the fly, unable to escape from the bottle, a striking self-portrait of Wittgenstein. (Wittgenstein was a Wittgensteinian case – just as Freud was a Freudian case.)

7. I do not see philosophy as a study of how to express things more precisely or exactly. Precision and exactness are not intellectual values in themselves, and we should never try to be more precise or exact than is demanded by the problem in hand.

8. Accordingly, I do not see philosophy as an attempt to provide the foundations or the conceptual framework for solving problems which may turn up in the nearer or the more distant future. John Locke did so; he wanted to write an essay on ethics, and considered it necessary first to provide the conceptual preliminaries.

His *Essay* consists of these preliminaries, and British philosophy has ever since (with very few exceptions, such as some of the political essays of Hume) remained bogged down in these preliminaries.

9. Nor do I see philosophy as an expression of the spirit of the time. This is a Hegelian idea, which does not stand up to criticism. Fashions there are in philosophy, as there are in science. But a genuine searcher for truth will not follow fashion; he will distrust fashions and even fight them.

VII

All men and all women are philosophers. If they are not conscious of having philosophical problems, they have, at any rate, philosophical prejudices. Most of these are theories which they take for granted: they have absorbed them from their intellectual environment or from tradition.

Since few of these theories are consciously held, they are prejudices in the sense that they are held without critical examination, even though they may be of great importance for the practical actions of people, and for their whole life.

It is an apology for the existence of professional philosophy that men are needed to *examine critically* these widespread and influential theories.

Theories like these are the insecure starting point of all science and of all philosophy. All philosophy must start from the dubious and often pernicious views of uncritical common sense. Its aim is to reach enlightened, critical common sense: to reach a view nearer to the truth; and with a less pernicious influence on human life.

VIII

Let me present some examples of widespread philosophical prejudices.

There is a very influential philosophical view of life to the effect that whenever something happens in this world that is really bad (or that we greatly dislike), then there must be somebody responsible for it: there must be somebody who has done it, intentionally. This view is very old. In Homer the envy and the anger of the gods were responsible for most of the terrible things that happened in the field before Troy and to Troy itself; and it was Poseidon who was responsible for the misadventures of Odysseus. In later Christian thought it is the Devil who is responsible for evil; in vulgar Marxism it is the conspiracy of the greedy capitalists that prevents the coming of socialism and the establishment of heaven on earth.

The theory which sees war, poverty and unemployment as the result of some evil intention, of some sinister design, is part of common sense, but it is uncritical. I have called this uncritical commonsense theory the conspiracy theory of society. (One might even call it the conspiracy theory of the world: think of Zeus' bolt of lightning.) It is widely held and, in the form of a search for scapegoats, it has inspired much political strife and has created the most frightful suffering.

One aspect of the conspiracy theory of society is that it encourages real conspiracies. But a critical investigation shows that conspiracies hardly ever attain their aims. Lenin, who held the conspiracy theory, was a conspirator, and so were Mussolini and Hitler. But Lenin's aims were not realized in Russia; nor were Mussolini's or Hitler's aims realized in Italy or in Germany.

All these conspirators become conspirators because they uncritically believed in a conspiracy theory of society.

It may perhaps be a modest but not quite insignificant contribution to philosophy to draw attention to the mistakes of the conspiracy theory of society. Moreover this contribution leads to further contributions such as to the discovery of the significance for society of the *unintended consequences* of human actions, and to the suggestion that we regard it as the aim of the theoretical social sciences to discover those social relations which produce the unintended consequences of our actions.

Take the problem of war. Even a critical philosopher of the status of Bertrand Russell believed that we have to explain wars by psychological motives – by human aggressiveness. I do not deny the existence of aggressiveness, but I am surprised that Russell did not see that most wars in modern times have been inspired by fear of aggression rather than by personal aggressiveness. They have been either ideological wars inspired by the fear of the power of some conspiracy, or wars which nobody wanted but which came about as the result of fear inspired by some objective situation. One example is the mutual fear of aggression which leads to an armaments race and thence to war; perhaps to a preventive war such as even Russell, who was an enemy of war and of aggression, recommended for a time, fearing (rightly) that Russia would soon have the hydrogen bomb. (Nobody wanted the bomb; it was the fear that Hitler would monopolize it which led to its construction.)

Or take a different example of a philosophical prejudice. There is the prejudice that a man's opinions are always determined by his self-interest. This doctrine (which may be described as a degenerate form of Hume's doctrine that reason is, and ought to be, the slave of the passions) is not as a rule applied to oneself (this was done by Hume, who taught modesty and scepticism with respect to our powers of reason, his own included); but it is as a rule only applied to the other fellow – whose opinion differs from our own. It prevents us from listening patiently to opinions which are opposed to our own, and from taking them seriously, because we can explain them by the other fellow's 'interests'. But this makes rational discussion impossible. It leads to a deterioration of our natural curiosity, of our interest in finding out the truth about things. In the place of the important question 'What is the truth about this matter?' it puts another question, less important by far: 'What is your self-interest, what are your hidden motives?' It prevents us from learning from people whose opinions differ from our own, and it leads to a dissolution of the unity of mankind, a unity that is based on our common rationality.

A similar philosophical prejudice is the thesis, at present immensely influential, that rational discussion is possible only between people who agree on fundamentals. This pernicious doctrine implies that rational or critical discussion about fundamentals is impossible, and it leads to consequences as undesirable as those of the doctrines discussed before.[6]

These doctrines are held by many people, but they belong to a field of philosophy which has been one of the main concerns of many professional philosophers: *the theory of knowledge.*

IX

As I see it, the problems of the theory of knowledge form the very heart of philosophy, both of uncritical or popular commonsense philosophy and of academic philosophy. They are even decisive for the theory of ethics (as Jacques Monod has recently reminded us).[7]

Put in a simple way, the main problem here as in other regions of philosophy is the conflict between 'epistemological optimism' and 'epistemological pessimism'. Can we have knowledge? How much can we know? While the epistemological optimist believes in the possibility of human knowledge, the pessimist believes that genuine knowledge is beyond the power of man.

I am an admirer of common sense, though not of all of it; I hold that common sense is our only possible starting point. But we should not attempt to erect an edifice of secure knowledge upon it, but rather criticize it and improve upon it. Thus I am a commonsense realist; I believe in the reality of matter (which I think is the very paradigm of what the word 'real' is meant to denote); and for this reason I should call myself a 'materialist', were it not for the fact that this term also denotes a creed that (a) takes matter as essentially irreducible, and (b) denies the reality of immaterial fields of forces and, of course, also of mind, or consciousness; and of anything else but matter.

I follow common sense in holding that there exist both matter ('world 1') and mind ('world 2'), and I suggest that there exist also other things, especially the products of the human mind, which include our scientific conjectures, theories and problems ('world 3'). In other words, I am a commonsense pluralist. I am very ready to have this position criticized and replaced by a sounder one, but *all the critical arguments against it which are known to me are, in my opinion, invalid.*[8] (Incidentally, I regard the pluralism here described as needed for ethics.)

All the arguments that have been advanced against a pluralistic realism are based, in the last instance, upon an *uncritical acceptance of the commonsense theory of knowledge*, which I regard as the weakest part of common sense.

The commonsense theory of knowledge is highly optimistic in so far as it equates *knowledge with certain knowledge*; everything conjectural is, so it holds, not really 'knowledge'. I dismiss this argument as merely verbal. I readily admit that the term 'knowledge' carries in all languages known to me the connotation of certainty. But science consists of hypotheses. And the commonsense programme of starting from what appears to be the most certain or basic knowledge available (observational knowledge), in order to erect on those foundations an edifice of secure knowledge, does not stand up to criticism.

It leads, incidentally, to two non-commonsensical views of reality, which stand in direct contradiction to each other.

1. Immaterialism (Berkeley, Hume, Mach)
2. Behaviourist materialism (Watson, Skinner)

The first of these denies the reality of matter, because the only certain and secure basis of our knowledge consists of our own *perceptual experiences*; and these remain, for ever, immaterial.

The second denies the existence of mind (and, incidentally, of human freedom), because all we can really *observe* is human behaviour, which is in every way like animal behaviour (except that it incorporates a wide and important field, 'linguistic behaviour').

Both these theories are based upon the invalid commonsense theory of knowledge which leads to the traditional but invalid criticism of the commonsense theory of reality. These theories are not ethically neutral, but pernicious: if I wish to comfort a weeping child, I do not wish to stop some irritating perceptions (of mine or of yours); nor do I wish to change the child's behaviour; or to stop drops of water from running down its cheeks. No, my motives are different – undemonstrable, underivable, but *human*.

Immaterialism (which owes its origin to the insistence of Descartes – who was of course no immaterialist – that we must start from an indubitable basis such as the knowledge of our own existence) reached its culmination at the turn of the century with

Ernst Mach, but has now lost most of its influence. It is no longer fashionable.

Behaviourism – the denial of the existence of mind – is very fashionable at present. Although it extols observation, it not only flies in the face of all human experience, but it also tries to derive from its theories an ethically horrible theory – the theory of conditioning;[9] although no ethical theory is, in fact, derivable from human nature. (Jacques Monod has rightly emphasized this point;[10] see also my *Open Society and Its Enemies*.[11]) It is to be hoped that this fashion, based upon an uncritical acceptance of the commonsense theory of knowledge whose untenability I have tried to show,[12] will one day lose its influence.

X

As I see philosophy, it never ought to be, and indeed it never can be, divorced from the sciences. Historically, all western science is an offspring of Greek philosophical speculation about the cosmos, the world order. The common ancestors of all scientists and all philosophers are Homer, Hesiod and the Presocratics. Central for them is the inquiry into the structure of the universe, and our place in this universe, including the problem of our knowledge of the universe (a problem which, as I see it, remains decisive for all philosophy). And it is the critical inquiry into the sciences, their findings and their methods, which remains a characteristic of philosophical inquiry, even after the sciences have broken away from it. Newton's *Mathematical Principles of Natural Philosophy* marks, in my opinion, the greatest event, the greatest intellectual revolution, in the whole history of mankind. It marks the fulfilment of a dream that was over two thousand years old; it marks the maturation of science, and its break away from philosophy. Newton himself, like all great scientists, remained a philosopher; and he remained a critical thinker, a searcher, and sceptical of his own theories. Thus he wrote in his letter to Bentley (25 February 1693) of his own theory, which involves action at a distance (italics mine):

> That gravity should be innate, inherent, and essential to matter, *so that one body may act upon another at a distance* . . . is to me so great an absurdity that I believe no man who has in philosophical matters a competent faculty of thinking can ever fall into it.

It was his own theory of action at a distance which led him to both scepticism and mysticism. He reasoned that if all the vastly distant regions of space can interact instantaneously with each other, then this must be due to the omnipresence at the same time of one and the same being in all regions – to the omnipresence of God. It was thus the attempt to solve this problem of action at a distance which led Newton to his mystical theory according to which space is the sensorium of God; a theory in which he transcended science and which combined critical and speculative philosophy and speculative religion. We know that Einstein was similarly motivated.

XI

I admit that there are some very subtle yet most important problems in philosophy which have their natural and indeed their only place in academic philosophy; for example, the problems of mathematical logic and, more generally, the philosophy of mathematics. I am greatly impressed by the astounding progress made in these fields in our century.

But as far as academic philosophy in general is concerned, I am worried by the influence of what Berkeley used to call the 'minute philosophers'. Criticism is the lifeblood of philosophy, to be sure. Yet we should avoid hairsplitting. A minute criticism of minute points without an understanding of the great problems of cosmology, of human knowledge, of ethics and of political philosophy, and without a serious and devoted attempt to solve them, appears to me fatal. It almost looks as if every printed passage which might with some effort be misunderstood or misinterpreted is good enough to justify the writing of another critical philosophical paper. Scholasticism, in the worst sense of the term, abounds; all the great ideas are buried in a flood of words. At the same time, a certain arrogance and rudeness – once a rarity in philosophical literature – seems to be accepted, by the editors of many of the journals, as a proof of boldness of thought and originality.

I believe it is the duty of every intellectual to be aware of the privileged position he is in. He has a duty to write as simply and clearly as he can, and in as civilized a manner as he can; and never to forget either the great problems that beset mankind and demand new and bold but patient thought, or the Socratic modesty of the man who knows how little he knows. As against the minute philosophers with their minute problems, I think that the main task of philosophy is to speculate critically about the universe and about our place in the universe, including our powers of knowing and our powers for good and evil.

XII

I might perhaps end with a bit of decidedly non-academic philosophy.

One of the astronauts involved in the first visit to the moon is credited with a simple and wise remark which he made on his return (I am quoting from memory): 'I have seen some planets in my day, but give me the earth every time.' I think this is not only wisdom, but philosophical wisdom. We do not know how it is that we are alive on this wonderful little planet – or why there should be something like life, to make our planet so beautiful. But here we are, and we have every reason to wonder at it, and to feel grateful for it. It comes close to being a miracle. For all that science can tell us, the universe is almost empty of matter; and where there is matter, the matter is almost everywhere in a chaotic, turbulent state, and uninhabitable. There may be many other planets with life on them. Yet if we pick out at random a place in the universe, then the probability (calculated on the basis of our dubious current cosmology) of finding a life-carrying body at that place will be zero, or almost zero. So life has at any rate the value of something rare; it is precious. We are inclined to forget this, and treat life cheaply, perhaps out of thoughtlessness; or perhaps because this beautiful earth of ours is, no doubt, a bit overcrowded.

All men are philosophers, because in one way or another all take up an attitude towards life and death. There are those who think that life is valueless because it comes to an end. They fail to see that the opposite argument might also be proposed: that if there were no end to life, life would have no value; that it is, in part, the ever-present danger of losing it which helps to bring home to us the value of life.

NOTES

1 F. Waismann, in H. D. Lewis (ed.), *Contemporary British Philosophy*, 3rd series, 2nd edn, George Allen & Unwin, London, 1961, pp. 447–90.

2 This idea comes to the fore in such remarks of Waismann's as 'Indeed, a philosopher is a man who senses as it were hidden crevices in the build of our concepts where others only see the smooth path of commonplaceness before them.' ibid., p. 448.

3 David Hume, *A Treatise on Human Nature*, 1739–40; ed. L. A. Selby-Bigge, Clarendon Press, Oxford, 1888 (and many later reprints), book II, part III, sec. III, p. 415.

4 Benedictus de Spinoza, *Ethics*, book V, proposition III.

5 The Vienna Circle was, in fact, Schlick's private seminar, and members were personally invited by Schlick. (The quoted words are from the concluding paragraphs, pp. 10 ff., of Moritz Schlick, 'Die Wende der Philosophie', *Erkenntnis*, 1, pp. 4–11.)

6 See also my paper 'The Myth of the Framework', in the Schilpp Festschrift, *The Abdication of Philosophy*, ed. E. Freeman, Open Court, La Salle, Illinois, 1976.

7 Jacques Monod, *Chance and Necessity*, Alfred Knopf, New York, 1971.

8 See, for example, K. R. Popper, *Objective Knowledge: An Evolutionary Approach*, Clarendon Press, Oxford, 1972, 1979; 7th impression, 1992 (especially chapter 2).

9 The conditioner's dream of omnipotence may be found in J. B. Watson's *Behaviourism* and also in the work of B. F. Skinner, for example, *Walden Two* (Macmillan, New York, 1948) or *Beyond Freedom and Dignity* (Alfred Knopf, New York, 1971). I may quote from Watson: 'Give me a dozen healthy infants . . . and I'll guarantee to take any one at random and train him to become any type of specialist I might select – doctor, lawyer, artist . . . [or] thief' (J. B. Watson, *Behaviourism*, 2nd edn, Routledge, London, 1931, p. 104). Thus everything will depend on the morals of the omnipotent conditioner. (Yet according to the conditioners, these morals are nothing but the product of conditioning.)

10 See note 7 above.

11 K. R. Popper, *The Open Society and Its Enemies*, 2 vols, Routledge & Kegan Paul, London, 1945; 5th edn, 1969; 14th impression, 1991–2; Princeton University Press, Princeton, NJ, 1950; and Princeton paperback, 1971.

12 See *Objective Knowledge: An Evolutionary Approach*, chapter 2.

14

TOLERATION AND INTELLECTUAL RESPONSIBILITY

(Stolen from Xenophanes and Voltaire)

I have been asked here today to repeat a lecture which I gave in Tübingen, on the theme 'Toleration and Intellectual Responsibility'. The lecture is dedicated to the memory of Leopold Lucas, a scholar, a historian, a man of toleration and humanity who became a victim of intolerance and inhumanity.

At the age of seventy, in December 1942, Dr Leopold Lucas and his wife were imprisoned in the Theresienstadt concentration camp, where he worked as a rabbi: an immensely difficult task. He died there ten months later. Dora Lucas, his wife, was kept in Theresienstadt for another thirteen months, but she was able to work as a nurse. In October 1944 she was deported to Poland, together with 18,000 other prisoners. There she was put to death.

It was a terrible fate. It was the fate of countless human beings; people who loved other people, who tried to help other people; who were loved by other people and whom other people tried to help. They belonged to families which were torn apart, destroyed, exterminated.

I do not intend, here, to talk about these dreadful events. Whatever one may try to say – or even to think – it always seems like an attempt to belittle events that defy the imagination.

Lecture delivered to the University of Tübingen on 26 May 1981 and repeated in Vienna in Spring 1982.

Translator's note: Translated from the German by Melitta Mew, with a few minor revisions for this volume by Laura J. Bennett. The verse translations are by the author.

14. TOLERATION AND INTELLECTUAL RESPONSIBILITY

I

But the horror continues. The refugees from Vietnam; the victims of Pol Pot in Cambodia; the victims of the revolution in Iran; the refugees from Afghanistan and the Arab refugees from Israel: time and time again, children, women and men become the victims of crazed fanatics.

What can we do to prevent these monstrous events? Can we do anything at all?

My answer is: yes. I believe that there is a great deal that we can do. When I say 'we', I mean the intellectuals, that is, human beings who are interested in ideas; especially those who read and, perhaps, write.

Why do I think that we, the intellectuals, are able to help? Simply because we, the intellectuals, have done the most terrible harm for thousands of years. Mass murder in the name of an idea, a doctrine, a theory, a religion – that is all *our* doing, *our* invention: the invention of the intellectuals. If only we would stop setting man against man – often with the best intentions – much would be gained. Nobody can say that it is impossible for us to stop doing this.

The most important of the Ten Commandments is: Thou shalt not kill! It contains nearly the whole of ethics. The way in which Schopenhauer, for example, formulates ethics is merely an extension of this most important commandment. Schopenhauer's ethics are simple, direct and clear. He says: *Hurt no one, but help all, as well as you can!*

But what happened when Moses came down for the first time with the stone tablets from Mount Sinai, before he could even announce the Ten Commandments? He witnessed a horrible heresy, the heresy of the golden calf. At this he forgot all about the commandment 'Thou shalt not kill!' and he shouted (Exodus 32):

> Who is on the Lord's side? Let him come unto me . . .
> And he said unto them, Thus saith the Lord God of Israel, Put every man his sword by his side, . . . and slay every man his brother, and every man his companion, and every man his neighbour . . .
>
> And there fell of the people that day about three thousand men.

That was, perhaps, the beginning. But what is certain is that things continued to go on in this way; in the Holy Land, and later here in the West. And in the West especially, after Christianity attained the status of an official religion. It became a terrible story of religious persecution, persecution for the sake of orthodoxy. Later – above all in the seventeenth and eighteenth centuries – still other ideologies competed in justifying persecution, cruelty and terror: nationalism, race, political orthodoxy and other religions.

Behind the ideas of orthodoxy and of heresy the pettiest of vices lie hidden; those vices to which the intellectuals are particularly prone: arrogance, smugness verging on dogmatism, intellectual vanity. All these are petty vices – not major vices like cruelty.

II

The title of my lecture, 'Toleration and Intellectual Responsibility', alludes to an argument of Voltaire's, the father of the Enlightenment; an argument in defence of toleration. Voltaire asks, 'What is toleration?' and he answers (I am translating freely):

> Toleration is the necessary consequence of realizing our human fallibility: to err is human, and we do it all the time. *So let us pardon each other's follies.* This is the first principle of natural right.

Here Voltaire is appealing to our intellectual honesty: we should admit our mistakes, our fallibility, our ignorance. Voltaire knows full well that utterly convinced fanatics do exist. But is their conviction truly honest? Have they honestly examined themselves, their beliefs and their reasons for holding those beliefs? And is not a self-critical attitude part of all intellectual honesty? Is not fanaticism often an attempt to drown our own unadmitted disbelief that we have suppressed and are therefore only half conscious of?

Voltaire's appeal to our intellectual modesty and above all his appeal to our intellectual honesty made a great impression on the intellectuals of his time. I should like to restate this appeal here.

The reason given by Voltaire in support of tolerance is that we should pardon each other's follies. But a common folly, that of *in*tolerance, Voltaire finds, quite rightly, is difficult to tolerate. Indeed, it is here that tolerance has its limits. If we concede to intolerance the right to be tolerated, then we destroy tolerance, and the constitutional state. That was the fate of the Weimar Republic.

But apart from intolerance there are still other follies that we should not tolerate; above all that folly which makes intellectuals follow the latest fashion; a folly which has caused many a writer to adopt an obscure, impressive style, that cryptic style which Goethe criticized so devastatingly in *Faust* (for example, the witch's multiplication table). This style, the style of big and obscure words, of words bombastic and incomprehensible, this manner of writing should no longer be admired, nor even tolerated by intellectuals. It is intellectually irresponsible. It destroys healthy common sense; it destroys reason. It makes possible the philosophy that has been described as *relativism*; a philosophy that amounts to the thesis that *all* theses are intellectually more or less equally defensible. Anything goes! So the thesis of relativism leads to anarchy, to unlawfulness; and to the rule of violence.

My theme, toleration and intellectual responsibility, has thus led me to the question of relativism.

At this point I would like to compare relativism with a position which is almost always confused with relativism, yet is in fact entirely different from it. I have often described this position as *pluralism*; but this has simply led to these misunderstandings. I will therefore characterize it here as *critical pluralism*. Whilst relativism, arising from a lax form of toleration, leads to the rule of violence, critical pluralism can contribute to the taming of violence.

In order to distinguish relativism from critical pluralism, the idea of *truth* is of crucial importance.

Relativism is the position that everything can be asserted, or practically everything, and therefore nothing. Everything is true, or nothing. Truth is therefore a meaningless concept.

Critical pluralism is the position that *in the interest of the search for truth*, all theories – the more, the better – should be allowed to compete with all other theories. This competition consists in the rational discussion of theories and in their critical elimination. The discussion should be rational – and that means that it should be concerned with the truth of the competing theories: the theory that seems to come closer to the truth in the course of the critical discussion is the better one; and the better theory replaces the inferior theories. It is therefore the question of truth which is at stake.

III

The idea of objective truth and the idea of the search for truth are of decisive importance here.

The first thinker to develop a theory of truth, and to link the idea of objective truth with the idea of our basic human fallibility, was the Presocratic Xenophanes. Born in 571 BC in Ionia, Asia Minor, he was the first Greek to write literary criticism; the first moral philosopher; the first to develop a critical theory of human knowledge; and the first speculative monotheist.

Xenophanes was the founder of a tradition, of a way of thinking, to which have belonged, among others, Socrates, Erasmus, Montaigne, Locke, Hume, Voltaire and Lessing.

This tradition is sometimes called the sceptical school. Such a description, however, can easily lead to misunderstandings. The *Concise Oxford Dictionary*, for example, says: 'Sceptic . . . person who doubts truth of . . . religious doctrines, agnostic, . . . atheist; . . . or who takes cynical views.' But the Greek word from which the word is derived means (as the *Oxford Dictionary* tells us) 'to look out', 'to inquire', 'to reflect', 'to search'.

Among the sceptics (in the original meaning of the word) there were certainly many doubting people and perhaps also distrustful people, but the fatal move of equating the words 'sceptical' and 'doubting' was probably a cunning move of the Stoic school, which wanted to ridicule its rivals. In any case, the sceptics Xenophanes, Socrates, Erasmus, Montaigne, Locke, Voltaire and Lessing were all theists or deists. What all the members of this sceptical tradition have in common – including Nicolas da Cusa, a cardinal, and Erasmus of Rotterdam – and what I also share with this tradition is that we stress our human *ignorance*. From this we can point to important ethical consequences: *toleration*, but *not* toleration of intolerance, of violence or cruelty.

Xenophanes was by profession a rhapsodist. He was a pupil of Homer and Hesiod, and he criticized them both. His criticism was ethical and pedagogical. He opposed Homer's and Hesiod's contention that the gods were stealing, lying and committing adultery. This led him to criticize Homer's doctrine of the gods. The important result of the criticism was the discovery of what would nowadays be called anthropomorphism: the discovery that the Greek stories of the gods were not to be taken seriously, because they represented the gods as human beings. At this point I may perhaps quote some of Xenophanes' arguments in verse form (in my nearly literal translation):

> The Ethiops say that their gods are flatnosed and black
> While the Thracians say that theirs have blue eyes and red hair.
> Yet if cattle or horses or lions had hands and could draw
> And could sculpture like men, then horses would draw their gods
> Like horses, and cattle like cattle, and each would then shape
> Bodies of gods in the likeness, each kind, of its own.

Xenophanes posed himself a problem with this argument: how should we think of the gods in the wake of such a criticism of anthropomorphism? We have four fragments which contain an important part of his answer. The answer is monotheistic although Xenophanes, like Luther when translating the First Commandment, takes refuge in using 'gods' in the plural in the formulation of his monotheism.

> One god, alone among gods and alone among men, is the greatest.
> Neither in body resembling the mortals, nor in his thinking.
> Always he stays fast in one place, without ever moving.
> Nor is it fitting for him to rove about, hither and thither.
> Effortless over the All he reigns by mere thought and intention.
> He is all sight; and he is all thought; and he is all hearing.[1]

These are the fragments which give an account of Xenophanes' speculative theology.

It is clear that this completely new theory was the solution to a difficult problem for Xenophanes. In fact it came to him as a solution to the greatest of all problems, the problem of the universe. No-one who knows anything about the psychology of knowledge can doubt that, to its creator, this new insight must have appeared like a revelation.

In spite of this, Xenophanes stated, clearly and honestly, that his theory was no more than conjecture. This was a victory of self-criticism without equal, a victory of his intellectual honesty and of his modesty.

Xenophanes generalized this self-criticism in a manner which, I think, was characteristic of him: it was clear to him that what he had discovered about his own theory – that it was nothing more than conjecture in spite of its intuitive power of persuasion – must be true of all human theories: everything is only conjecture. This seems to me to reveal that it had not been easy for him to view his own theory as conjecture.

Xenophanes formulated his critical theory of knowledge – everything is conjecture – in six beautiful lines of verse:

> But as for certain truth, no man has known it,
> Nor will he know it; neither of the gods,
> Nor yet of all the things of which I speak.
> And even if by chance he were to utter
> The perfect truth, he would himself not know it:
> For all is but a woven web of guesses.

These six lines contain more than a theory of the uncertainty of human knowledge. They contain *a theory of objective knowledge*. For Xenophanes tells us here that, whilst something I say may be true, neither I nor anybody else will *know* that it is true. This means, however, that truth is objective: truth is the correspondence of what I say with the facts; *whether or not I actually know* that the correspondence exists.

In addition, these six lines contain another very important theory. They contain a clue to the difference between objective *truth* and the subjective *certainty* of knowledge. For the six lines affirm that, even when I proclaim the most perfect truth, I cannot know this with certainty. For there is no infallible criterion of truth: we can never, or almost never, be quite sure that we have not been mistaken.

But Xenophanes was not an epistemological pessimist. He was a searcher; and during the course of his long life he was able, by way of critical re-examination, to improve many of his conjectures, and more especially his scientific theories. These are his words:

> The gods did not reveal, from the beginning,
> All things to us; but in the course of time,
> Through seeking, we may learn, and know things better.

Xenophanes also explains what he means by 'to know things better': he means the approximation to objective truth: closeness to truth, similarity to truth. For he says of one of his conjectures:

> These things, we may well conjecture, resemble the truth.

It is possible that in this fragment the word 'conjecture' alludes to Xenophanes' monotheistic theory of deity.

In Xenophanes' theory of truth and of human knowledge we may find the following points:

1. Our knowledge consists of statements.
2. Statements are either true or false.
3. Truth is objective. It is the correspondence of the content of a statement with the facts.
4. Even when we express the most perfect truth, we cannot know this – that is, we cannot know it with certainty.
5. Since 'knowledge' in the usual sense of the word is 'certain knowledge', there can be no knowledge. There can only be *conjectural knowledge*: 'For all is but a woven web of guesses.'
6. But in our conjectural knowledge there can be progress to something better.
7. Better knowledge is a better approximation to the truth.
8. But it always remains conjectural knowledge – a web of guesses.

For an understanding of Xenophanes' theory of truth it is important to stress that Xenophanes differentiates clearly between objective *truth* and subjective *certainty*. Objective truth is the correspondence of a statement with the facts, whether we know this – know it for certain – or not. Thus, *truth must not be confused with certainty or with certain knowledge*. He who knows something for certain is he who knows the truth. But it often happens that someone conjectures something without knowing it for certain; and that his conjecture is actually true since it corresponds to the facts. Xenophanes implies quite correctly that there are many truths – and important truths – which nobody knows for certain; and that there are many truths which nobody can know, even though they may be conjectured by some. And he further implies that there are truths which nobody can even conjecture.

Indeed, in any of the languages in which we are able to speak of the infinite sequence of natural numbers, there exists an infinite variety of clear and unambiguous statements (for instance: $17^2 = 627 + 2$). Each of these statements is either true or, if it is false, its negation is true. There are, therefore, infinitely many different true propositions. And from this it follows that there exist infinitely many true propositions which we shall never be able to know – infinitely many unknowable truths.

Even today there are many philosophers who think that truth can be of significance for us only if we possess it; that is, know it with certainty. Yet the knowledge of the existence of conjectural knowledge is of great importance. There are truths which we can only approach by laborious searching. Our path, nearly always, winds its way through error. And without truth there can be no error (and without error there is no fallibility).

IV

Some of the views which I have just described were more or less clear to me, even before I read Xenophanes' fragments; perhaps I would not have understood them otherwise. It had become clear to me through Einstein that our best knowledge was conjectural, that it was a woven web of guesses. For he pointed out that Newton's theory of gravity – just like Einstein's own gravitational theory – is conjectural knowledge, despite its immense success; and, just like Newton's theory, Einstein's own theory appears to be only an approximation to the truth.

I do not believe that the significance of conjectural knowledge would ever have become clear to me without the work of Newton and Einstein; and so I asked myself how it could have become clear to Xenophanes 2,500 years ago. Perhaps the answer to this question is this: Xenophanes first accepted Homer's picture of the universe, just as I accepted Newton's picture of the universe. His first belief was shattered for him just as it was for me: for him through his own criticism of Homer; for me by Einstein's criticism of Newton. Xenophanes, just like Einstein, replaced the criticized picture of the universe with another; and both were aware that their new picture of the universe was merely conjecture.

The realization that Xenophanes had anticipated my theory of conjectural knowledge by 2,500 years taught me to be modest. But the idea of intellectual modesty was likewise anticipated for nearly as long. It comes from Socrates.

Socrates was the second, and much more influential, founder of the sceptical tradition. He taught: only he is wise who knows that he is not.

Socrates and, at about the same time, Democritus made the same ethical discovery quite independently of each other. Both said, in very similar words: 'It is better to suffer injustice than to commit an injustice.'

One can claim that this insight – at least if combined with the knowledge of how little we know – leads, as Voltaire taught much later, to toleration.

V

I shall now turn to the contemporary significance of this self-critical philosophy of knowledge.

First, we must discuss the following important objection. It is true, somebody may say, that Xenophanes, Democritus and Socrates did not know anything; and it was indeed wise that they recognized their own lack of knowledge; and perhaps even wiser that they adopted the attitude of seeking or searching for knowledge. We – or more precisely our scientists – are still searchers, researchers. But today scientists are not only seeking but also finding. And they have found a great deal; so much indeed that the very volume of our scientific knowledge has become a problem. Is it right, therefore, that we should continue even now in all sincerity to build up our philosophy of knowledge upon the Socratic thesis of lack of knowledge?

The objection is correct, but only in the light of four very important additional points.

First, when it is suggested that science knows a great deal, this is correct, but the word 'knowledge' is used here, apparently unconsciously, in a sense which is completely different from that intended by Xenophanes and Socrates, and also from the meaning given to the word 'knowledge' in current everyday usage. For by 'knowledge' we usually mean '*certain* knowledge'. If someone says 'I *know* that today is Tuesday but I am *not sure* that today is Tuesday,' he is contradicting himself, or retracting in the second half of his statement what he is saying in the first half.

But our scientific knowledge is still *not* certain knowledge. It is open to revision. It consists of testable *conjectures*, of hypotheses – at best, of conjectures that have been subjected to the most stringent tests, yet, still, of *conjectures* only. This is the first point, and it is in itself a complete justification of Socrates' emphasis on our lack of knowledge, and of Xenophanes' comment that, even when we speak the perfect truth, we could not know that what we have said is true.

The second point, which must be added to the objection that we know so much nowadays, is this: with almost every new scientific achievement, with every hypothetical solution of a scientific problem, both the number of the unsolved problems and the degree of their difficulty increase. In fact, they increase much faster than the solutions. One might well say that whilst our hypothetical knowledge is finite, our ignorance is infinite. But not only that: for the genuine scientist with a feeling for unsolved problems, the world is becoming, in a very concrete sense, more and more of a riddle.

My third point is this: when we say that today we know *more* than Xenophanes or Socrates did, it is probably incorrect if we take 'know' in a subjective sense. Presumably none of us know *more*; we simply know *different* things. We have replaced particular theories, particular hypotheses, particular conjectures by others; admittedly, in most cases by better ones: better in the sense of being a better approximation to the truth.

The *content* of these theories, hypotheses, conjectures may be called *knowledge in the objective sense*, as opposed to subjective or personal knowledge. For example, the content of an encyclopaedia of physics is impersonal or objective – and of course hypothetical – knowledge: it far exceeds what the most learned physicist can possibly know. What a physicist knows – or, more exactly, conjectures – may be called his personal or subjective knowledge. Both – the impersonal and personal knowledge – are mainly hypothetical and capable of improvement. Yet not only does the impersonal or objective knowledge currently go far beyond the personal knowledge of any human being, it also advances so rapidly that personal or subjective knowledge can only keep up with it in small areas and for short periods of time and is, in the main, constantly becoming outdated.

This is the fourth reason why Socrates is still right. For this outdated knowledge consists of theories which have been found to be false: outdated knowledge is not knowledge, at least not in the ordinary sense of the word.

VI

So we have four reasons that show even today that the Socratic insight, 'I know that I know almost nothing, and hardly this', is still highly relevant – possibly even more so than in Socrates' time. And we have good reason, in the defence of toleration, to derive from this insight those ethical consequences which Erasmus, Montaigne, Voltaire and later Lessing derived from it. But there are still other consequences.

The principles that form the basis of every rational discussion, that is, of every discussion undertaken in the search for truth, are in the main *ethical* principles. I should like to state three such principles.

1. The principle of fallibility: perhaps I am wrong and perhaps you are right. But we could easily both be wrong.
2. The principle of rational discussion: we want to try, as impersonally as possible, to weigh up our reasons for and against a theory: a theory that is definite and criticizable.
3. The principle of approximation to the truth: we can nearly always come closer to the truth in a discussion which avoids personal attacks. It can help us to achieve a better understanding; even in those cases where we do not reach an agreement.

It is worth noting that these three principles are both epistemological and ethical principles. For they imply, among other things, toleration: if I hope to learn from you, and if I want to learn in the interest of truth, then I have not only to tolerate you but also to recognize you as a potential equal; the potential unity and equality of all men somehow constitute a prerequisite of our willingness to discuss matters rationally. Of importance also is the principle that we can learn much from a discussion, even when it does not lead to agreement: a discussion can help us by shedding light upon some of our errors.

Thus ethical principles form the basis of science. The idea of truth as the fundamental regulative principle – the principle that guides our search – can be regarded as an ethical principle.

The search for truth and the idea of approximation to the truth are also ethical principles; as are the ideas of intellectual integrity and of fallibility, which lead us to a self-critical attitude and to toleration.

It is also very important that we can *learn* in the field of ethics.

VII

I should like to demonstrate this by looking at the example of an ethics for the intellectuals, especially for the intellectual professions: an ethics for scientists, for doctors, lawyers, engineers, and for architects; for civil servants and, most importantly, for politicians.

I should like to put before you some principles for *a new professional ethics*, principles closely connected with the concepts of toleration and intellectual honesty.

For this purpose I will first characterize the old professional ethics, perhaps even drawing a bit of a caricature, in order to compare it with the new professional ethics I am proposing.

Both the *old* and the *new* professional ethics are based, admittedly, upon the concepts of truth, of rationality and of intellectual responsibility. But the old ethics was based upon the idea of personal knowledge and of certain knowledge and, therefore, upon the idea of *authority*; whereas the new ethics is based upon the idea of objective knowledge and of uncertain knowledge. This signifies a fundamental change in the underlying way of thinking and, consequently, in the way that the ideas of truth, of rationality and of intellectual honesty and responsibility function.

The old ideal was to *possess* truth – certain truth – and, if possible, to *guarantee* truth by means of a logical proof.

This ideal, widely accepted to this day, is the idea of wisdom in person, the sage; not of 'wisdom' in the Socratic sense, of course, but in the Platonic sense: the sage who is an authority; the learned philosopher who claims power: the philosopher king.

The old imperative for the intellectuals is: Be an authority! Know everything in your field!

Once you are recognized as an authority, your authority will be protected by your colleagues; and you must of course protect the authority of your colleagues.

The old ethics I am describing leaves no room for mistakes. Mistakes are simply not allowed. Consequently, mistakes must not be acknowledged. I do not need to stress that this old professional ethics is intolerant. Moreover, it always has been intellectually dishonest: it leads (especially in medicine and in politics) to the covering up of mistakes for the sake of protecting authority.

VIII

This is why I suggest that we need a *new* professional ethics, mainly, but not exclusively, for scientists. I suggest that it be based upon the following twelve principles, with which I shall conclude this lecture.

1. Our objective conjectural knowledge goes further and further beyond what any *one* person can master. So there simply cannot be any 'authorities'. This holds true also within specialized subjects.

2. *It is impossible to avoid all mistakes*, or even all those mistakes that are, in themselves, avoidable. All scientists are continually making mistakes. The old idea that one can avoid mistakes and is therefore duty bound to avoid them, must be revised: it is itself mistaken.

3. *Of course it remains our duty to avoid mistakes whenever possible*. But it is precisely so that we can avoid them, that we must be aware, above all, of how difficult it is to avoid them and that nobody succeeds completely. Not even the most creative scientists who are guided by intuition succeed: intuition may mislead us.

4. Mistakes may be hidden even in those theories which are very well corroborated; and it is the specific task of the scientist to search for such mistakes. The observation that a well-corroborated theory or a technique that has been used successfully is mistaken may be an important discovery.

5. *We must therefore revise our attitude to mistakes*. It is *here* that our practical ethical reform must begin. For the attitude of the old professional ethics leads us to cover up our mistakes, to keep them secret and to forget them as soon as possible.

6. The new basic principle is that in order to learn to avoid making mistakes *we must learn from our mistakes*. To cover up mistakes is, therefore, the greatest intellectual sin.

7. We must be constantly on the look-out for mistakes. When we find them we must be sure to remember them; we must analyse them thoroughly to get to the bottom of things.

8. The maintenance of a self-critical attitude and of personal integrity thus becomes a matter of duty.

9. Since we must learn from our mistakes, we must also learn to accept, indeed accept *gratefully*, when others draw our attention to our mistakes. When in turn we draw other people's attention to their mistakes, we should always remember that we have made similar mistakes ourselves. And we should remember that the

greatest scientists have made mistakes. I certainly do not want to say that our mistakes are, usually, forgivable: we must never let our attention slacken. But it is humanly impossible to avoid making mistakes time and again.

10. We must be clear in our own minds that *we need other people to discover and correct our mistakes (as they need us)*; especially those people who have grown up with different ideas in a different environment. This too leads to toleration.

11. We must learn that self-criticism is the best criticism; but that *criticism by others is a necessity*. It is nearly as good as self-criticism.

12. Rational criticism must always be specific: it must give specific reasons why specific statements, specific hypotheses, appear to be false, or specific arguments invalid. It must be guided by the idea of getting nearer to objective truth. In this sense it must be impersonal.

I ask you to regard these points as suggestions. They are meant to demonstrate that, in the field of ethics, too, one can put forward suggestions which are open to discussion and improvement.

NOTE

1 This note is a defence of my translation of D–K (= Diels–Kranz, *Die Vorsokratiker*), Xenophanes B 25:

> Effortless over the All he reigns by mere thought and intention.

I am here translating the Greek verb *kradainō* (= *kradaō*) as 'to reign', whilst previously I translated it as 'to swing', following Hermann Diels, who was supported by the dictionaries (which do not give the meaning 'to reign' or 'to hold sway', etc.). By 'to swing the All', I obviously thought of some pre-Aristotelian theory of a first mover. But any such theory was rejected by Karl Reinhardt in his book *Parmenides*, where he opted for the dictionary meaning 'to shake', which was accepted by D–K and, under its influence, by Kirk and Raven, pp. 168 f. (p. 169: '. . . he shakes all things by the thought of his mind'), and by Guthrie (*History of Greek Philosophy*, volume I, p. 374: '. . . he makes all things shiver by the impulse of his mind'). These suggestions seemed to be impossible and led me, first, to search for the best meaning from the context. After deciding that 'he reigns' would fit best, I found that one of the basic meanings of *kradainō* was 'to brandish or shake a spear', and of *kraiainō* (or *kraainō*) 'to brandish or shake the staff of rule' (the *skeptron* or sceptre); see Sophocles, *Oedipus Coloneus*, line 449), and therefore 'to hold sway' or 'to reign'. So it seems that *kradainō* and *kraainō* had (sometimes) the same fundamental meaning: to shake or brandish a (long) stick. I suggest that both words may be sometimes translated by 'to hold sway' and 'to reign'. Because of the many misunderstandings of Xenophanes against which Galen had already protested in vain, I wish to propose here a translation of fragment B 28. (It was, unbeknown to me, proposed by Felix M. Cleve in *The Giants of Pre-Sophistic Greek Philosophy*, 2nd edition, 1969, volume I, pp. 11 ff.)

> At our feet we see how the Earth with its uppermost limit Borders on Air; with the lower, she reaches Apeiron.

'Apeiron' (the 'Unlimited' or the 'Indeterminate') is here, obviously, Anaximander's principle – the indeterminate or formless stuff that fills what we now call 'space', the world. 'Apeiron' was replaced, by Anaximenes, by 'Air': Xenophanes was present in Miletus when this problem was debated – when Anaximenes asserted, against Anaximander, that Air was not only on top of the earth, but also supported it from below. B 28 clearly takes sides in this quarrel, for Anaximander and against Anaximenes: it is most unlikely that Xenophanes uses the juxtaposition *Air – Apeiron* in any other sense than in the sense of this quarrel. That this was not understood is due to the authority of Aristotle who (demonstrably) did not know fragment B 28 when he wrote (or spoke) *De Caelo* 294a21, but quoted with approval Empedocles who, for his part, had misinterpreted our fragment – with far-reaching consequences. (See a forthcoming paper of mine.)

15

WHAT DOES THE WEST BELIEVE IN?

(Stolen from the author of *The Open Society*)

I am sorry to say that I must begin with an apology: an apology for the title of my lecture. This title reads: 'What Does the West Believe In?' When I think of the history of the expression 'the West', I wonder whether I should not have avoided it. This expression has gained currency in England primarily through the translation of Spengler's *Untergang des Abendlandes*, for the English title of this book is *The Decline of the West*. Yet I do not, of course, want to associate myself with Spengler, whom I regard not only as a false prophet of an alleged decline, but also as a symptom of a real decline, even though this is not a decline of the West: what his prophecies actually illustrate is the decline of the intellectual conscience of many western thinkers. They illustrate the victory of intellectual immodesty, of the attempt to beguile a public that is thirsty for knowledge by using bombastic words, in short, the victory of Hegelianism and of that Hegelian historicism which Schopenhauer exposed as the intellectual plague of Germany more than a century ago and against which he fought.

My choice of title and the echoes of Hegelianism it may arouse compel me to begin my lecture by drawing a clear distinction between myself, on one side, and Hegelian philosophy, together with prophecies of decline and of progress, on the other.[1]

In the first place, therefore, I should like to introduce myself. I am the last laggard of the Enlightenment, a movement outmoded long since, whose shallowness and, indeed, silliness has been demonstrated *ad nauseam*. This means that I am a rationalist

A lecture given in Zürich in 1958 at the invitation of Albert Hunold. First published in German in: *Erziehung zur Freiheit. Sozial Wissenschaftliche Studien für das Schweizerische Institut für Auslandsforschung*, ed. Albert Hunold, vol. 7, Erlenbach-Zürich/Stuttgart, 1959.

and that I believe in truth and in human reason. It does not mean, of course, that I believe in the omnipotence of human reason. A rationalist is by no means what our antirationalist opponents try to make us believe: a person who would like to be a purely rational being and who would like to turn others into purely rational beings. That would be most irrational. Any reasonable person, and therefore, I hope, any rationalist, knows quite well that reason plays a very modest role in human life: it is the role of critical consideration, of critical discussion. What I mean when talking of reason or rationalism is nothing more than a conviction that we can learn through criticism, that is, through critical discussion with others and through self-criticism: that we can learn from our mistakes. A rationalist is a person who is willing to learn from others, not simply by accepting their opinions, but by allowing them to criticize his ideas and by criticizing theirs: in other words by critical discussion. The true rationalist does not believe that he or anyone else has a monopoly on wisdom. He knows very well that we constantly need new ideas and that criticism does not produce them. But he believes that criticism can help us to separate the wheat from the chaff. He is also aware of the fact that the rejection or acceptance of an idea can never be a purely rational matter. But only critical discussion can help us to see an idea from many sides and to judge it fairly. A rationalist will, of course, not assert that all human relations can be fully explored by critical discussion; that again would be most unreasonable. But a rationalist may perhaps point out that the attitude of give and take, which is at the bottom of critical discussion, is also of the greatest importance in purely human relations. For the rationalist will easily be able to see that he owes his rationality to other men. He will recognize that the critical attitude can only be the result of criticism by others, and that one can become self-critical only by criticism of and by others. Perhaps the rational attitude can best be expressed by saying: You may be right, and I may be wrong; and even if our critical discussion does not enable us to decide definitely who is right, we may still hope to see matters more clearly after the discussion. We may both learn from each other, as long as we do not forget that what really matters is not who is right, but rather that we come nearer to the objective truth. After all, it is objective truth for which we both are striving.

This is, briefly, what I mean if I declare myself a rationalist. I have something more than this in mind, however, when I speak of myself as the last laggard of the Enlightenment. I have in mind the hope that inspired Pestalozzi, that knowledge may make us free – that we may free ourselves through knowledge from economic and spiritual bondage; and I have in mind the hope that we may rouse ourselves from our dogmatic slumber, as Kant called it. And I have in mind a serious obligation, one which most intellectuals have tended to forget, particularly since certain philosophers like Fichte, Schelling and Hegel have begun to undermine intellectual honesty. I am alluding to *the obligation never to pose as a prophet*.

Against this duty the German philosophers in particular have sinned grievously. They did so undoubtedly because they were *expected* to appear as prophets, as something like religious innovators, capable of revealing the deepest secrets of the universe and of life. Here as elsewhere, the constant demand produces, unfortunately, the supply. Prophets and leaders were sought; prophets and leaders were found. What this reaction produced, particularly in the German language, is scarcely credible. Happily, these things are less popular in England. If I compare the situation in the literature of the two languages my admiration for England becomes boundless. In this connection it is worth remembering that the Enlightenment started with Voltaire's *Letters Concerning the English Nation*, with an attempt to transfer to the European continent the intellectual sobriety of England – that dryness of the intellectual climate of England, which contrasts so oddly with its physical climate. This dryness, this sobriety, is simply a product of the respect for one's fellow man: one does not try to sell him one's ideas, nor does one try to impose them on him.

In the German domain it is unfortunately not so. There every intellectual wants to show that he is in possession of all the ultimate secrets of the world. There not only philosophers, but also economists, physicians, and particularly psychologists and psychiatrists become founders of religions.

Is there a distinguishing characteristic of these two attitudes – that of a follower of the Enlightenment, and that of the self-appointed prophet? Yes: it is their different way of speaking, of using the language. Prophecy speaks deeply, darkly, grandly; while a follower of the Enlightenment speaks as simply as possible: he wants to be understood. In this respect Bertrand Russell is our great master. Even when one cannot agree with him, one must always admire him. He always speaks clearly, simply and forcefully.

Why does the Enlightenment value simplicity of language so highly? Because it wants to enlighten, not to sway. The genuine disciple of the Enlightenment, the true rationalist, does not even want to persuade, nor even to convince. He remains always aware that he may err. Thus he esteems too highly the independence of the other person to try to sway him in important matters; rather he wants objections and criticisms. He wants to arouse and stimulate the cut and thrust of argument. This is what is valuable to him. Not only because we may approach truth better with the free exchange of opinion, but also because he values this process as such. He respects it even if the opinion thus formed appears to him mistaken.

One of the reasons why a follower of the Enlightenment wants neither to sway nor to persuade is this: he knows that only in the narrow confines of logic and mathematics is it possible to give logical proofs. Oversimplifying somewhat, one may say: *nothing can be proved*. One may sometimes offer strong arguments and one can always investigate various views critically; yet excepting mathematics, our arguments are *never* conclusive. We must always assess the weight of arguments and of reasons; we must always decide or judge which of them have greater weight; those for a given view, or those against it. Therefore, the search for truth and the formation of opinion always contain an element of free decision; and it is this free decision which makes human opinion valuable.

The philosophy of the Enlightenment adopted this high regard for free personal opinion from the philosophy of John Locke. It was, one may conjecture, the direct result of the English and Continental religious wars and conflicts. These conflicts produced in the end the idea of religious tolerance, which is by no means a negative idea, as is often maintained (for example by Arnold Toynbee). It is not only the expression of weariness and of the recognition that the attempt to enforce religious conformity by terror is a hopeless undertaking. On the contrary, religious tolerance is a product of the positive insight that enforced religious conformity is worthless, that only freely accepted faith can be valuable. This insight induces us to respect every honest belief, and to respect the individual and his opinion. It leads finally, in the words of Immanuel Kant – the last great philosopher of the

Enlightenment – to the recognition of the dignity of the human being.

The principle of the dignity of the individual means, according to Kant, the duty to respect every man and his convictions. Kant related this principle closely to what in English is called, with good reason, the Golden Rule. He also recognized the close connection of this principle with the idea of freedom: the freedom of thought, as demanded by the Marquis Posa from Philip II (in Schiller's *Don Carlos*); the freedom of thought which Spinoza, who was a determinist, believed to be an inalienable freedom, one of which the tyrant tries to rob us, but cannot.

On this last point, I believe we can no longer fully agree with Spinoza. It is probably true that freedom of thought can never be suppressed completely, but it can be suppressed at least to a very great extent, because without free exchange of thought there can be no true freedom of thought. We need others in order to put our thoughts to the test to find out which of our ideas are valid. Critical discussion is the foundation of the free thought of the individual. But this means that true freedom of thought is impossible without political freedom. Political freedom becomes thus a condition for the full use of his reason by each individual person.

Political freedom, however, cannot be secured except by tradition, by the traditional readiness to defend it, to fight for it and to make sacrifices for it.

It has often been maintained that rationalism is in conflict with all tradition. It is true that rationalism feels free to discuss critically each and any tradition, but ultimately rationalism itself is founded on tradition: the tradition of critical thinking, of free discussion, of simple clear language and of political freedom.

I have tried to explain here what I mean by rationalism and enlightenment, and since I wanted to disassociate myself from Spengler and other Hegelians, I had to declare myself a rationalist and admirer of the Enlightenment, one of the last laggards of a long abandoned and totally unfashionable philosophical movement.

But you may well ask whether this is not a somewhat lengthy introduction. What does all this have to do with our subject? You have come here to hear about the West and what the West believes in. Yet instead I am just talking about myself and what I believe in. You may wonder how much longer I am going to abuse your patience.

Yet in fact, I am already in the midst of our subject matter. As I have just said, I know very well that rationalism and the philosophy of enlightenment are unfashionable ideas and that it would be ridiculous to maintain that the West believes in these ideas, either consciously or unconsciously. But although today most intellectuals treat those ideas with scorn, rationalism, at least, is an idea without which the West could not even exist. For nothing is more characteristic of our western civilization than the fact that it is inextricably linked with science. It is the only civilization which has produced a science of nature, and in which this science is playing a decisive role. But the natural sciences are a direct product of the rationalism of the classical Greek philosophers: the Presocratics.

Please do not misunderstand me: it is by no means my thesis that western civilization believes in rationalism either consciously or unconsciously. I shall say more about the beliefs of the West later on. Here I want only to state, as others have done before me, that our western civilization is, historically speaking, largely a product of that rationalist mode of thought which our civilization has inherited from the Greeks. It seems to me quite obvious that whenever we talk of the West, Spengler's West or ours, we have in mind mainly the fact that there is a rationalist element in our western tradition.

In trying to explain rationalism, my motive was not only the wish to distance myself from certain fashionable anti-rationalist movements, but to attempt to place before you the much abused rationalist tradition, which has so decisively influenced our western civilization; so much so that one may very well characterize western civilization as the only one in which the rationalist tradition has played a dominant part. In other words, I had to talk of rationalism in order to explain what I mean when I talk of the West. And at the same time, I had to defend rationalism since it is so often perverted and misrepresented.

Thus I have perhaps clarified what I mean when I talk of the West. But I must add that in talking of the West I am thinking primarily of Britain. Perhaps this is so only because I live in Britain, but I believe that there are other reasons. Britain is the country which did not capitulate when it was facing Hitler alone. And if I now turn to the question 'What does the West believe in?' I shall mainly be inclined to think of those things in which my friends, and other people in Britain, believe. Surely not in rationalism; surely not in science, though it was created by Greek rationalism. On the contrary: rationalism seems obsolete to many; and as for science, it has become to many westerners first something strange and later, after the atom bomb, something monstrous and inhuman. Thus what is it we believe in today? What does the West believe in?

If we seriously contemplate this question and try to answer it honestly, most of us will probably have to confess that we do not quite know what we may believe in. Most of us have realized, at one time or another, that we believed in the one or the other false prophet and, through these false prophets, also in some false god. We all have gone through upheavals in our beliefs. And even the few whose beliefs have remained firm through all these upheavals will have to admit that it is not easy today to know what we in the West may believe in. These remarks perhaps sound very negative. I know many good people who consider it a weakness of the West that it has no unified supporting idea, no unified belief which we could proudly oppose to the Communist religion of the East. This popular view is very understandable but I think it is entirely wrong.

We ought to be proud that we do not have *one* idea but *many* ideas, good ones and bad ones; that we do not have a *single* belief, not *one* religion but many: good ones, and bad ones. It is a sign of the supreme strength of the West that we can afford that. The agreement of the West on a *single* idea, on a *single* belief, *one* religion, would be the end of the West, our capitulation, our unconditional surrender to the totalitarian idea.

Not so long ago, Mr Macmillan, now prime minister of Great Britain, but then still foreign secretary, was asked by Mr Khrushchev about what we of the West really believe in. He replied: 'In Christianity.' From a historical point of view one cannot disagree with him: apart from Greek rationalism nothing has influenced the history of the ideas of the West as much as Christianity and the long conflicts and fights within Christendom.

Nevertheless, I think that Macmillan's answer was mistaken. Surely there are good Christians among us; but is there a country, is there a government, is there a policy, which can honestly and seriously be called Christian? Can there be such a policy? Is not rather the long fight between ecclesiastical and secular power and the defeat of the ecclesiastical claim to worldly power one of those historical facts which have most deeply influenced the traditions of the West? And is Christianity a single, well-defined idea? Are there not many incompatible interpretations of this idea?

But perhaps even more important than these questions is the reply which Khrushchev must have had ready like every Marxist since Karl Marx. 'You are not Christians at all,' every Communist will answer, 'you only call yourselves Christians; the true Christians are we, we who do not call ourselves Christians but Communists. For you adore Mammon, while we fight for the oppressed, for those that labour and are heavy laden.'

It is not by chance that such answers have always impressed genuine Christians, and that there always existed and exist Christian Communists in the West. I do not doubt the honest conviction of the Bishop of Bradford when, in 1942, he described our western society as a work of Satan and called on all faithful servants of the Christian religion to work for the destruction of our society and for the victory of Communism. Since then the satanism of Stalin and his torturers has been admitted by the Communists themselves, and, going even further, for some time the thesis of Stalin's satanism was an integral part of their general party line. Nevertheless, there are sincere Christians who still think the same way as the former Bishop of Bradford. I do not think that we can, like Macmillan, rest our case on Christianity. Ours is not a Christian society, any more than it is a rationalist society.

This is quite understandable. The Christian religion demands from us a purity of action and thought that only saints can attain. This is why so many attempts to build a society imbued with the spirit of Christianity have been failures. They have always, and inevitably, led to intolerance, to fanaticism. Not only Rome and Spain can tell a tale of this but also Geneva and Zürich and numerous American Christian-Communist experiments. Marxist Communism is but the most terrible example of all those attempts to realize heaven on earth: it is an experiment which teaches us how easily those who presume to realize heaven on earth can achieve hell.

It goes without saying that it is not the idea of Christianity that leads to terror and inhumanity. Rather it is the idea of the one unified idea, the belief in one unified and exclusive belief. And since I have called myself a rationalist I regard it as my duty to point out that the terrorism of rationalism, of Robespierre's religion of reason, was, if possible, even worse than that of

Christian or Mohammedan or Jewish fanaticism. A genuinely rationalist social order is just as impossible as a genuinely Christian one; and the attempt to realize the impossible must here lead to at least equally abominable outrages. The best one can say about the Terror of Robespierre is that it did not last long.

Those well-meaning enthusiasts who have the wish and feel the need to unify the West under the leadership of one inspiring idea know not what they are doing. They are unaware of the fact that they are playing with fire – that it is the totalitarian idea which attracts them.

No, it is not the unity of an idea, but the diversity of our many ideas, of which the West may be proud: the pluralism of its ideas. To our question 'What does the West believe in?' we can now find a first and preliminary answer. For we can say proudly that we in the West believe in many and different things, in much that is true and in much that is false; in good things and in bad things.

My first and preliminary answer is thus to point out an almost trivial fact: we believe in a great variety of things.But this trivial fact is most significant.

Of course, there are many who have denied the western tolerance of opinion. Bernard Shaw, for example, asserted time and again that our age and our civilization are just as intolerant as any other. He tried to prove that only the *content* of our superstition and of our dogmas has changed: in place of the religious dogma we now have the scientific dogma; and whoever would dare to oppose the scientific dogma would be burned at the stake like Giordano Bruno in days past. But although Bernard Shaw did everything he could to shock his fellow beings by his opinions, they tolerated him. Nor is it true that he was not taken seriously, or that his was merely the freedom of the court-jester. On the contrary, although he amused his contemporaries he was taken very seriously by many of them; in particular, his theory about western intolerance was quite influential. I do not doubt that Shaw's influence was far greater than Giordano Bruno's, yet he died, more than ninety years old, not at the stake, but of a broken hip.

I propose thus to accept my first preliminary answer to our question and to turn to the many different things which different people believe in throughout our West.

There are good things and bad things, at least that is how they appear to me. And since I want to treat the good things in more detail, I want first to get the bad part out of the way.

We have many false prophets in the West, and many false gods. There are people who believe in power and in enslaving others. There are persons who believe in historical necessity; in a law of history, which we can guess and which allows us to foresee the future and to jump on the bandwagon in time. There are prophets of progress and prophets of reaction, and they all find faithful disciples. There are also prophets of, and believers in, the goddesses of *Success*, and of *Efficiency*, and especially believers in the growth of production at any price, in the economic miracle, and in man's power over nature. But the largest influence among intellectuals seems to belong to the *moaning prophets of pessimism*.

Nowadays, it seems as if all contemporary thinkers – at least those who care for their good reputation – are agreed on one point: that we live in a rather miserable time – in a positively criminal time, possibly even in the worst of all times; that we are walking on the rim of an abyss; and that it is our wickedness, perhaps even original sin, which has brought us to this. We have become, says Bertrand Russell (whom I esteem very highly), clever – perhaps too clever; but as far as morality is concerned, we are not good enough. It is our misfortune that our intelligence has developed faster than our moral consciousness. Thus we were clever enough to construct atom bombs and hydrogen bombs; but morally we were too immature to build a world state, which alone can save us from an all-annihilating war.

I have to confess that I believe this fashionable pessimistic view of our time to be mistaken. It is, I think, a dangerous fashion. I certainly do not want to speak against a world state or a world federation of states. But it seems to me quite wrong to blame any failure of the United Nations on a lack of morality on the part of the individual citizens of these nations. On the contrary, it is my conviction that nearly every one of us in the West would be ready to make any possible sacrifice to assure peace on earth, if we could only see how to make such a sacrifice serve our purpose. I personally expect there are few people who would not readily give their lives if by this sacrifice they could assure peace for mankind. I do not want to deny that there may be some who would not be ready to do this; but I do want to assert that they are comparatively rare. We surely all want peace. But that does not mean that we want *peace at any price*.

It is not my intention to devote this talk to the problem of atomic weapons. There is little talk about these questions in Britain, and although everybody loves and admires Bertrand Russell, even he hardly succeeded in getting these things seriously discussed. My students, for example, invited him to give a lecture on this topic and he was received with ovations. They were enthusiastic about the man, they listened to his talk with great interest, they even spoke during the discussion period, but, as far as I know, they then dropped the subject. In my seminar – where there is the freest possible discussion of any imaginable problem from natural philosophy to political ethics – no student has ever touched on Russell's problem. I realize that on the Continent the situation is quite different.

You might be interested to hear that I heard Russell's arguments for the first time in the United States, eight years ago [that is, in 1950] from an atomic physicist, who himself has done perhaps more than any other individual to bring about the decision to make the atomic bomb. His viewpoint was: capitulation is preferable to an atomic war. Admittedly, mankind would have to live after capitulation through its worst times; but, he said, sometime in the future, liberty may be won again. But an atomic war would be the end of everything. The same idea has been expressed by others in the following way: it would be better and even more honourable to live under the Russian dictatorship than to be killed by atomic bombs.

While respecting this opinion I think that the alternative is wrongly put. It is wrong because it does not consider the possibility of avoiding atomic warfare without capitulating. We *do not know*, after all, that atomic war is inevitable, and in fact we cannot know this. Nor do we know whether capitulation will lead to atomic war or not. The true alternative before us is thus: Shall we capitulate, to diminish the possibility or probability of an atomic war, or shall we, *if necessary*, defend ourselves with all means? Even this alternative involves a most difficult decision. But it is not the decision between a peace-party and a war-party. Rather it is a decision between a party that thinks it can estimate with sufficient precision the *degree of probability* of an atomic war and thinks the risk too great – so great that capitulation is preferable – and on the other side, a party that also wants peace yet also remembers that it was never possible to defend liberty without taking risks; that Churchill, when his position was almost hopeless, did not capitulate before Hitler; that nobody considered capitulation when Hitler announced his V-weapons, although those in the know had reason to fear that he was alluding to atomic weapons; and that, for instance, little Switzerland succeeded, in spite of her obvious military weakness, in keeping Hitler out, by her determined armed neutrality.

What I want to point out here is that both parties in this discussion are opposed to war. They also agree in that they do not oppose war *unconditionally*. And finally both parties believe not only in peace but also in liberty.

All this both parties have in common. The disagreement starts with the question: Shall we calculate, and rely upon, degrees of probability or shall we follow our tradition?

We have here therefore an antithesis between rationalism and tradition. Rationalism, so it seems, is for capitulation; the tradition of liberty is against it.

I have introduced myself here as a rationalist who is also a great admirer of Bertrand Russell. But in this conflict I do not choose rationalism but tradition. I do not believe that in such questions we can estimate degrees of probability. We are not omniscient; we know only a little, and we should not pose as being omniscient. Just because I am a rationalist I believe that rationalism has its limits, and that it is, in fact, impossible without tradition.

I should like to avoid polemics, which have already produced many bitter words. I could not well avoid telling where I stand. Whilst I do not think it is my task here to defend my position, I wish to analyse the differences of opinion and to find what the parties have in common, for here we can learn what the West believes in.

Returning now to our main question, 'What does the West believe in?' we can say perhaps that the most important answer of the many correct ones we could give is the following. We hate despotism, suppression and force and we all believe in fighting them. We are against war and against blackmail of any kind and especially also against blackmail by threat of war. We believe the invention of the atom bomb to be a terrible calamity. We want peace and we believe that it is possible to realize this aim. We all believe in liberty and that only liberty makes life worth living. Our ways part only at the question whether or not it is right to yield to blackmail and to endeavour to buy peace at the price of liberty.

The fact that we in the West want peace and liberty, and that we are all ready to make the greatest sacrifice for both, seems to me more significant than the discord between the two parties which I have described. And I believe that this fact allows me to offer you a very optimistic picture of our time. It is so optimistic that I hardly dare to submit it to you for fear of losing your confidence. For my thesis is this:

I assert that, in spite of everything, our time is the best of which we have any historical knowledge and that the kind of society in which we live in the West, despite its shortcomings, is the best that has existed so far.

In saying this I am thinking by no means primarily of our material wealth, although it is, after all, quite significant that during the short time since the Second World War, poverty has nearly disappeared from Northern and Western Europe, while in my youth and even between the two world wars, poverty (especially as a consequence of unemployment) was still *the* one great social problem. The disappearance of poverty (unfortunately only in the West) has several causes, of which increased production may be the most important. But here I should like to point mainly to three causes, all of which are significant for our problem. For they show very clearly what we in the West believe in.

1. Our time has established it as an article of faith, even as morally self-evident, that no one must go hungry as long as there is food enough for all. And we also have made up our minds that *the struggle against poverty must not be left to chance*, but that it must be considered as an elementary duty of all, particularly of those who are well off.

2. Our time believes in the principle of giving everybody the best possible chance in life ('equality of opportunity'). Like the Age of Enlightenment, our time believes in self-liberation through knowledge, and with Pestalozzi in fighting want through knowledge, and it believes therefore, rightly, that higher education ought to be accessible to all who have the necessary abilities.

3. Our time has stimulated in the masses new needs and the ambition for possession. This is obviously a dangerous development, but without it mass-misery is unavoidable. This was recognized early by the reformers of the eighteenth and nineteenth centuries. They saw that the problem of poverty could not

be solved without the active support of the poor, and that the desire and the will to improve their lot must be awakened before their support could be enlisted. This insight was clearly formulated for example by George Berkeley, Bishop of Cloyne (this is one of those truths which Marxism has adopted and exaggerated beyond recognition).

These three articles of public faith – the struggle against poverty, education for all, and the awareness of needs and the increase of demand – have led to very doubtful developments. The fight against poverty has produced in some countries a welfare state with a monstrous bureaucracy engulfing for example the hospitals and the entire medical profession, with the obvious result that only a fraction of the money spent for welfare actually benefits those who need it.

But even though we criticize the welfare state – and we should be critical of it – we must never forget that it originates in a most humane and most admirable moral conviction, and that a society which is ready for severe material sacrifices in fighting poverty thereby testifies to the sincerity of its conviction.

And a society which is ready to make such serious sacrifices for its moral convictions has the right to put its ideas into practice. Thus, our criticism of the welfare state must be aimed at showing better ways for realizing these ideas.

The idea of equal opportunity and of equal access to higher education has produced similar undesirable effects in some countries. For the impecunious student of my own generation the struggle for knowledge was an adventure, demanding self-denial and sacrifice, which gave the knowledge attained a unique value. I am afraid that this attitude is on the wane. The new right to education has created a different attitude. This right is taken for granted; and what we receive as our due, without sacrifice, we value but little. By making the right to education a gift to the student, society has deprived him of a unique experience.

As you see from my remarks on these two points, my optimism does not mean that I admire all the solutions which we have found, but rather that I admire the motives for trying these solutions. It is part of the fashionable pessimism to debunk these motives as basically hypocritical and egotistical. The pessimists forget, however, that even the moral hypocrite testifies by his very protestations that he believes in the moral superiority of those values which he pretends to accept. Even our great dictators were forced to talk as if they believed in liberty, in peace and in justice. Their hypocrisy was an unconscious and involuntary acknowledgement of those values, and an unintentional compliment to the masses who believed in them.

I am coming now to my third point: the increase in the material demands of the masses. Here the harm appears obvious since this idea is in direct conflict with another ideal of freedom: the Greek and Christian ideal of freedom from material desires and of self-liberation through self-denial.

Apart from this, the increase in material demands has had many undesirable consequences; for example the ambition to keep up with and surpass others, instead of enjoying what one has attained. It has led to dissatisfaction and envy instead of satisfaction. But, in this context, one should not forget that we are at the start of a new development and that learning takes time. The new and newly widespread economic ambition of the masses is perhaps morally not very admirable and certainly not very pretty; but it is, after all, the only way to overcome poverty through the effort of the individual. And this economic mass-ambition is also the most promising means of counteracting one of the most questionable features of a welfare state: the growth of bureaucracy and its growing tutelage of the individual. Only individual economic ambition can make poverty so unusual that it will become nonsensical to make the fight against poverty the main purpose of the state. Only the realization of a high standard of living can solve the ancient problem of poverty by making it so rare a phenomenon that limited social work can take care of it, thus avoiding the danger of a numerous and powerful bureaucracy.

In the light of these considerations the effectiveness of our western economic system appears to me very important: if we do not succeed in making poverty a rare exception, we may easily lose our freedom to the bureaucracy of the welfare state. Yet I must take issue here with a doctrine voiced time and again in various forms: I mean the doctrine that the decision between the western and the eastern economic systems will ultimately depend on the economic superiority of one of the two. Personally, I believe that a free market economy is more efficient than a planned economy; but I consider it entirely wrong to base the rejection of tyranny on economic arguments. Even if it were true that a centrally planned state economy is superior to that of the free market, I should oppose the planned economy; for the simple reason that it is likely to increase the power of the state to the point of tyranny. It is not the inefficiency of Communism that we are fighting, but its lack of liberty and of humanity. We should not despise our freedom nor sell it for a pottage of lentils (*Genesis* 25:34); norfor the highest possible productivity, not even if it were possible to purchase efficiency at the price of liberty.

I have used the word 'masses' several times, especially in order to point out that the increase of the demand and the economic ambition of the masses is something new. It is for this reason necessary to dissociate myself from those who emphasize the character of our society as a 'mass-society'. This label and similarly the expression 'uprising of the masses' have become slogans which seem, indeed, to have fascinated masses of intellectuals and semi-intellectuals.

I believe that these slogans describe nothing whatever in our social reality. Our social philosophers' vision, and their description of this reality, has been faulty for the simple reason that they have seen it through the spectacles of the Platonic-Marxist theory of society.[2]

Plato was the theorist of an aristocratic form of absolute government. As the *fundamental problem of political theory*, he posed the following questions: '*Who should rule?* Who is to govern the state? The many, the mob, the masses, or the few, the elect, the elite?'

Once the question 'Who should rule?' is accepted as fundamental, then obviously there can be only one reasonable answer: Not those who do not know, but those who do know, the sages; not the mob, but the few best. That is Plato's theory of the rule by the best, of aristocracy.

It is somewhat odd that great theorists of democracy and great adversaries of this Platonic theory – such as Rousseau – adopted Plato's statement of the problem instead of rejecting it as inadequate, for it is quite clear that the fundamental question in political theory is not the one Plato formulated. The question is not 'Who should rule?' or 'Who is to have power?' but 'How much power should be granted to the government?' or perhaps more precisely, 'How can we develop our political institutions in such a manner that even incompetent and dishonest rulers cannot do too much harm?' In other words, the fundamental problem of political theory is the problem of checks and balances, of institutions by which political power, its arbitrariness and its abuse can be controlled and tamed.

I do not doubt that the kind of democracy in which we in the West believe is no more than a state in which power is, in this sense, limited and controlled. For the kind of democracy in which we believe is by no means an ideal state; we know perfectly well that much happens that should not happen. It is childish to strive after ideals in politics, and any reasonable mature man in the West knows that '*All political action consists in choosing the lesser evil*' (to quote the Viennese poet Karl Kraus).

For us there are only two types of government: those in which the governed can get rid of their rulers without bloodshed, and those in which the governed can, if at all, get rid of their rulers only by bloodshed. The first of these types of government we call democracy, the second tyranny or dictatorship. But the names do not really matter here, only the facts do.

We in the West believe in democracy only in this sober sense: as *the least evil form of government*. This is also how the man described it who has done more than anyone to save democracy and the West: 'Democracy is the worst form of government,' Winston Churchill said once, 'except of course all those other forms of government that have been tried from time to time.'

Thus we believe in democracy, but not because it is the rule of the people. Neither you nor I rule; on the contrary, both you and I are being ruled, and sometimes more than we like. Yet we believe in democracy as the form of government which is compatible with peaceful and effective political opposition, and therefore with political freedom.

I have mentioned above the unfortunate fact that Plato's misleading question 'Who is to rule?' was never clearly rejected by the philosophers of politics. Rousseau asked the same question, but gave the opposite answer: 'The will of the people shall rule – the will of the many, not of the few'; a dangerous answer indeed, since it leads to the mythological deification of 'The People' and 'The Will of the People'. Marx too asks, quite in Plato's vein: 'Who shall rule, the capitalists or the proletarians?' And he too gave the answer: 'The many; not the few; the proletarians should rule, not the capitalists.'

Contrary to Rousseau and to Marx we see in the majority decision of a vote or of an election only a method of producing decisions without bloodshed, and with the least possible restriction of freedom. Of course, majorities often arrive at mistaken decisions, and we must insist that minorities have rights and freedoms which no majority decision can overrule.

What I have said may support my suggestion that the fashionable terms 'mass', 'elite' and 'uprising of the masses' originate from the ideologies of Platonism and Marxism.

Just as Rousseau and Marx simply inverted the Platonic answer, so some opponents of Marx inverted the Marxist answer: they want to counteract the 'revolt of the masses' by a 'revolt of the elite', thereby reverting to the Platonic answer and the claim of the elite to rule. But this whole approach is mistaken. God save us from that anti-Marxism which simply inverts Marxism: we know it only too well; even Communism is no worse than the anti-Marxist 'elite' which ruled Italy, Germany and Japan and which it took a global war to remove.

'But', the educated and also the half-educated keep asking, 'can it be right that my vote should carry no more weight than that of any road sweeper with no education at all? Is there not an educational elite that sees farther than the mass of the uneducated and should therefore have a greater influence on important political decisions?'

The answer is that the educated and semi-educated do have a greater influence anyway. They write books and papers, they teach and lecture, they talk in discussions and they can make their influence felt as members of their political party.

By this I do not mean to say that I approve of the greater influence of the educated, compared with the 'road sweeper'. For the Platonic idea of the rule of the wise and good should, I believe, be rejected unconditionally. Who, after all, decides between wisdom and folly? Have not the wisest and best been crucified – and precisely by those who were acknowledged as wise and good?

Are we to burden our political institutions with the task of judging wisdom and goodness, integrity and unselfish achievement? Are we to make a political problem of this task? As a matter of practical politics the problem of the elite is hopelessly insoluble: in actual practice elites and cliques can never be told apart.

Yet in fact there is hardly a grain of truth in all this balderdash about masses and elites, simply because these 'masses' do not really exist. Those masses by which we all are confronted – and bothered – are not concrete masses of people but, say, of motorcars and motorcycles. Yet neither the driver of a car nor the rider of a motorcycle is a member of the mass; quite the contrary, he is an incorrigible individualist who, one might almost say, comes close to struggling for existence, single-handed, against everybody else. The individualistic image *homo-homini-lupus* has never been more appropriate.

No, we are not living in a mass society. On the contrary: there never was a time when so many individuals were ready for sacrifice and willing to bear the burdens of responsibilities. Never before was there so much spontaneous and individual heroism as in the inhuman wars of our times; in spite of the fact that there has never been less social and material inducement for heroism.

The monument of the Unknown Soldier to which western nations pay homage is a symbol of what the West believes in – a symbol of our faith in the ordinary unknown man. We do not ask whether he belonged to the mass or to the elite: he was a man, take him for all in all.

It is this belief in our fellow men, and the respect for them, which makes our time the best we know. The sincerity of this belief is proved by the readiness to make sacrifices for it. We believe in freedom, because we believe in our fellow men. This is why we have abolished slavery. And our social order is the best of which we have historical knowledge, because it is the one most favourably disposed towards improvement.

If we look to the East from this point of view, perhaps, we can conclude with a conciliatory thought:

It is true that Communism has reintroduced slavery and torture; and this we must not condone and cannot forgive. Yet we must not forget that all this happened because the East believed in a theory which promised freedom – freedom for all mankind. We must not forget, in this bitter conflict, that even Communism, this worst evil of our time, was born out of the desire to help others and to make sacrifices for others.

NOTES

1 Translator's note: The rest of this text is based upon a previous translation by the author with some minor revisions by the present translator for this edition.

2 For the following compare my books: *The Poverty of Historicism*, 1957 (14th impression, Routledge, London, 1991), and *The Open Society and Its Enemies*, 1945 (revised edn, Routledge & Kegan Paul, London, 1966); especially the first volume, chapter 8, and the second volume: 'The High Tide of Prophecy: Hegel and Marx and the Aftermath'.

16

CREATIVE SELF-CRITICISM IN SCIENCE AND IN ART

(Stolen from Beethoven's sketch books)

I should like first of all to express my thanks for the kind invitation to give the opening address at the Salzburg Festival. This is a great honour. The invitation came as a complete surprise, and it was even somewhat disturbing. Ever since 1950 my wife and I have led a secluded life in our house in the Chiltern Hills. We have no television and no newspaper, and we are completely absorbed by our work. My work is concerned mainly with an abstract subject: the problem of human knowledge and, in particular, of scientific knowledge. That hardly qualifies me to give an opening address at the Salzburg Festival.

So I wondered why I had been invited. First I thought that I had been confused with somebody else. Or was it perhaps because of my love for this city, which sprang from a childhood love, when I was about 5 or 6 years old, well over 70 years ago? Yet no one knew of this. And nobody knew about an adventure I had here on an icy cold night, more than half a century ago. It was midnight, and I was on my way home from skiing, when, in the beautiful light of a full moon, I happened to slip into one of Salzburg's two famous horseponds . . . Indeed there must have been other reasons for choosing me as your guest speaker. Then something occurred to me. In one respect I am really quite unique: you see, I am an optimist. I am an optimist in a world where among the intelligentsia it has become a strict rule that one must be a pessimist if one wants to be 'in'. But I do believe that our age is not so bad as is generally maintained. I do believe that it is better and more beautiful than its reputation. A quarter of a century ago, I gave a lecture, the title of which sounds today even more provocative than it did then: 'The History of our Time: An Optimist's View'.[1]

So if there is anything that qualifies me to give this address, then it is perhaps the reputation of being an incorrigible optimist.

Allow me to say a few words about this optimism of mine which also pertains to things connected with the Salzburg Festival. For many years – at least since the time of Adolf Loos and Karl Kraus, both of whom I knew – our intellectuals have strictly adhered to the principle that our so-called culture is a commercialized industry, and therefore just kitsch and vulgarity. Especially in what this industry offers to the masses as culture, the pessimist sees nothing but depravity and tastelessness. But an optimist also sees the other side: millions of records and tapes of the most beautiful works by Bach, Mozart, Beethoven and Schubert – the greatest musicians of all – are being bought; and the number of people who have come to love these great musicians and their wonderful music has become incalculable.

Of course I must agree with the pessimists when they point out that we almost deliberately educate our children to become accustomed to cruelty and violence by exposing them to cruel and violent films and television. Unfortunately almost the same holds for modern literature. As an optimist, however, I can say that in spite of all our attempts to propagate violence, there are still many good and helpful people in the world. And in spite of everything the cultural pessimists have to say about the hatefulness of our time – and sometimes it is quite convincing – there are still many people who are happy to be alive.

The pessimists point to the moral and political decline, to the disregard for human rights which we all thought secure. They are right. But are they also right when they blame this on science and its use in technology? Certainly not. And the optimist remarks that science and technology have brought modest prosperity to the peoples of Europe and America and that the appalling poverty and the suffering of the previous century have almost been banished from large areas of the world.

Ladies and gentlemen, I am not a believer in progress or in a law of progress. In the history of mankind there are ups and downs. Great wealth can concur with great depravity, and a flowering of the arts may concur with a decline of humanity and of good will. More than forty years ago I wrote a few things against the belief in progress and against the influence of fashions and the cult of modernity upon art and upon science. Only quite recently we were called upon to believe in the idea of modernity and of progress and today we are to be injected with cultural pessimism. What I want to say to the pessimists is that in my long life, I have seen not only retrogression but also very clear evidence of progress. The cultural pessimists who do not want to admit that there is anything good about our age and our society are blind to this, and they make others blind. I believe that it is harmful when leading and admired intellectuals continually tell people that they are in fact living in hell. In this way they make people not only dissatisfied – that would not be so very bad – but they make them also unhappy. Their joy in living is taken away from them. How did Beethoven, who in his personal life was deeply unhappy, end his work? With Schiller's *Ode to Joy*.

Beethoven lived in a time of disappointed hopes of freedom. The French Revolution had perished in a reign of terror and in the Empire of Napoleon. Metternich's Restoration suppressed the idea of democracy and sharpened class antagonism. The misery of the masses was terrible. Beethoven's *Hymn to Joy* is a passionate protest against the class antagonism by which mankind is divided; 'sharply divided' (*'streng geteilt'*), says Schiller, Beethoven alters these words in one place, for an outburst by the choir, writing: 'insolently divided' (*'frech geteilt'*).[2] Yet he knows no class hatred; he knows only the love of his fellow men. And almost all his works end either in a spirit of solace, as does the *Missa Solemnis,* or jubilant, as do the symphonies and *Fidelio*.

Many of our contemporary productive artists have become victims of pessimistic propaganda about our culture. They believe that it is their task to present what they regard as a gruesome world or a gruesome historical period in a gruesome manner. It is true that even some great artists of the past did just this. I am thinking of Goya or Käthe Kollwitz. Such criticism of society is necessary, and it should be deeply disturbing. But its significance should not lie in lament; rather, it should be a call to overcome suffering, as in *The Marriage of Figaro* which is packed with criticism of its period. It is full of wit, satire, and irony; but it also contains a deeper significance. There is plenty of seriousness and even grief in this great work, but also much joy and overflowing vitality.

Ladies and gentlemen, I have said too much about my optimism, and it is high time to come to the theme I have announced, 'Creative Self-criticism in Science and in Art'.

This theme is closely related to what I said in my introduction. Even though only briefly, I should like to speak about some of the similarities and differences between the creative work of the great natural scientists and that of the great artists, partly in the hope of combatting the propaganda of the cultural pessimists against the natural sciences, an issue that has recently become topical.

Great artists always have one central interest: their work; the work on which they are engaged. That is the meaning of the saying 'Art for art's sake': for this means: art for the sake of the *work of art*. But the same is true of the great scientists. It is quite wrong to think that the inducement for doing natural science lies in its applications. Neither Planck nor Einstein, neither Rutherford nor Bohr, thought of a possible application of the atomic theory. On the contrary, until 1939 they thought that any such application was impossible; they relegated the idea to the realm of science fiction. These men were searching for the sake of the search; seeking the truth for its own sake. They were physicists, or, perhaps better, cosmologists, inspired by the desire that Goethe's Faust expresses when he says:

To know what forces there might be
That hold this world in unity.

This is an ancient dream of mankind, a dream of poets and of thinkers. Cosmological speculation can be found in all the ancient civilizations. It is found in Homer's *Iliad* (8, 13–16) and in Hesiod's *Theogomy* (720–5).

There are still some scientists and of course many amateurs who believe that the natural sciences just collect facts – perhaps in order to make use of them in industry. I see science differently. Its beginnings are to be found in poetical and religious myths, in human fantasy that tries to give an explanation of ourselves and of our world. Science develops from myth, under the challenge of rational criticism: a form of criticism that is inspired by the idea of truth; by the search for truth, and by the hope of attaining it. The basic questions underlying this criticism are: Can this be true? And is it true? Thus I come to the first thesis of my address: poetry and science have the same origin. They originate in myths.

My second thesis is as follows: we can distinguish two kinds of criticism, one that has aesthetic and literary interests and one that has rational interests. The first leads from myth to poetry, the second leads from myth to science; or to be more precise, to natural science. The former evaluates the beauty of the language, the energy of the rhythm, the radiance and vividness of the images, the dramatic tension and its persuasive power. This kind of critical judgement leads to poetry, especially to epic and dramatic poetry; to poetic song, and with it to classical music.

Rational criticism, by contrast, asks whether the mythical report is true; whether the world really evolved in the manner asserted: whether it could have been created as Hesiod tells us or, perhaps, in according with *Genesis*. Under the pressure of such questions myth becomes cosmology, the science of our world, of our environment; it turns into natural science.

My third thesis is that there are still many traces left over from the common origin of poetry and music on the one hand and of cosmology and science on the other. I am not asserting that all poetry is mythical in character, or that all science is cosmology. But what I wish to say is that in poetry – one only has to think of Hofmannsthal's *Jedermann* – and in science, the creation of myths still plays an unexpectedly large role. Myths are our attempts, naive and inspired by our imagination, to explain ourselves and our world to ourselves. A large part not only of poetry but also of science can still be described as a naive attempt, inspired by imagination, at explaining our world to ourselves.

Poetry and science – and therefore also music – are blood relations. They stem from the attempt to understand our origin and our fate, and the origin and the fate of our world.

These three theses can be described as historical hypotheses, although for Greek poetry, especially for Greek tragedy, the mythical source can hardly be doubted. For the enquiry into the beginnings of Greek natural philosophy, the three hypotheses have shown their fruitfulness. Our western natural science and our western art are both the rebirth – the renaissance – of their Greek predecessors. Yet although art and science have a common origin, there are of course essential differences between them.

In science there is progress. That has to do with the fact that science has an aim. Science is the search for truth and its aim is the approximation to the truth. In art too there may be aims, and in so far as the same aim is pursued for some length of time, one can indeed sometimes talk about progress in art. For a long time, the imitation of nature was an aim in painting and in sculpture; although it was certainly never their only aim. And indeed we can speak of progress relative to this aim, for instance in the treatment of light and shade. Perspective can also be mentioned here. But aims like this were never the only driving forces in art. Great works of art often affect us quite independently of the artist's mastery of such skills and other means that are subject to progress.

It has often been seen and has often been emphasized that there is no general progress in art. Primitivism has perhaps over-emphasized this fact. Yet where there certainly is progress, and of course also decline, is in the creative power of the individual artist.

Every artist has to learn his art, even an incredible genius like Mozart. Every artist, or nearly every artist, has his teacher; and every great artist learns from his own experiences, from his own work. Oscar Wilde, a great poet not unknown in Salzburg, says: 'Experience is the name every one gives to their mistakes.'[3] And John Archibald Wheeler, a great physicist and cosmologist says: 'Our whole problem is to make the mistakes as fast as possible.'[4] My own comment on this is: And it is our task to discover our mistakes, and to learn from them. Even Mozart made radical changes and improvements to some of his works, for example to an early work of his, the first string quintet in B flat major. Mozart's greatest works were produced in the last decade of his short life, from about 1780 to his death in 1791, between the ages of 24 and 35. This shows indeed that he must have learnt through self-criticism, and astonishingly quickly. It is still quite incredible that he wrote the *Seraglio* at the age of 25 or 26, and *Figaro* at the age of 30.

Yet the title of my present address, 'Creative Self-criticism in Science and in Art' was inspired by the work of Beethoven; more precisely, it was inspired by an exhibition of Beethoven's sketch books, organized by the *Gesellschaft der Musikfreunde* (Society of the Friends of Music) in Vienna; an exhibition which I visited many years ago.

Beethoven's sketch books are documents of his creative self-criticism; of his constant reconsideration of his ideas, and of the often relentless corrections which he made to them. This attitude, an attitude of ruthless self-criticism, makes it perhaps a little easier to comprehend Beethoven's astonishing personal development, from the time he began composing, influenced by Haydn and Mozart, to his last works.

There are different kinds of artists and of writers. Some do not seem to work with the method of error elimination. They are, it seems, capable of creating a perfect work, without any preliminary attempts; they achieve perfection immediately. Amongst philosophers, Bertrand Russell was a genius of this kind. He wrote the most beautiful English; and in his manuscripts there was perhaps just one single word changed, in three pages, or perhaps in four pages. Others work in a totally different way. Their method of writing is the method of trial and error, the method of making mistakes and of correcting them.

Mozart belonged to the first group of creative artists, it seems, although he rewrote some of his works. But Beethoven certainly belonged to the second, to those whose work sometimes grows out of many corrections.

It is of interest to contemplate the methods of work adopted by these artists who belong to the second group. I should like to stress that everything I say about this is speculative and conjectural. I conjecture that these artists start with a problem, or a task; for example with the task of writing a violin concerto or a mass or an opera. I suppose that it is part of the task to have some idea about the size of the work, its character and its structure – say, its sonata form – and perhaps also about some of the themes to be used. Or the plan may be much more detailed, especially in the case of a mass or an opera.

Yet when it comes to the execution, to actual work, to the realization of the idea and to transferring it onto paper, then even the artist's plan begins to change under the influence of the execution of his work, which embodies his self-critical corrections and the elimination of errors. The plan becomes more concrete, its outlines become more definite. Each part, each detail, is judged as to whether or not it fits in with the ideal picture of the whole. And vice versa: the ideal picture of the whole is constantly corrected as the work proceeds to be realized in its details. There is a feedback effect here, a give and take between the plan, the ideal picture, as it becomes clearer and more definite on the one hand, and on the other the emerging concrete work, in the process of being completed through the correction of errors.

All this can perhaps be seen most clearly in the case of a painter working on a portrait; that is, in the case of an artist who tries to build up his interpretation of a natural object. He plans, he sketches, he starts to correct. Here he adds a speck of colour and stands back to test the effect. The effect of the added speck of colour greatly depends on the context, on everything which is already there. And vice versa, the new speck of colour in its turn affects the whole. Everything is changed by it, everything becomes different, better or worse. And with the effect on the whole, the ideal picture at which he aims, and which is never quite fixed in his mind, is also changed. And in the particular case of the painter of portraits, the likeness that the artist tries to attain, and his interpretation of the character of the subject, are also changing.

The important thing here is that the act of painting, that is, an attempt at realization, must of course come before any act of critical comparison and of correction ('Making comes before matching', says Ernst Gombrich.[5]) On the other hand there must be an idea, approaching an ideal picture, with which the artist can compare the work so far achieved, since anything like a correction is only made possible by a comparison with such an ideal object. When, in the particular case of the painter of portraits, an object to be represented is present to the artist, then the problem may be somewhat less pressing. It is probably similar in music where self-criticism and the correction of errors may be easier if a text is to be set to music. In any case, the correction of errors is like a comparison, a comparison between what has been achieved and what is being aimed at, the ideal picture of the work which is continuously changing under the impact of the work actually done. The work that has been done influences the creative process more and more powerfully. In the case of a great work this can go so far that the artist who wrote it can hardly recognize it any longer as his own work. It has become greater than his conception. This happened with Haydn's *Creation* and, in a completely different way, with the symphony that Schubert himself abandoned: the *Unfinished*.

Let me now turn in conclusion to a comparison of the arts with the sciences which are maligned rather than understood by the cultural pessimists. In science the work is the hypothesis, the theory; and the aim of the activity is truth, or approximation to the truth, and explanatory power. This aim is largely constant; and this is the reason why there is progress. It is a progress that can last for centuries: the progress towards ever better theories. In art, the most important criticism is the creative self-criticism of the artist; in science however, criticism is not just self-criticism but also co-operative criticism: when a scientist overlooks a mistake or tries to conceal it – something that fortunately happens only rarely – this mistake is as a rule discovered by other scientists. For the method of science is self-criticism and mutual criticism. The criticism judges the theory by its attainments in the search for truth. It is that that makes the criticism rational.

The theory, that is to say, the work of the creative scientist, has therefore much in common with the work of art; the creative activity of the scientist resembles that of the artist – at least the activity of those artists to whom Beethoven belonged, those artists who begin with a bold conception and who can raise their work by means of creative criticism to heights unthought of; so that, as a result, the beautiful *Choral Fantasia* grows into the still more beautiful *Ode to Joy*.

In science, the great theoretician corresponds to the great artist, and, like the artist, he is guided by his imagination, his intuition and his sense of form. Einstein said of the model of the atom developed by Niels Bohr in 1913 – a revolutionary theory that was soon afterwards greatly improved – that it was a work of the 'greatest musicality'. Yet in contrast to a great work of art, the great theory always remains subject to further improvement.

The scientist knows this and he also knows that his imagination, his intuition, and even his sense of form lead him more often astray than to his aim; that is, to a better approximation to the truth. This is why, in science, a permanent critical examination not only by the creator of a theory but also by other scientists is essential. In science there is no great work based merely on inspiration and a sense of form.

Ladies and gentlemen, I want to close with a quotation from one of the greatest of scientists, Johannes Kepler, the great cosmologist and astronomer who died in the year 1630, the twelfth year of the Thirty Years War. In this quotation, Kepler takes as his starting point his theory of the movement of heavenly bodies, and he compares it to music, especially to the divine music of the spheres. Yet almost unintentionally, Kepler concludes with a hymn of praise to the music created by man, to the polyphonic music that was then still a fairly recent discovery. Kepler writes:[6]

> Thus the heavenly motions are nothing but a kind of perennial concert, rational rather than audible or vocal. They move through the tension of dissonances which are like syncopations or suspensions with their resolutions (by which men imitate the corresponding dissonances of nature), reaching secure and pre-determined closures, each containing six terms like a chord consisting of six voices. And by these marks they distinguish and articulate the

immensity of time. Thus there is no marvel greater or more sublime than the rules of singing in harmony together in several parts, unknown to the ancients but at last discovered by man, the ape of his Creator; so that, through the skilful symphony of many voices, he should actually conjure up in a short part of an hour the vision of the world's total perpetuity in time; and that, in the sweetest sense of bliss enjoyed through Music, the echo of God, he should almost reach the contentment which God the Maker has in His Own works.

NOTES

1 *Conjectures and Refutations*, chapter 19, pp. 364–76; Routledge, London, 1991 (first reprint of the fifth edition).

2 Schiller's wording ('*streng geteilt*') occurs several times in the first edition of Beethoven's Ninth Symphony; Beethoven's change ('*frech geteilt*') occurs once. (I once possessed the first edition, and when I drew the attention of Dr Zeller, the then Director of the Schiller-Museum in Marbach am Neckar, to this change, he checked and confirmed my information.)

3 Oscar Wilde, *Lady Windermere's Fan*, Act 3.

4 J. A. Wheeler, *American Scientist*, vol. 44, 1956, p. 360.

5 E. H. Gombrich, *Art and Illusion*, Phaidon Press, London 1986 (fourth impression of the fifth edition), part I, chapter 1. (See also the index on p. 378 for other passages.)

6 Joannis Keppleri, *Harmonices Mundi*, *Lib*. V, end of *Caput* VII, p. 212 (misprinted 213); Lincii Austriae 1619. Kepler's Latin text is translated by the author.

APPENDIX

This appendix contains the German texts of the Habermas quotations and the author's 'translations' in chapter 6, 'Against Big Words'.

[*Quotations from Habermas' essay*]	[*My 'translation'*]
Die gesellschaftliche Totalität führt kein Eigenleben oberhalb des von ihr Zusammengefaßten, aus dem sie selbst besteht.	Die Gesellschaft besteht aus den gesellschaftlichen Beziehungen.
Sie produziert und reproduziert sich durch ihre einzelnen Momente hindurch.	Die verschieden Beziehungen produzierten *irgendwie* die Gesellschaft.
So wenig jenes Ganze vom Leben, von der Kooperation und dem Antagonismus des Einzelnen abzusondern ist,	Unter diesen Beziehungen finden sich Kooperation und Antagonismus; und da (wie schon gesagt) die Gesellschaft aus diesen Beziehungen besteht, kann sie von ihnen nicht abgesondert werden;
so wenig kann irgendein Element auch bloß in seinem Funktionieren verstanden werden ohne Einsicht in das Ganze, das an der Bewegung des Einzelnen selbst sein Wesen hat.	aber das Umgekehrte gilt auch: keine der Beziehungen kann ohne die anderen verstanden werden.

System und Einzelheit sind reziprok und nur in der Reziprozität zu verstehen.	(Wiederholung des Vorhergehenden.)

(Bemerkung: Die hier vorgetragene Ganzheitslehre ist unzählige Male, und sehr oft besser, vorgetragen worden; aber mit jedem Male werden die Worte eindrucksvoller.)

Now Professor Habermas himself writes:

Adorno begreift die Gesellschaft in Kategorien, die ihre Herkunft aus der Logik Hegels nicht verleugnen.	Adorno verwendet eine an Hegel erinnernde Ausdrucksweise.
Er begreift Gesellschaft als Totalität in dem streng dialektischen Sinne, der es verbietet, das Ganze organisch aufzufassen nach dem Satz: es ist mehr als die Summe seiner Teile;	Er sagt daher (sic) nicht, daß das Ganze mehr ist als die Summe seiner Teile;
ebensowenig aber ist Totalität eine Klasse, die sich umfangslogisch bestimmen ließe durch ein Zusammennehmen aller unter ihr befaßten Elemente.	ebensowenig ist (sic) das Ganze eine Klasse von Elementen.

And so on. For example, further down the page we find

die Totalität der gesellschaftlichen Lebenszusammenhänge . . .	wir alle stehen irgendwie untereinander in Beziehung . . .

or on page 157

Theorien sind Ordnungsschemata, die wir in einem syntaktisch verbindlichen Rahmen beliebig konstruieren.	Theorien sollten nicht ungrammatisch formuliert werden; ansonsten kannst Du sagen, was Du willst.

Sie erweisen sich für einen speziellen Gegenstandsbereich dann als brauchbar, wenn sie ihnen die reale Mannigfaltigkeit fügt.

Sie sind auf ein spezielles Gebiet dann anwendbar, wenn sie anwendbar sind.

NAME INDEX

SUBJECT INDEX